The Ethnography of Moralities

The social construction of morality is a complex and challenging topic which is central to the anthropological discipline. Until recently, however, it has received little direct attention from anthropologists. With the growing interest in indigenous notions of self and personhood and related questions regarding human rights, issues pertaining to moral and ethical groundings of social life have become increasingly relevant. So far, however, few anthropologists have concerned themselves with disentangling 'moralities' and how one might set about studying them in empirical settings.

The focus for *The Ethnography of Moralities* was chosen precisely in order to raise a debate around the empirical study of different moral discourses and how these are related to social institutions, to indigenous concepts of human nature (male and female), to cosmology, and to the nature of good and evil.

These questions are addressed in their theoretical context and discussed with reference to a wide array of ethnographic studies from: Argentina, Mongolia, Melanesia, Yemen, Zimbabwe, Mexico, England, and the Old Testament. *The Ethnography of Moralities* will be of considerable interest to students of anthropology, sociology and cultural studies as well as, in some aspects, to law students.

Signe Howell is Professor of Social Anthropology at the University of Oslo.

European Association of Social Anthropologists

The European Association of Social Anthropologists (EASA) was inaugurated in January 1989, in response to a widely felt need for a professional association which would represent social anthropologists in Europe and foster co-operation and interchange in teaching and research. As Europe transforms itself in the nineties, the EASA is dedicated to the renewal of the distinctive European tradition in social anthropology.

Other titles in the series:

Conceptualizing Society
Adam Kuper

Revitalizing European Rituals
Jeremy Boissevain

Other Histories
Kirsten Hastrup

Alcohol, Gender and Culture
Dimitra Gefou-Madianou

Understanding Rituals
Daniel de Coppet

Gendered Anthropology
Teresa del Valle

**Social Experience and
Anthropological Knowledge**
*Kirsten Hastrup and
Peter Hervik*

Fieldwork and Footnotes
*Han F. Vermeulen and Arturo
Alvarez Roldan*

Syncretism/Anti-Syncretism
*Charles Stewart and
Rosalind Shaw*

Grasping the Changing World
Václav Hubinger

Civil Society
Chris Hann and Elizabeth Dunn

Nature and Society
*Philippe Descola and
Gísli Pálsson*

The Ethnography of Moralities

Edited by Signe Howell

London and New York

First published 1997
by Routledge
11 New Fetter Lane, London EC4P 4EE

Simultaneously published in the USA and Canada
by Routledge
29 West 35th Street, New York, NY 10001

Typeset in Times by Routledge
Printed and bound in Great Britain by
Clays Ltd, St Ives PLC

British Library Cataloguing in Publication Data
A catalogue record for this book is available from the British Library

Library of Congress Cataloguing in Publication Data
The ethnography of moralities / edited by Signe Howell.
p. cm.–
'European Association of Social Anthropologists.'
Includes bibliographical references and index.
1. Ethics–Cross-cultural studies. 2. Values–Cross-cultural studies
I. Howell, Signe. II. European Association of Social Anthropologists.
GN468.7.E83 1997
170–dc20   96–21563
                                                                    CIP

ISBN 0–415–13358–0 (hbk)
ISBN 0–415–13359–9 (pbk)

Contents

Notes on contributors   vii
Preface   ix

Introduction   1
Signe Howell

Part I   Discourses on morality

1 **Exemplars and rules: aspects of the discourse of moralities in Mongolia**   25
Caroline Humphrey

2 **'I lied, I farted, I stole ...': dignity and morality in African discourses on personhood**   48
Anita Jacobson-Widding

3 **The morality of locality: on the absolutism of landownership in an English village**   74
Nigel Rapport

4 **The moralities of Argentinian football**   98
Eduardo P. Archetti

Part II   The gendering of moralities

5 **Double standards**   127
Marilyn Strathern

6 Inside an 'exhausted community': an essay on case-
reconstructive research about peripheral and other
moralities   152
Andre Gingrich

7 The troubles of virtue: values of violence and suffering
in a Mexican context   178
Marit Melhuus

8 Eve: ethics and the feminine principle in the second and
third chapters of Genesis   203
T.M.S. Evens

Index   229

Notes on contributors

Eduardo P. Archetti is Professor of Social Anthropology at the University of Oslo. He has carried out fieldwork in Argentina and Ecuador. His publications include *El mundo social y simbolico del Cuy* (1991) and *Exploring the Written: Anthropology and the Multiplicity of Writing* (ed., 1994).

T.M.S. Evens is Professor of Anthropology at the University of North Carolina, Chapel Hill. His fieldwork areas are Israel and the Sudan. His publications include 'Two concepts of "society as a moral system"' (1989) and 'Rationality, hierarchy, and practice' (1992).

Andre Gingrich is Senior Lecturer in Social Anthropology at the University of Vienna. He has done extensive fieldwork in Syria, Saudi Arabia and the Yemen. His publications include *Beiträge zur Ethnographie der Provinz Sa'ada*, with J. Heiss (1986) and *Studies in Oriental Culture and History* (1993).

Signe Howell is Professor of Social Anthropology at the University of Oslo. She has done fieldwork in Malaysia and Indonesia. Her publications include *Society and Cosmos: Chewong of Peninsular Malaysia* (1984/89) and *For the Sake of our Future: Sacrificing in Eastern Indonesia* (ed., 1996).

Caroline Humphrey is Lecturer in Social Anthropology and Director of the Mongolia and Inner Asia Research Centre at the University of Cambridge. She has done fieldwork in Mongolia, India, the Soviet Union and Nepal. Her publications include *Karl Marx Collective: Economy, Society and Religion in a Soviet*

Collective Farm (1985) and *The Archetypal Actions of Ritual* with J. Laidlaw (1994).

Anita Jacobson-Widding is Professor of Cultural Anthropology at the University of Uppsala. She has carried out fieldwork in the Congo, Nigeria and Zimbabwe. Her major publications include *Red-white-black as a Mode of Thought* (1979) and *Body and Space: Symbolic Models of Unity and Division in African Cosmology and Experience* (ed., 1991).

Marit Melhuus is Senior Lecturer in Social Anthropology at the University of Oslo. She has carried out fieldwork in Argentina, Norway and Mexico. Her publications include 'Gender and the problem of hierarchy' (1990), and *The Power of Latin American Gender Imagery* with K.A. Stølen (ed., 1996).

Nigel Rapport is Professor of Social Anthropology at the University of St Andrews. He has done fieldwork in Israel, Newfoundland and England. Among his publications are *Talking Violence: An Anthropology of Conversation in the City* (1987) and *Diverse World-views in an English Village* (1993).

Marilyn Strathern is Professor of Social Anthropology at the University of Cambridge. She has done fieldwork in Papua New Guinea and in England. Among her major publications are *The Gender of the Gift* (1988) and *After Nature: English Kinship in the Twentieth Century* (1992).

Preface

This book derives from of the plenary session entitled 'The ethnography of moralities' that I convened at the 1994 conference of the European Association of Social Anthropologists. The conference was held in Oslo and the overall title was *Perspectives on Moralities, Knowledge and Power*.

The topic of the conference, and of this particular session, was chosen in order to encourage debate on the empirical study of different moral discourses and discursive practices. The underlying agenda was a desire to find a new starting point for examining familiar anthropological topics, such as social organization, kinship, cosmology, ritual, symbolism, gender, exchange and hierarchy. Despite an initial unease among many of the members of EASA when asked to consider issues connected to moral and ethical principles and values, the conference itself attracted more than 450 participants and more than 200 papers were presented. Clearly, anthropologists found that they had something to say about questions pertaining to morality.

The original four invited speakers, Eduardo P. Archetti, Andre Gingrich, Caroline Humphrey and Anita Jacobson-Widding, have all prepared their manuscripts for publication in this volume. T.M.S. Evens and Marilyn Strathern both presented papers to the plenary session entitled 'Morality and gender'. Their papers were equally apposite to the theme of the ethnography of morality, and I invited them to publish them in this volume. Marit Melhuus, who organized the roundtable discussion entitled 'The nature of anthropological endeavour in situations of heightened public concern', and Nigel Rapport, the convenor of the workshop on 'Questions of consciousness', were asked to write chapters specifically for this book.

I wish to take this opportunity to thank the Social Science Faculty and the Department and Museum of Anthropology at the University of Oslo for their generous financial and administrative support. Without this we would not have been able to host the conference. I further wish to thank the Norwegian Science Research Council, as well as the anthropology departments of the universities of Bergen, Trondheim and Tromsø for their financial support.

Signe Howell
Department and Museum of Anthropology
University of Oslo

Introduction

Signe Howell

A headline from the science section of the *New York Times*, dated 24 May 1944, reads 'Old accident points to brain's moral center'. Briefly, the article concerns a railwayman who, in 1848, was struck by a long metal rod which entered under his left cheek, went behind his left eye and exited through the top of his brain. He survived and remained able to take rational decisions, but he was 'a different man' in the sense that he had become 'unable to make moral judgements'. A philosopher and a cognitive scientist had examined the skull with the aid of 'advanced computer brain-imaging techniques' and stated that it offers

> compelling evidence that the human brain has a specialized region for making personal and social decisions and that this region, located in the frontal lobes at the top of the brain, is connected to deeper brain regions that store emotional memories. When this higher brain region is damaged in a certain way ... a person undergoes a personality change and can no longer make moral decisions.

They are further reported as saying that 'we will need to re-examine our notions about moral character, empathy and the determinants in choosing right over wrong, foolish over sensible'.

This report reflects a long-standing tradition within Western academic discourse to make claims concerning human nature from within some kind of natural science mode. It is yet another example of a desire to anchor human capabilities firmly within biology. The information is indeed intriguing, but how can we as anthropologists use it? Should we deconstruct the scientists' claims along familiar definitional and theoretical grounds, or should we gratefully embrace their findings as one further step in the search for cognitive hard wiring? While few anthropologists would accept such a positivistic approach to the sensitive and complex questions concerning human cognition, reasoning, emotionality or morality, the example does, nevertheless, raise issues concerning human universals and primordial characters. It also raises issues concerning to what extent one may delineate something called 'morality' from within the whole gamut of human endeavour, thought and values, and whether there can be an anthropology of morality.

Although this book does not attempt to answer all these questions, the authors address theoretical and methodological problems involved in the study of indigenous moralities. They try to delineate arenas suitable for empirical investigations which can yield pertinent material for the understanding of moral orders. They debate various approaches towards interpretations of their own ethnographic material. No attempts at grand theorizing are provided in this book. However, important questions are posed that go to the heart of the anthropological ambition of eliciting not only alternative realities, but the implicit and explicit premises that make such realities meaningful and desirable for those who live them. For these reasons alone, I maintain that this volume represents an important first step in an empirical and comparative study of moral discourses and discursive practices.

MORALITY: AN 'ODD-JOB' WORD?

The overall focus of this book is methodological. While no general definition will be put forward, questions will be posed as to what we might mean by morality or moral discourse; how we as anthropologists may set about studying such phenomena; and how our studies may enhance our understanding of some significant indigenous concepts, pertaining, for example, to human nature (both male and female), to cosmology and to the nature of right and wrong (to say nothing of good and bad). An overriding concern is how such knowledge might provide a potential for fresh approaches in the interpretation of social institutions and practices more generally.

From an anthropological point of view, there are few useful definitions of morals, morality or ethics. A pioneering work entitled *Anthropology and Ethics* appeared in 1959. It was written by May and Abraham Edel, she the anthropologist, he the moral philosopher. It had little impact in anthropological circles, although, once it was brought to the attention of the contributors to this volume, several of them have in fact made use of it. Edel and Edel start by stating, 'Of course in one sense we all know what we are talking about when we talk about morality', but, they continue, 'By what mark shall we know "the moral"?' (Edel and Edel 1959: 7). While not making a distinction between morals and ethics, their suggestion is that we distinguish between 'ethics wide' and 'ethics narrow'. Briefly, ethics wide assumes that moralities are part and parcel of the whole field of human endeavour and striving. It implies a widest possible empirical investigation and assumes that accounts of virtues, obligations, sanctions, feelings and so forth will in the long run reveal human values and modes of achieving them. Ethics narrow, on the other hand, limits the scope. Conceptually, it pushes to the fore the idea of *obligation* or *duty*. Values, they insist, are 'far too broad, far too promiscuous'. According to ethics narrow, only those notions that *ought to be* or *ought to be realized* come within the scope of morality (ibid.: 8–11, my emphasis). Perhaps today we would regard the former as too wide and the latter as too narrow.

More recently, there have been a few anthropological attempts at tackling the issue of definition and delimitation. In his introduction to the edited volume *The Anthropology of Evil*, Parkin considers the possibility for an anthropological study of morality. While not actually offering a definition of morality, he debates possible ramifications of such a concept and asks whether the study of evil would not be better if carried out as the study of morality (Parkin 1985: 3). He concludes, however, that until anthropologists can reach some kind of consensus as to what would be involved in such studies, 'the approach to the study of evil is ... signposted more directly than simply to morality' (ibid.: 6).

Edel and Edel's definition of ethics wide is similar to the more familiar anthropological concept of culture. It is also open to similar criticisms: namely those of reification, of discrete bounded static universes of shared customary practices and beliefs, of totalizing conformity, of implicit agency. (cf. Borofsky 1994). Whether or not we agree with the anthropological hard-line anti-culture lobby, is it legitimate to ask whether, by introducing 'moralities', we are doing nothing more than taking the pressure off culture; and whether moralities might not equally be subjected to the same analytical and theoretical attacks to which culture has been subjected? Perhaps; but since I would argue that human beings are inherently cultural (as well as social and moral), and that the job of anthropologists is to study the many different cultural processes and forms that exist, to drop culture from our vocabulary just because some have used it unwisely, would be to throw the baby out with the bath-water. The same argument applies to morality. The use of the term 'moralities' in the unusual plural form is a deliberate choice: first, because it opens for plurality – a prerequisite for anthropological comparison; second, whether in the singular or the plural form, it is a more inclusive term than 'morals'. Moralities can be made to contain and express both discourse and practice. Just as emotions act on the self and on the world (cf. Archetti this volume), the argument is that morality constitutes the self and makes for action in the world.

The challenge for anthropologists lies precisely in discerning the link between values which are derived from a larger metaphysical whole and actual behaviour and practices. The relationship between moral values and practice is a dynamic one. Values are continuously changing and adapting through actual choices and practices, while, at the same time, they continue to inform and shape choices and practices.

The contributors were asked to anchor their discussion firmly within their own particular ethnographic area and consider the dynamic interaction between abstract ideals and empirical realities. They were further asked to consider problems in connection with the *doing* of fieldwork which seeks to elicit indigenous morality, and about the subsequent *writing* of anthropological texts in which the ethnographic material is analysed. My aim through such an approach has been to raise some general points concerning definitions and methodology. In particular, I feel that we need to deliberate where and how to direct our ethnographic gaze when seeking to discover and interpret the moralities, the moral discourse and practices, of a particular social group. We need to consider what might be used as data for eliciting underlying moral assumptions and premises as well as explicit moral values.

The methodological challenge may, in part, be met by addressing some of the following questions: How is ethical knowledge grounded? What constitutes an ethical breach and what can breaches, or active dissent, tell us about reigning orthodoxies? What is the force of 'the ought', and how are the various morally prescriptive discourses formulated and legitimated? Who defines and enforces what is right and wrong? Which social domains most profoundly articulate moral values and which are most (or least) affected by such? These, and related questions, are variously deliberated by the authors of this volume. They seek meaningful answers by isolating selected socio-cultural arenas which throw some important constituting moral values into sharp relief. Each, then, has identified arenas which they consider highlight local morality. These include the moral significance of: the use of exemplars; of sexuality; of cross- and same-sex relations; of gossip; of guilt, honour and shame; of showing respect; and of passages from scriptural texts.

How we deal with the existence of apparently different moralities being operative according to context, or to the social personhood of the actors, within any one indigenously defined social group, becomes an important issue. Should we treat such multiplicities of meaning as pieces in a complex puzzle which may add up to some overall moral order, or should we be satisfied to explicate upon the apparent paradoxes? There can be no final answers, but I regard it as important to identify as many arenas as possible which may serve as 'pegs' for analysis for future anthropological studies of moralities.

Some of the complexity may best be expressed in terms of two different levels. First, there is the challenge of discerning conflicting premises and values within any one moral community, such as those pertaining to men and women, to nobles and commoners. Second, conflicts of premises and values may emerge at the meeting of different moral orders, such as, for example, between a modern Western one based on principles of democracy and human rights and Hinduism based on a hierarchical caste system.

However one chooses to approach the empirical study of moralities, it is a domain where extreme definitional caution must be exercised, and where it is prudent to think polythetically (Needham 1975). Having brought a previously unexplored concept into anthropology, it would be a great mistake if we immediately hypostesize it.

The fact that few anthropologists have attempted the empirical study of different moral discourses does not mean that such studies should not, or could not, be undertaken. Nor should the fact that it is difficult to pin down exactly what indigenous morality might mean, prevent us from trying to glean moral principles and values in our fieldwork. Such arguments are not sufficient justification for abandoning the theoretical and ethnographic quest to approach morality as a field of cultural predispositions informing and creating, rather than supporting social relations between groups and persons (cf. Parkin 1985: 4). Indeed, it is the underlying premise of this volume that not only are such studies possible, they are potentially very fruitful, opening new paths for interpretation. Rather than leaving indigenous moral precepts and values unexplored, it is suggested that a head-on confrontation with them might reveal previously unperceived depths about why people act the way they do. At the very least, in this book, we have begun to identify some methods to approach the empirical study of morality, and to discuss the ramifications of various possible approaches.

INDIGENOUS MORALITIES AND SOCIAL ANTHROPOLOGY

It might be argued that anthropologists have, ultimately, always been studying the variety of social constructions of morality with a more or less explicit aim of eliciting premises for comparative ethics. Yet the topic of morality as such has hardly ever been directly addressed. Many earlier studies of indigenous religious concepts might also be characterized as studies of indigenous moralities. For example, Evans-Pritchard's and Lienhardt's studies of, respectively, Nuer (1956) and Dinka (1961) religious concepts and practices, Leenhardt's study *Do Kamo* (1979) about personhood among the Kanaq of New Caledonia, and the work by Griaule (e.g. 1965) and Dieterlin (e.g. 1973) on the Dogon cosmology would qualify. However, these authors never presented their work in terms of the exploration of indigenous moralities. Similarly, the extensive debates about the interpretation of Mediterranean concepts of honour and shame (starting with the classical studies in Peristiany 1966) were carried out without any attempt to locate these concepts within a wider moral schema. As Melhuus, Gingrich and Jacobson-Widding show (this volume), honour and shame can fruitfully be examined as expressions of profound moral values.

Within the anthropology of law it is possible to discern implicit references to moral codes, or moral orders, but, again, the issues are not framed in such terms. In *Crime and Custom in Savage Society* (1926), Malinowski posed questions about why people behave as they should. He asks whether they are constrained by fear of punishment, or whether the answer lies elsewhere, in 'the nature of bonding forces' (ibid.: 15). Gluckman and the Manchester School, in their work on judicial systems, focused on principles of social control, less on underlying moral values. Moral codes were treated as expressing sanction and as maintaining and reinforcing the *status quo*, not as shaping epistemological and judicial concerns, nor as constituting a universe of meaning.

One major exception to the above approaches is Read's 'Morality and the concept of the person among the Gahuku-Gama', first published in 1955. Read begins by stating that it is primarily an essay in comparative ethics; in this case a comparison between ethical categories of Western European philosophical traditions and those of the Gahuku-Gama of the New Guinea Highlands. While his argument in this respect may be faulted today, primarily because he is not comparing like with like, his general plea for focusing upon indigenous notions of personhood as a way to learn about non-literate people's moralities is to the point – as is his exposition of Gahuku-Gama's conceptions of body, 'soul' and other qualities of personhood which leads him to suggest that therein lies the springboard for their ethical understandings. Today, most would agree that a scholarly pursuit of the moral system of any one social group must in some way take account of indigenous perceptions about the human being; about personhood, agency and sociality.

A project that occupied Durkheim during his last years was to develop a sociology of ethics. Although he never published a major work on the topic, he did write several articles, some of which were recently reissued (Durkheim 1992). In many ways unsatisfactory, not least because of their sometimes moralizing stance, the essays, nevertheless, show us Durkheim both as the analytical and methodological sociologist, and Durkheim as the socially engaged citizen seeking solutions to what he regarded as the rising utilitarianism of modern society (cf. Turner 1992). (See also the discussion below on embodied concepts.) Certainly, the essays on 'Civic morals' and 'Professional ethics' (ibid.) can still be read with profit by anthropologists. His discussion about the delineation of a moral domain, about the relationship between individual and collective responsibility and justice, and about contextualized morality, succinctly debates the implications of various possible theoretical positions. Parkin expresses a common, but perhaps unfair, reaction to Durkheim when he states that 'Durkheim so conflated the moral with the social that ethnographers could not isolate for analysis those contemplative moments of moral reflexivity that, rather than strict and unambiguous rules, so typify human activity and predicaments' (Parkin 1985: 4–5). Lukes suggests that towards the end of his life, Durkheim began to shift his investigations from 'the obligatory to the "desirability" aspect of morality, and from the rules people follow to the moral beliefs expressed by the rules' (Lukes 1975: 419). This reading of Durkheim (see also Archetti this volume) opens for fruitful contemporary anthropological investigations.

While anthropologists have, by and large, ignored the theoretical challenges of the empirical study of moralities, moral philosophy has a long intellectual tradition. Philosophers, however, do not concern themselves with locating the moral subject within social and cultural worlds. As a result, anthropologists tend not to draw upon philosophical writings. Three levels of moral philosophy are commonly identified: first, that of meta-ethics, whereby general questions are asked about what might be moral principles or moral beliefs, what kind of sense is a moral sense, etc.; second, that of moral theory, which is concerned with how to explain principles used to solve concrete problems of applied ethics. The third level concerns issues of applied ethics whereby arguments about concrete moral dilemmas, such as euthanasia or capital punishment, are tested with a view to reach defensible positions (Thompson and Harman 1996). Anthropologists could have something to contribute to debates on all these three levels. They can widen the scope of enquiry from one searching for a single truth, to one questioning the basis of the very propositions in each instance by demonstrating alternative, but viable, rationalities, approaches and solutions.

David Pocock, paying tribute to the book by Edel and Edel, cites their explanation for the anthropological lack of interest in moral issues, namely their overarching preoccupation with 'describing empirical facts and [with] causal investigation to the neglect of the analysis of concepts' (Pocock 1986: 3). However, as my comments above suggest, an interest in indigenous concepts does not necessarily lead to an interest in moral issues. Interestingly, as the work of Dumont demonstrates (e.g.1986), a theoretical concern with value in anthropology doe not lead to a concern with moral issues either. Dumont appears to link morality as an intellectual reality only to the Western philosophical tradition in which the bounded individual is the focal analytic entity. In this tradition, he argues, an inevitable separation between fact and value, between is and ought stands central. However, I would argue that outside the logic of academic philosophy, such separations are not made, and that facts and values are inevitably entangled. Moral principles, I suggest, express simultaneously an inherent dynamic relationship between the 'ought' and the 'is.' If this is so, then they are worthy of special attention in the study of social and cultural life.

THE HIDDEN TRAPS OF EMBODIED CONCEPTS AND VALUES

> The trouble with you people [he meant the West] is that you see everything through sex and politics. These are your imperatives. And, incidentally, this makes it almost impossible for you to understand the past when people had quite different priorities.
>
> (Lessing 1995: 188)

An African historian once said the above to Doris Lessing. The criticism may equally be directed to our (i.e. Western intellectuals') failure to understand the priorities of our contemporaries who live in different social worlds from ours and who orient themselves according to different moral priorities. It is an anthropological truism to say that we study social and cultural life in terms of indigenous ideas and practices. The continuous reflexive probing of our own ideas, values and practices is heralded as an integral part of the process of interpreting alien forms of human life. Despite this, certain domains have gained an unquestioned centrality in the analysis of social life. The African historian was probably right in identifying sex and politics to be among them. (See also p. 18 below.) As a result, it is notoriously difficult to shed our Western a priori assumptions where these matters are concerned; they represent perhaps a prime example of entangled fact and value within the 'modern' world.

Although of a somewhat different order, I would like to add morality to the list of relatively unexamined Western social domains. We appear unable to stand completely outside our core moral values, values so naturalized, so intellectually and emotionally embodied that they are integral parts of our sense of self. Our sense of morality is, after all, what constitutes our sociality, the very basis for relating. Humans are, I suggested at the outset, inherently moral. But unless we exercise rigorous checks on our own moral imaginations (Johnson 1993), we easily fall victim to socio-centric evaluations of situations involving people whose moral worlds and moral imaginations draw on different sources (see also Howell

1995). Anthropologists are well aware that the *Declaration of Human Rights* is of little relevance to the majority of the world's population, and that it represents a clear expression of socio-centric assumptions (cf. American Anthropological Association 1947). Nevertheless, that humans everywhere are cognitively and emotionally predisposed towards moral sensibility is the underlying argument of this book. This, of course, is just a starting point; it can tell us nothing about the content of any moral sensibility.

I do not wish to revive the old debate about moral relativism. I only wish to argue that the long-standing deep concern about the *possibility* of moral relativism is a peculiarly Western (moral) dilemma. I suggest that debates in European moral philosophy since the eighteenth century, whether about moral principles or about applied ethics, have predisposed anthropologists and others to worry about the basis for taking moral stands (cf. Thompson and Harman 1996, Taylor 1992). In our fieldwork it is at times difficult to avoid taking a moral stand. Our deeply felt sense of right and wrong is put severely to the test when we observe socially sanctioned physical violence, or manifestations of exploitative relationships between unequal social persons, such as between parents and children, husbands and wives, rich and poor, masters and servants, nobles and commoners, etc. Anthropologists can easily find themselves in situations where their disinterested role is severely challenged. This, in turn, may result in a reluctance towards conducting a disinterested analysis of the moral system in question on a par with an analysis of the kinship system, exchange relations or any of the more traditional anthropological themes. However, in my view, this ought to act as a spur to investigation, reflexivity and interpretation, not as a damper.

SOME EMERGENT GENERAL ISSUES

The anthropologists in this volume represent a wide geographical spectrum, having done fieldwork in Mongolia, East Africa, Argentina, Mexico, England, Papua New Guinea and the Middle East. In contrast to these traditional ethnographic studies is the chapter by the last contributor who bases his discussion not on fieldwork, but on the Old Testament.

There clearly are difficulties in deciding what constitutes 'data' in the quest to bring to light the principles of a particular moral order. Where to look for relevant material? What may count as relevant material? What sorts of questions to ask? Who to ask? What kind of legitimacy to place on different people's answers? These are just some of the questions that immediately arise. I asked the anthropologists writing here to pay particular attention to these and to other questions of methodology. None of them had explicitly taken morality as a topic for investigation during their fieldwork, although all them have been concerned with the study of indigenous concepts and values.

One insight derived from this collection of papers is that it is possible for two or more moral discourses to exist within any one society, each predicated upon a specific kind of sociality. In Chapters 4, 5, 6 and 7 this is explicit, in others more implicit. By contrast, Jacobson-Widding (Chapter 2) found that, despite initial impressions to the contrary, the same moral code can be found to underpin social relations of different orders. What is clear, however, is that within any one society two or more moral discursive practices may coexist and be made operational according to context. Of course, this does not mean that people themselves perceive the situation in terms of contested meanings.

I turn now to a consideration of the eight chapters and start by seeking to isolate each individual anthropologist's approach and contribution to the empirical study of moralities. The eight authors vary widely in how they choose to interpret 'morality', where they focus their interpretative gaze, and how they set about building up an argument about the morality (the moral order, values and practices) in their particular given socio-cultural setting. I will give a brief summary of each, before proceeding to a discussion of some themes that may be identified across the chapters. It is important to bear in mind that, not only are we presented with material from eight different societies, we are also invited to interact with eight (nine if I include myself) different anthropologists, each of whom is a product of his or her relationship to one or more 'interpretative communities' (Howell 1994), and has a particular vision of the discipline and the kinds of question that are important. This fact is, I suggest, particularly relevant in the present case because, as discussed above, moral issues and moral values are embodied knowledge which make us act in the world in ways that render the separation of fact and value – subject and object – especially difficult. For these reasons also, I asked the contributors to self-consciously debate questions of definitions and what might constitute suitable empirical material.

Defining and locating moralities

All the authors seek to delineate the field for investigation; to identify some manageable domain(s) of socio-cultural life that can give some clues to moral imperatives.

From his study of a rural community in the north of England, Nigel Rapport suggests that morality here is manifested 'in terms of a sense of righteous indignation'. He is interested in the discourses employed by the locals in moralizing about outsiders to the village. His chosen *entrée* is gossip – speech acts uttered in a self-righteous form by local inhabitants.

Eduardo Archetti maintains that since the field of morality covers such a vast arena of actions and evaluations, it is impossible to deal with all of these. Rather, we need to direct our concern to particular concrete activities. In his paper, therefore, he focuses on male Argentinian attitudes to the national sport of football which, he argues, may be considered as a kind of microcosm for moral values. His 'pegs' for analysis are male virtues, the importance of local traditions for understanding the present, the significance of different styles of playing football and ideas of happiness. His data are a mixture of historical material from newspapers and studies about the history of football, juxtaposed with informants' comments and reactions to events.

Caroline Humphrey points out that there is no single term in the Mongolian language that corresponds, however loosely, to the European concept of morality. Choosing to interpret the meaning of morality as 'the evaluation of conduct in relation to esteemed or despised human qualities', she finds that the most appropriate way to elicit these in the Mongolian context is to examine the range of exemplars to good behaviour that individuals choose for themselves. The most common type of exemplars are sayings of famous personages – either historical, legendary or contemporary. She thus distinguishes between commonly accepted 'rules of order, reason and custom' (*yos*) and the much more personal 'things that are taught' (*surtakhuun*) which she treats as exemplars.

In her work with the Shona of Zimbabwe, Anita Jacobson-Widding also fails to find local words that she can satisfactorily translate into 'moral' or 'morality'. The word *tsika* that her informants gave when asked, means 'to show respect'. At first she refused to equate this with morality, but later she came to accept a semantic equivalence. She employs a method of using 'cultural scripts'. This involves identifying simple sentences that both capture indigenous norms and universal concerns, and which lay bare the clear dominant social values of a group. She further seeks out 'muted structures' of values that 'lurk behind the façade of "dominant structure" of social personhood and morality'. She suggests that in her own ethnographic case, relevant cultural scripts would need to focus upon guilt, shame and dignity. She finds, to her surprise, that there is a correspondence between the two analytical levels of muted and dominant structures. In other words, we do not find parallel moral discourses operating dependent upon context or category of actors. Rather, the Shona cultural script of hierarchical relationships between different social personages is mirrored throughout society.

Marilyn Strathern takes her cue from the feminist critic Carol Smart who argues that the law's claims (in Euro-American legal traditions) to operate according to objective and neutral criteria do not reflect reality, since men's and women's interests are differentially protected in it. Drawing on her material from the Hagen people of New Guinea, Strathern examines moral reasoning from a gender perspective and asks whether double standards may be discerned here also. She uses several case studies which concern the killing of close kin to elicit what moral considerations may be discerned from people's manipulation of, and reactions to, such events.

Marit Melhuus also examines the operation of relative gender values as the main means to understand the moral universe of meaning among Catholic rural Mexican mestizos. She suggests that one may not separate morality from gender. She draws on some case studies from her own field material as well as on story lines of Mexican films in order to bring out some dominant moral themes and evaluations, and focuses upon local notions of honour and shame as these are expressed in relation to sexual behaviour.

Terry Evens seeks to connect our contemporary Western moral thinking firmly to its roots, namely the Bible and, more precisely, the chapters that deal with the Fall in the Book of Genesis. His interpretation also draws heavily on various exegetical texts. He makes clear that he approaches biblical criticism as a social anthropologist, not as a biblical scholar. He is concerned with eliciting explicit and implicit meanings. He treats the analysis of Genesis on a par with any other anthropological analysis of myth, projecting the 'logic' of a particular socio-cultural tradition.

Andre Gingrich, who worked with an Arab Muslim community in the Yemen, draws on scriptural texts, as well as on local notions of *haram*. He states that collective moralities which are the forms by which communities 'establish normative ordering for individual behaviour ... cannot be studied independently of legal orders and social practice'. In addition, he argues that the religious moral tenets must be incorporated in any empirical study of morality. His overall theoretical frame is that of an 'exhausted community'. Through this interpretative category, he seeks to explain what can only be described as a moral collapse within Islamic communities, when *haram* ideals of respecting women are breaking down in the attack on women and children of other Islamic communities.

Moral reasoning

One question that arises in the study of moralities is whether moral codes and values must necessarily involve individual self-awareness in some form or another, and whether moral reasoning is performed by every individual regardless of socio-cultural conditions and ideological constructs. Ultimately, we are dealing with moral reasoning, judgements and moral dilemmas. The moral philosopher Mary Midgley makes a helpful suggestion, namely that we shift away from 'the content and object of morality to the way of reasoning'. To ask what kind of reasoning a person (or a group of people) conducts in order to justify a particular decision in a situation of a moral dilemma can be, she says, a useful way to elicit moral values (Pocock 1986: 9–12). It is hard to believe that something recognizably like moral dilemmas are not found everywhere. Some might maintain that moral dilemmas experienced in more holistic societies might be more predictable than those of the industrial modern West (cf. ibid.: 11). It would, however, be wrong to conclude that they are any less difficult to handle. This is where Midgley's proposed focus on the processes of reasoning might come in useful. According to Pocock, by shifting the focus from moral content to moral thinking, or reasoning, Midgley opens the path for anthropological, i.e. comparative, studies of moral systems. The argument is that it is not a question of whether the Homeric Greeks (or the Nuer, the Hagen or whoever) had moral standards or not; loosely speaking they clearly had. Whether they had '*alternatives* to their own evaluations, rather than the quality of their evaluations' has led commentators to hesitate to call them moral (ibid.: 12, original emphasis). I suggest that insisting on this criterion may help us to identify the nub of 'Western' dilemmas in studying other moralities. We do operate with some prerequisites for what may be accepted as a moral system, and central to these are demands for alternatives, for moral reasoning and for choice. Much of the difference between Western intellectuals and the highlanders of New Guinea may, I suggest, be found precisely in posited alternatives and, hence, the degree of reflexivity involved in the reasoning.

If self-conscious reasoning is ubiquitous, then how do people regard responsibility for immoral acts? Several of the contributors address this question. Strathern, taking her material from the Hagen area of Papua New Guinea, makes explicit her own Euro-American position that takes it for granted that the moral person acts knowingly, and that this necessitates a conscious positing *vis-à-vis* possible different courses for action. However, she maintains that the ethnography from the Highlands demonstrates that there also 'people sift through different types of information in a knowing way'. She suggests that some morally deviant behaviour, such as killing kin, is explained locally by the actor having been rendered 'unknowing' and hence 'amoral' through the application of poison. This results in a special kind of madness which accounts for the deviant moral behaviour. There is linguistic support for such an interpretation. This madness is called *wulya*, and the sorcery substance applied is *wulya wulya*. A mad person does not reason according to the same moral norms as does a normal person – which would also be a Western argument. Thus, through focusing on Hagen perceptions about the person, Strathern addresses questions about moral reasoning and responsibility, and highlights contextual differences in these with regard to same-sex and cross-sex relations (see also below).

Emotionality may play a part in moral reasoning. Archetti shows how Argentinian male football players and fans are torn between the desire to win and the desire to create beautiful football. According to local aesthetic values, the players have to play brutishly in order to win against foreign teams. But it is only elegant playing that produces a feeling of happiness. Archetti makes an interesting distinction between 'feeling happy' and 'being happy'. The former is transient, but strong, and is provoked by good football. Concomitantly, to lose to a foreign team produces a feeling of despair. Archetti shows how football is intrinsically part of male Argentinians' sense of personal and national identity, and how football also orchestrates feelings of honour and shame. The failure of the national team to win in the 1958 World Cup after many years' refusal to participate, produced a moral crisis among football players and fans. Informants told him that 'for many years [afterwards] we could not distinguish right from wrong'. Brutish football gets the goals, but does not produce happiness. The choice involved in choosing the style of playing takes on moral dimensions for fans and players alike. To play in order to win would, according to Argentinian supporters of the old values, mean a betrayal of deeply felt values about themselves, each other, and the social and moral world in which they live.

The moral person

With a recent shift in interest towards indigenous notions of self and personhood, questions pertaining to the moral grounding of ideas and values concerning what it means to be a human being are highly pertinent (Heelas and Lock 1981, Carrithers *et al.* 1985). Several of the authors address such questions in seeking a 'peg' on which to hang their analysis. Some collectively held views on human nature are present in every known socio-cultural group. A useful distinction may be made between qualities perceived as inherently part of different categories of social persons – such as men, women, chiefs, Brahmins, slaves – and those that are perceived as attainable (in both positive and negative directions) and, as such, potentially subject to training and socialization. From such a starting point one may explore questions concerning, *inter alia*: responsibility and rights; laws, rules, and sanctions; crime and punishment; right and wrong; good and evil; sin and forgiveness or redemption; notions of causality; intentionality; possibility for choice; notions of conscience.

Evens interprets Genesis as an endeavour of 'self-construction'. The ultimate existential question of 'who am I' is, he suggests, a practical question, the answer to which Jewish and Christian individuals can find in this text. Genesis informs its readers that they, as humans, are 'those creatures who are especially given to giving themselves their own identity'. If this interpretation is correct, it certainly helps to explain the old and persistent value placed on individualism in these religions, culminating in the democratic ideal and the notion of universal human rights.

Jacobson-Widding centres her essay around a proposition that the concept of morality is a Western one and depends upon an individualistic, egalitarian conception of personhood. She questions whether obeying norms for good behaviour 'in so far as this behaviour affects the well-being of any other person than the actor him- or herself' must necessarily imply notions of bounded and equal individuals. If so, how then can one approach the study of moralities in those places, as in much of Africa, where hierarchical categories of social persons are the norm, where ideas about unique and bounded individuals are not meaningful? The Shona social person, like the Hagen one, is a function of the relative position that he or she occupies in any one social context. However, having elaborated Shona notions of social, not personal, personhood and associated values, she finally accepts that showing respect in the way that Shona themselves understand this behaviour, may indeed coincide with the way that people orient themselves morally in the world. Failure to behave accordingly provokes feelings of shame rather than guilt.

The Mongolians, like the peoples of Zimbabwe, also operate with different, and hierarchically placed, categories of social persons each associated with different behavioural (moral) expectations, but to different effect. Humphrey makes an interesting distinction between Mongolian basic premises and Western ones. She suggests that in Western philosophy a basic premise has been that 'at the very least a sympathy for others has been considered ... as a *sine qua non* for entering in the world of morality'. This contrasts sharply with Mongolian precepts where 'the core of morality is essentially referred to the self, adjudicating one's own actions as good and bad *for oneself*' (original emphasis). Thus, the very quality of personhood and responsibility differs radically between the two cultural traditions. Altruism (so heralded in the West) is, she suggests, 'weakly internalized' among the Mongols.

Rapport's analysis of how individual discourses form different subject positions highlights some common features about constructing and expressing identities. He is primarily interested in the construction of the 'outsider' in different contexts. He points out, however, that each such construction simultaneously constructs the self in its role as 'insider'. Identities, he says, 'are intrinsically comparative ... implicitly admitting their own negativity'. Employing Boon's ideal types of tribal and scribal 'nay-saying', Rapport discerns a tension in the English village that he studied, between what, he suggests, may be a changeover from a 'scribal' tendency of mutual exclusions to a 'tribal' one of complementary opposites; from clear-cut notions of good and bad, right and wrong, to demands of relativism which is following in the wake of regional, national and international intrusions into the local.

Sex and morality

Debates about right or wrong behaviour inevitably involve morality. Certain kinds of behaviour are, in the West, singled out for moral debates more often than others. These include sexual behaviour. Foucault makes this point when he asks in the introduction to Volume Two of *The History of Sexuality*,

> why is sexual conduct, why are the activities and pleasures that attach to it, an object of moral solicitude? Why this ethical concern – which, at certain times, in certain societies and groups, appears more important than the moral attention that is focused on other, likewise essential, areas of individual or collective life, such as alimentary behaviour or the fulfilment of civic duties?
>
> (Foucault 1986: 10)

Foucault rightly, in my view, seeks the answer in the history of thought, not in circular arguments about rules and regulations. The method he pursues is to pose the question 'how, why, and in what forms was sexuality constituted as a moral domain?' (ibid.). Sexuality then becomes part of a wider field of gender, one that focuses directly upon sexual behaviour and its constituting values.

However, as every anthropologist knows, not all moralities are particularly concerned with sexual conduct. The papers in this collection that explicitly take up sexuality as one *entrée* into the study of indigenous morality are based on societies anchored within Christian or Islamic traditions. Melhuus, in her study of a Catholic mestizo peasant community in Mexico, shows how women as sexual beings can, through their behaviour, shame or honour the significant men in their lives: husbands, fathers and brothers. Through an ideology of *machismo*, men's own honour as men is vulnerable to the conduct of their women. Male identity is constructed along a scale of more or less male, the criteria for which are dependent upon a paradox. By seducing other men's women they enhance their masculinity, while they lose their honour when other men seduce their own women. Within this harsh value system, women represent a moral barometer for men while, at the same time, their own femaleness becomes classified as either good or bad. Thus good women are both asexual and mothers. Bad women are characterized by dint of sexual activities. Melhuus shows how these conflicting ideals are reflected through different levels of Mexican society, from the pious pilgrim at the site of the Virgin of Guadelupe, to the man who violently confronts another who has made his sister into a bad woman. These images are reiterated in popular films and serious literature. Honour and shame, good and bad, married and unmarried, sexual and asexual, male and female, virginity and promiscuity, Church and home are all lived concepts that create the overall moral discourse for rural Mexicans. This discourse is articulated through images derived from values about sexual conduct.

Evens relies on written texts alone to debate similar issues. His purpose is to elicit the foundations for Christian moral values about sexuality, and he returns for this to Eve's part in the Fall. Eve, as the representative of biblical female principles, may, he argues, be regarded as the ultimate temptress; but as part of Adam, she is 'no more than Adam's temptation of himself, the seduction of his spiritual by his carnal nature'. Echoes of this interpretation can be found in the Mexican situation described by Melhuus. This becomes striking when we consider that Evens suggests that, despite all appearances to the contrary, a primacy of the female principle may be discerned in Genesis. Again, we are faced with a paradox: spirituality versus materiality in which the explicit moral storyline emphasizes the former at the expense of the latter. However, while the conjugal relationship opposes Adam to 'God, his maker, the fundamental association of marriage and creativity makes it "next to godliness"'. Genesis may thus serve as an exemplar (cf. Humphrey this volume) for the Catholic Church's teaching about sexuality and marriage.

By contrast, such moral central concern with sexuality is not part of the Hagen situation. Strathern, however, stresses that gender values and differences still may be regarded as constituting a significant moral force. She suggests that in the New Guinea Highlands, people evaluate possible courses of action open to them, but that their room for manoeuvring and for acting is 'crucially affected whether they find themselves acting with *others of their sex or with those of opposite sex*'(my emphasis). She further makes a distinction between mediated and unmediated relations and, although Strathern is concerned to analyse the Hagen situation, the following point is, I suggest, pertinent more widely: 'Women did not have the same access to such objects of mediation [as men], as they also lack oratorical skills or unambiguous claims to support. But they *had relationships at their disposal*.'

If we now look at the example from northern Yemen as discussed by Gingrich, we find that he provides an interesting complement to Evens' and Melhuus's papers. Gingrich also draws on authoritative religious texts, in this case Islamic ones, but he supplements these with observations from fieldwork in a Muslim community in the Yemen. Indeed, he argues forcibly that to analyse local concepts of moral concepts, such as *haram* ('forbidden', 'sacrosanct' – a term applied most frequently to the segregation and seclusion of women and children from public life) in isolation from their scriptural traditions is 'to cut one segment of a moral, legal, and political system from its other elements'. Gingrich shows how the dominant Islamic ideology of male honour is intimately linked to the way that their significant women behave. This is not unlike much of what Melhuus describes for rural Mexico. According to Gingrich, 'The moral location of women and children as a protected appendage to men's honour certainly represents one powerful and effective local concept.' However, he is not satisfied just to explore the semantics of this social fact, but wishes to take it one step further and elucidate how women themselves, in their segregated interactions, refer to the concept of *haram*. He argues that the female-centred idea of 'modesty' may be interpreted as serving as a second, parallel concept for women's behaviour. On the other hand, he reports that in some tribal periphery of the Arab-speaking Muslim world 'women often have the right to, and the burden of, an honour of their own'. In sharp contrast to other Muslim areas, here women who defend themselves are 'good and honourable'.

CONCLUDING REMARKS

In this text I have been pursuing paths that have led in many different directions. The aim, however, has been to start to clear the ground for some novel approaches to old problems experienced and debated in social anthropology. The aim has not been to provide clear answers as to how that ground be defined or operationalized, nor to define an anthropology of moralities . At the outset, I made a long list of possible questions that could be posed in the pursuit of eliciting indigenous moral discourses and discursive practices. Some of these have been addressed in this book. Many remain for future studies to engage with. From their very varied positions, the authors of these papers have raised a range of theoretical and methodological problems and issues. Common to them all, however, is a willingness to grapple with the same central topic and to present their ethnographic material from an angle that they would otherwise not have chosen. For this reason alone, I feel that the exercise has been worthwhile. The range and quality of the papers in this volume do, I believe, bear witness to the rich potentiality inherent in a focus on morality.

Anthropology can indeed contribute to the understanding of indigenous moral discourses and discursive practices and, on the bases of such understandings, to comparative ethics.

REFERENCES

American Anthropological Association (1947) 'Statement on human rights', *American Anthropologist* (n.s.) 49 (4): 539– 543.

Borofsky, R. (ed.) (1994) *Assessing Cultural Anthropology*, New York: McGraw-Hill.

Carrithers, M., Collins, S. and Lukes, S. (eds) (1985) *The Category of the Person: Anthropology, Philosophy, History*, Cambridge: Cambridge University Press.

Dieterlin, G. (1973) *La notion de la personne en Afrique noire*, Paris: Centre National de la Recherche Scientifique.

Dumont, L. (1986) *Essays on Individualism: Modern Ideology in Anthropological Perspective*, Chicago: University of Chicago Press.

Durkheim, E. (1992) *Professional Ethics and Civic Morals*, London: Routledge.

Edel, M. and Edel, A. (1959) *Anthropology and Ethics*, Springfield, Ill.: Charles C. Thomas.

Evans-Pritchard, E.E. (1956) *Nuer Religion*, Oxford: Clarendon Press.

Foucault, M. (1986) *The History of Sexuality, Volume Two: The Use of Pleasure*, New York: Vintage Books.

Griaule, M. (1965) *Conversations with Gotemméli: An Introduction to Dogon Religious Ideas*, London: Oxford University Press.

Heelas, P. and Lock, A. (eds) (1981) *Indigenous Psychologies: The Anthropology of the Self*, London: Academic Press.

Howell, S. (1994) 'Reading culture: or how anthropological texts create fieldwork expectations and shape future texts', in E. P. Archetti (ed.) *Exploring the Written: Anthropology and the Multiplicity of Writing*, Oslo: Scandinavian University Press.

——(1995) 'Whose knowledge and whose power? A new perspective on cultural diffusion', in R. Fardon (ed.) *Counterworks: Managing the Diversity of Knowledge*, London: Routledge.

Johnson, M. (1993) *Moral Imagination: Implications of Cognitive Science for Ethics*, Chicago: University of Chicago Press.

Leenhardt, M. (1979) *Do Kamo: Person and Myth in the Melanesian World*, Chicago: University of Chicago Press.

Lessing, D. (1995) *Under My Skin: Volume One of My Autobiography, to 1949*, London: Flamingo.

Lienhardt, R.G. (1961) *Divinity and Experience: The Religion of the Dinka*, Oxford: Clarendon Press.

Lukes, S. (1975) *Emile Durkheim: His Life and Work, A Historical and Critical Study*, London: Allen Lane.

Malinowski, B. (1926) *Crime and Custom in Savage Society*, London: Kegan Paul.

Needham, R. (1975) 'Polythetic classification: convergence and consequences', *Man* (n.s.) 10: 349–369.

Parkin, D. (1985) 'Introduction', in D. Parkin (ed.) *The Anthropology of Evil*, Oxford: Blackwell.

Peristiany, J.G. (ed.) (1966) *Honour and Shame: The Values of Mediterranean Society*, Chicago: University of Chicago Press.

Pocock, D.F. (1986) 'The ethnography of morals', *International Journal of Moral and Social Studies* 1 (1): 3–20.

Read, K.E. (1955) 'Morality and the concept of the person among the Gahuku-Gama', *Oceania* XXV (4): 233–282.

Taylor, C. (1992) 'Inwardness and the culture of modernity', in A. Honneth, T. McCarthy, C. Offe and A. Wellmer (eds) *Philosophical Interventions in the Unfinished Project of Enlightenment*, Cambridge, Mass.: MIT Press.

Thompson, J.J. and Harman, G. (1996) *Moral Relativism and Moral Objectivity*, Cambridge, Mass.: Blackwell.

Turner, B.S. (1992) 'Preface to the second edition', in E. Durkheim, *Professional Ethics and Civic Morals*, London: Routledge.

Part I
Discourses on morality

Chapter 1

Exemplars and rules
Aspects of the discourse of moralities in Mongolia

Caroline Humphrey

It is not an immediately easy task to locate 'morality' in Mongolian culture. There is no single term in Mongol that corresponds with the European concept, which itself is complex even in everyday usage. I shall adopt a base-line understanding of the word 'morality' in this paper, referring to the evaluation of conduct in relation to esteemed or despised human qualities. The combination of terms used by the Mongols to translate the European idea, *yos surtakhuun*, seems to be of rather recent origin. I shall argue that each of these two terms does, however, denote an area of moral activity which is important in Mongolian culture. *Yos* means the commonly accepted rules of order, reason and custom, while *surtakhuun* (literally 'those things that have been taught') refers to personal ethics. The two are not unconnected, but I shall argue that, as practices of evaluating conduct, they work in different ways. Through living in Mongolia and talking with Mongols I became aware that, while they of course do have rules, for them the more important arena of morality appears in the relation between persons and exemplars or precedents, that is the general sphere of *surtakhuun*. The concern here is with cultivation of the self as a moral subject in relation to individually chosen ideals. Morality in this sense is not simply the affirmation of existing cultural ways of life; there needs to be a social space for deliberation about ways of life, amid the pressures that circumscribe the instantiation of personal ideals. The suggestion here is that this is successfully achieved primarily in the discourse of exemplars, despite the fact that Communist governments have attempted to hijack exemplary precedents to their own ends. The sophistication of the relational space constructed in the indigenous discourse of exemplars has enabled Mongols to withstand simplistic party-inspired variants, as will be described later in the paper.

In their emphasis on the exemplar-focused way of thinking about morality, the Mongols can be aligned in a very general way with the Chinese, for whom, especially in Confucian traditions, a prominent discourse of historical exemplars counteracts the learning of right conduct through performing ritual and etiquette. The contrast that I have drawn emerged from considering morality in Mongolia, and I subsequently became aware from the work of Foucault that a distinction somewhat like it could be seen even more broadly as characteristic of morality in general. Foucault (1987: 29) writes: 'Every morality, in the broad sense, comprises the two elements ... codes of behaviour and forms of subjectivation' (by the latter term he refers to moral practices of the self).[1] Foucault likewise suggests that moralities of different societies will vary in their emphasis on one or another of these modes. Whether it is right to divide moralities in general in this way may be a matter of debate, but it does seem significant that in this case a distinction arising from native categories meets theory arrived at on a different basis and in a different context. Thus what this paper attempts is an initial discussion of the ways in which the unfamiliar moral world of the Mongols can be understood, in the hope that this may illuminate the constructions of morality more generally.

To give an idea of what I mean by an exemplar, I shall immediately describe one such case. A Mongolian friend of mine, living in Inner Mongolia, which is a large province of China, had fallen in love. The object of his affections was a young Chinese girl from a very influential family. But the question of marriage with her was a moral dilemma for him. The Mongols in this region are culturally hard-pressed, outnumbered ten to one by a huge population of Chinese, and in danger of losing their language and identity. To marry a Chinese, especially someone from an important family, is not only to take the radical step of betraying one's ancestors, of extinguishing the possibility of contributing to the Mongol nation by having 'pure Mongol' descendants, but is also a step into the camp of those – in some sense contemptible collaborators – who 'side with the Chinese' and thereby advance their careers. However, in the end, my friend decided to marry the girl, and taking this decision he thought to himself, 'The great Emperor Chingghis Khaan, in his strategy for Mongol greatness, married princesses of different nationalities.' And he told me that he thought he could, by thinking of his marriage in this light, become a better person, and overcome in himself the belittling divisiveness of ethnic exclusivity.

I suggest that using an ideal exemplar like this can be contrasted with the moral issues raised by following rules. The matter is not simple, however, as the idea of 'rules' is used in several senses by anthropologists and philosophers. Writing of social rules in general, Wittgenstein noted how they could in principle, in the abstract as it were, always be misunderstood, and he stressed the unarticulated, perhaps even unarticulable, nature of the understanding necessary to follow rules or directions: ' "Obeying a rule" is a practice', he wrote (Wittgenstein 1973: 202), and 'My reasons will soon give out. And then I shall act, without reason' (Wittgenstein 1973: 211). If Kripke interprets this to mean that the background knowledge necessary to follow a rule consists of *de facto* links, such that we are conditioned to react in this way, Taylor (1993: 47–48) argues against this that the background is an *understanding*, a 'grasp on things that, although unarticulated, may allow us to formulate reasons and explanations when challenged'.[2] Taylor goes on to question the supposition that rules are always explicit representations, or rather, he writes that it does not matter much whether they are or not. In either case, what we are dealing with is understanding located in practices and largely unexpressed.

> This understanding is more fundamental [than formulated representations] in two ways: first, it is always there, whereas sometimes we frame representations and sometimes we do not; and, second, the representations we do make are only comprehensible against the background provided by this inarticulate understanding. ... Rather than representations being the primary locus of our understanding, they are similarly islands in the sea of our unformulated practical grasp on the world.
>
> (Taylor 1993: 50)

Taylor uses Bourdieu's idea of *habitus* to argue that it is an intellectualist mistake to see consciously laid-down rulings as the effective factor in 'following rules'. This is a mistake equivalent to ignoring the difference between a two-dimensional map of a terrain and our situated, embodied familiarity with the land which allows us to make out way around it.

The problem with such an argument as regards morality, however, is that it seems resigned to the givenness of social structures and inherited practices (a point to which I shall return). Furthermore, this particular discussion of Taylor's makes no contribution to the problem of the explicit rulings of political powers which might violate ordinary people's ways of life, nor to that of the wider forces of social change or domination that operate behind the backs of the followers of rules. In effect Taylor is using Bourdieu's argument against the distortion created by anthropologists' models, presented to readers as 'rules' which 'they', the studied people, follow, to slip sideways into the idea that it makes little difference whether *indigenous* moral ideas are expressed overtly or not, and hence whether they are discussable by the people or not. But the effect of this is to glide past Bourdieu's discussion of power (let alone that of Foucault or Habermas).

At first sight, however, an approach like that suggested by Taylor might seem appropriate for the case of the Mongols. They make a distinction between rules as socially accepted customs (*yos, zanshil*) and as edicts (*zarlig*) of temporal rulers. However, there is a certain cosmological elision between the two, which suggests that both can be taken by Mongols to be largely concerned with power, and there seems to be a sense in which both are thereby removed from the sphere of morality as conceived by the Mongols. From the seventeenth until the early twentieth century the successive edicts through the centuries of khans or feudal rulers curiously took the form of specifying the different penalties applied to various social categories for not observing them. Rather than saying 'It is forbidden to steal', such a law would state that if a noble of such-and-such a rank steals horses he must repay X times the number, if a commoner steals horses he must repay Y times the number, and so forth. Rulers regularly let off people from such penalties on account of some counterbalancing positive service they had performed (Jagchid 1988: 58). This then was a world of temporal and historical give-and-take, an arena of contingent actions, with very little accent on general values of 'right' or 'wrong'.

The same can be said, perhaps more controversially, about religious customs (*yos, zanshil*) in the context of shamanism and the respect paid to objects in nature. Accepted rules such as 'You must not wash in rivers' contain some idea of polluting flowing water, but even here the ways that Mongols talk about this show that the action can be considered as much dangerous as wrong. If you pollute the water, the river spirit will take revenge and punish you, so it is better not do it; or alternatively, people might say that you would be lucky to get away with it. The spirits of nature, existing in trees, mountains, rivers, springs, etc., are known as *ezen* (lord, proprietor). This is the same term as that used for temporal rulers, ranging from the Bogd Ezen Khaan (the Manchu Emperor) and in later times, more colloquially, Communist rulers, to local chiefs, officials and even household heads.

What is unclear is whether all these rulers are understood to have the right to rule, thus delineating a moral universe, or whether the fact of there being rulers is seen simply as part of the general, amoral inequality of the way things are. It seems to me that both understandings are available in Mongol culture. Let us look first at the idea that there is a moral sense of the rightness of the *order* of power. In the allusive way that Mongols often talk about such matters I have to admit that in some respects they do seem to bear out Taylor's idea of following rules based on a background understanding that is principally embodied rather than rationalized. An example of this is the following saying, which alludes to the order of power as intrinsically ranked:

If there are two people one of them is senior
If there is one person his hat is senior
(Gaadamba and Tserensodnom 1967: 8)

One might imagine this to be ironic, were it not for the fact that Mongolians do in fact pay respect to hats – the hat being the material objectification of the idea of 'above humanity' in the vertical cosmology that places the person under heaven. In the seventeenth-century chronicle *Altan Tobchi* we read:

Holy Chingghis Khaan spoke in reverence to Heaven on high [the sky], 'You have made me, by means of your own government, so powerful that there is no-one other than I who is powerful on the face of the earth. Only my hat is above me.' So saying, he took off his hat, placed it on the seat of honour, prostrated himself before it, and drank wine that day until he was very hot. Thus did Chingghis speak to his brothers and sons, after granting them subject people, instructing them (*zarlig bolugsan*) on the support of nations and the gist of government in summary.
(Okada 1993: 231–232)

This passage establishes precisely that continuity between human and 'natural' powers alluded to above, and shows how the sense of 'above' is physically expressed in Chingghis's prostrations. The language used ('holy', 'respectfully', 'honour') indicates an implicit moral evaluation.

More equivocal, however, is the following saying:

> Man follows customary rules [*yos*]
> [As] dog follows bone
> (Gaadamba and Tserensodnom 1967: 9)

This saying plays with the two meanings of 'follow', which, in Mongolian even more clearly than in English, combine 'submission' with 'going after'. The sense here *is* perhaps ironic, since it seems to mock people in the enjoyment and satisfaction that they take in following rules. The analogy is with an 'embodied' *habitus* so deep that it is virtually an instinct, and the sense is conveyed – since people, after all, are not dogs – that things should not be this way. There should be reasons for following rules; or, to put this another way, as some Mongols have explained to me, the idea of 'rules' (*yos*) contains the idea of reasons. This sense of *yos* appears, for example, in the sentence, 'Ene xün yosoor xeldeg xün' (This person gives reasons for what he says). *Yos*, in this way of thinking, are not simply there to be followed unconditionally, but have to be learned, together with their reasons. The process of learning implies acquiring an explicit rational understanding which can be argued for and debated. In a Buddhist religious context this is particularly developed in *nom xeleltsex*, the regular disputations about sacred texts by lamas learning them. I was told that learning *yos* in this sense implies discovering and explaining the intrinsic patterns of the way that things ideally are, providing one's understanding of these patterns as reasons in one's argument. To illustrate this idea indirectly I was given an example, namely the intricate grain of wood, which should be studied before one cuts it, and which gives a reason for cutting it in a certain way.

The complexity of the relations between the various ideas briefly outlined here runs against any orientalist tendency to construct Mongols simply as 'despots' on the one hand, or thoughtless followers of prevailing political hierarchies on the other. Historically it seems that the value of 'reasonableness' as applied to the cases of actual rulings was mostly forced negatively into the open by the abuses of power by rulers. During the eighteenth and nineteenth centuries there were a number of petitions of grievances submitted by serfs about the intolerable activities of local lords, presented to higher princes in the hope that the rules would be correctly applied from the senior level. Most of these were complaints about local rulers' demands for payments or services in the guise of legitimate taxation when they were in fact used to cover the ruler's personal debts. 'Reasonableness' in these practical documents refers to the justification of actions in terms of publicly well-known norms of taxation and the separation of state ('official') business from that of the princes acting as private persons. In the midst of the flow of detail about numbers of sheep and ounces of silver, moral ideas like 'justice', 'right', 'loyalty' and 'truth' occasionally make their appearance:

> When we spoke to Jayisang [an official] Shagdar about the tax I was the only one who argued with him. People who have good connections with Jayisang Shagdar would never complain about him. Is this oppression of the humble people supposed to be only my concern? In spite of the injustice of the penalty inflicted on me because I protected the loyal people, I believe I did right, didn't I? Even though I was dismissed from my office, I am still a citizen of the district. I dare to say that our people cannot stand it any longer if the taxes remain this way. The people suffer as much as I do, but they are afraid to say anything. I am inflamed with indignation and must make this accusation and let the truth be known at any risk, even if it costs me my head. Therefore, I beg of you my great lords and honourable superiors, to give me orders and I will follow them.
>
> (Rashidondog and Veit 1975: 9)

However, despite this evidence that moral arguments surfaced in public life, it still seems to me that this was not the main arena of morality for the Mongols. My reasons for this conclusion require referring again to ideas held in the past which nevertheless still have salience today. For one thing, the public arena revealed by some of the eighteenth- to early twentieth-century petitions of grievances as a space for disagreement about values (what it is to be just, for example) could shrink to something virtually devoid of moral content if people simply reckoned that rules should be followed and the 'dogs following bones' attitude prevailed. In most of the documents individuals simply compared conduct to a set of unquestioned rules. For another, even if questions of justice, right, etc., were sometimes raised, such discussions were constantly undercut by another simultaneously available view which saw powers as inevitably pitted against one another. In this view the notion of a morally ordered universe was virtually absent. In this case it was not that social institutions and laws themselves were regarded as immutable. On the contrary, they could be seen as passing affairs. However, there always would be rulings of some kind, and this was because the exercise of power of differently situated beings, with their own necessities for reproducing their existence, was seen as part of nature (the way things are). Thus to summarize, the very same action, a ruler's excess, could be seen in moral terms, but it could alternatively be seen as both inevitable and arbitrary. The world might be peopled by seniors and juniors, and 'rightly so', but this idea was countered by another which acknowledged that any kind of existence had its own force of being, and that each of these existent beings would exercise its own ('amoral', we could say) conflictual power. Among human beings this could appear as 'rebelliousness' and 'punishment', but such actions could simply be seen as akin to the clashes among beings in the world in general. The result of this way of thinking was that Mongols before the Communist period could punish a mountain, for not bringing rain in the way that it was supposed to do, in much same way that they could punish a man for not delivering state dues.

There are, however, domains, notably kinship, where following rules seems to have an irreducible moral aspect. To be in the right, one has not only to respect one's senior kin, but to feel this respect. However, kinship is also the domain of the power of the lord of the household (*ger-ün ezen*) and so here the overlapping between the arbitrary 'way things are', the right 'way things should be' and the ethical 'way I should be' is at its most dense. Between these three aspects, which conflate the rulings given by the household head with the accepted customary behaviour of gendered and hierarchized persons and with the interiorized self-awareness of values attributed to actions, there is a great density of possible dilemmas. However, even in kinship the idea of a rule does not offer much discursive space, since the subject is constantly tripped up by the fiat-like nature of one or another ruling. Such a space is opened, by contrast, in the idea of the exemplar.

Implicit in the above discussion is the weighting given by Mongols to personal, as opposed to impersonal, social values. I having been using the term 'morality' at the most pared-down level, to refer simply to evaluation of actions, that is, judging them better or worse. But the very great difference with the European concept is that for Mongols the core of morality is primarily referred to the self, adjudicating one's own actions as good or bad *for oneself*, whereas in the West at the very least a sympathy for others has been considered by most recent philosophers as a *sine qua non* for entering in the world of morality (Williams 1993: 12). In Mongolian culture it is your responsibility to improve yourself – at the very least to place yourself rightly in the world – before addressing the lives of others (the sense in which this can be regarded as moral is also discussed in Humphrey 1992). Altruism is also a value for the Mongols, but particularly among those with a Buddhist education it tends to be seen as an outcome of the cultivation of virtues in the self. In general, perhaps it can be said that social values, such as justice or altruism, are weakly internalized, compromised, as I have suggested above, by the existence of alternative understandings of how the world works. It is impossible to deal adequately with this subject here, that is in a paper more concerned with locating the moral discourse of the Mongols than describing its content. However, it does seem important to point out that even communist ethics, which was notably inspired by social values, was also assimilated by the Mongols to their preference for the morality of the self, resulting in images of a world inhabited by people 'good-in-themselves'. This is illustrated by the final words of the autobiography of Academician Shirendev, who was for much of his life in charge of propaganda for the Mongolian government:

> Kind-hearted ones,
> Let us make this a country of good workers;
> If flowers can adorn the wide world
> Then good people can decorate the nation.

The social rules discussed above can be contrasted with universalized ethical precepts, which appear in the Mongolian context in both Buddhism and in communism. As Carrithers (1992: 92–116) has pointed out, precepts, which he associates with the rather patchy appearance of generalizing paradigmatic thought in any culture, are not free-floating and timeless, however abstract they may appear, and they must be understood in the form of discourse and social context of their appearance. The point to be appreciated here is that in Mongolia, unlike in Europe, in practice almost no space is given to general ethical precepts as emanations of God or society. Rather, such precepts tend to be *authored*, and they then appear in relationships as tied to the personalities of both the mentor and the follower. So what I am arguing is that precepts tend to be assimilated into the exemplary mode. Therefore, rather than contrasting precepts and moral stories, as Carrithers does, I attempt, as a first step, to try to understand the nature of exemplary morality by employing the tactic of contrasting it with Western moral rules.

European rules and codes, such as the Catholic catechism or the French and American constitutions, have at least three characteristics:

1 They are the same for everyone, or for everyone of a designated category; they suppose the sameness of the subject, i.e. human equality, or they are designed to promote such equality.
2 Rules and codes must be in principle consequential and consistent, such that if you obey one rule you do not thereby disobey some other rule in the code.
3 The discourse of rules aims at maximum clarity, eliminating ambiguity, such that the subject knows immediately what is a right action and what is wrong.

None of these characteristics apply to morality by exemplars, and with this realization we step into another world.

The device of clarification by negative contrast with European moral rules suggests three conclusions about the ethics of exemplars: (a) it constructs a particular kind of individuality, or culturally specific concept of the person (cf. Jacobson-Widding this volume), which relates in a very interesting way to assumptions of individual difference and social hierarchy; (b) it contributes to the crystallization of a variety of different 'ways of life' (cf. Archetti this volume), which acknowledges rather than denies social conflict; and (c) it requires that the subject do some 'work', that is ponder the meaning of the exemplar for him- or herself, and in this sense exemplars as moral discourse are open-ended and unfinished. Everything I have said here implies that, as far as 'the ethnography of moralities' is concerned, we can only proceed rather cautiously as people from outside, since the mode of exemplars is interiorized and subjective, permeating someone's action in general rather than single acts, and thus the 'case' that I gave at the beginning should be seen as a somewhat artificial example for the sake of exposition.

Let me, however, proceed to elaborate the three points summarized above.

1 In Mongolia exemplars are not the same for everyone, but chosen by subjects in their own particular circumstances. How does this actually work? Everyone, at some time in their life, should have a 'teacher' (*bagshi*). This applies to a herder or clerk just as much as to someone with religious concerns like a Buddhist monk. A person with no teacher is 'no-body', Mongols said to me. Teachers are often Buddhist lamas, but they can also be inspired women, scholars, statesmen, or indeed anyone who is held to have perfected an admired quality. The teacher is someone who advanced and improved him- or herself in relation to some moral principle, such as 'bravery', 'purity of thought' or 'compassion'. In the case of religious people, behind the teacher there may lie a saint or god, to whose qualities the teacher also aspires. However, this does not amount to a genealogy of teachers, unlike in the case of a Buddhist reincarnation. The reincarnation is different from the exemplar, because the new incarnation *is* (in a sense) the earlier one, whereas the relation with a teacher or exemplar is dyadic, implying difference of status between the two and mutual obligations that are in fact different on either side.

The first thing to point out is the extraordinary variety of these teachers, ancestors and gods that stand in a teacher-like relation to the subject. And someone is not, of course, limited to having only one exemplar in their life. A Mongolian friend of mine, an admirer of Chingghis Khaan, was a little shocked to find that in a composite portrait, a friend of his had joined together in one frame a picture of the great warrior and the friend's own teacher, a still-living master of *chi-gong* (a kind of magic of vitality widely practised in China). This was shocking not because the two exemplified such different qualities (that was only to be expected), but because Chingghis in his view was too great to be amalgamated with the *chi-gong* master. The portraits should have been separate and in some way hierarchically marked.[3] A Mongolian household then invariably has an altar, or honoured space, where the representations of the exemplars are placed. These altars are as diverse as the people in the family are diverse, and people will point out: this is my father, this is my teacher, that is the god that my husband worshipped when X happened, this is the saint that I particularly revere, and so on.

A Mongolian child is not given a definite exemplar to follow (in contrast to the case of rules, which are taught to children by their parents). Rather, a young child is exposed to a great variety of moral stories and precepts and he or she then develops as a personality to the point where a teacher or an exemplar can be intentionally chosen. Thus, the subject in the morality of exemplars is already someone, already a moral person. In principle people are held to have individuality even from birth, although the accomplishing of moral qualities has yet to happen, since Mongols are born already marked as people. They emerge from a given *töröl* (kin-group), on an astrologically marked day (which also has qualitative implications), they are washed at birth with the water of the birth-place, and then they are nourished by its special air, water, milk and meat, and they are given a name which must not be the same as that of any known person – all of which establishes people as different and perpetuates this difference in the course of life.

If these differences of social origin and symbolically significant geography begin to constitute children as persons, the development of the personality – that is of a source conscious of awareness, knowledge, reason and moral judgement – constitutes a self. Mauss (1985) was wrong to say that there is no idea of the self except in the West, and to see in China 'an Orient that has never made the self into a sacred entity ... a fundamental form of thought and action' (quoted in Elvin 1985). In Mongolia, I suggest, it is as oneself that one searches for and chooses a teacher. It is common for people to look for many years until they find the one teacher they can truly admire.[4]

Finding exemplars is part of discovering and cultivating oneself. In Inner Mongolia (China) adolescents in particular choose wise sayings (*tsetsen üg*) that they particularly admire from the thousands available in the culture. They write these on pieces of paper which are kept in personal spaces (in one's desk drawer, under the pillow, in an inner pocket). Sometimes the wise words are written on the back of photographs of film-stars – not that they are the sayings of these film-stars, but two kinds of ideal are combined in this way. Young people often exchange papers with wise words, as a way of indicating to one another what kind of person they truly are.

The relation of teacher (*bagshi*) and disciple (*shabi*) is a hierarchical one, in the sense that it is the teacher's role to give advice and wise words, and the disciple's to listen and learn.[5] The relation between teacher and disciple is, of course, one between socially defined persons, but it is also one between selves. This, I think, emerges from the nature of the discourse between teacher and disciple. To get at this we must think about what exactly it is that the moral subject strives after in putting him- or herself in the position of disciple. The chosen teacher simply is someone who has the qualities that one admires. However, what is important here is that it is not just the teacher as a social person that is the exemplar. In fact, more than the teacher, the exemplar is constituted by the 'discourse' of the teacher, which may be sayings or actions.

The word that the Mongols mostly use for exemplar is *üliger*, which at first might seem like a homonym, since it means what initially appear to be two quite different ideas. *Üliger* means example, model or precedent, e.g. when a mother says, 'You should be an example (*üliger*) to your younger brother.' But *üliger* also means an oral or written text of some kind, usually a story, and in different parts of Mongolia also an epic, or a riddle, precept or proverb. However, the exemplary words are not just something that has been said by the teacher. This is true even though Mongols do regard anything said as having more consequence than we do. For example, they have a rather negative attitude to just chatting, and if you ask a Mongol about something they often will not reply directly but retort, '*Why* did you ask that?' It is as though all sayings should have an intentional meaning, that is a meaning beyond their overt sense. So people may avoid dealing with the sense unless they can also see the intentional point, and this gives almost all talk a kind of weight, or directedness, which one might see as the grounds for a pervasiveness of morality in their culture. In any case, *üliger* stand out beyond such ordinary talk and sayings, that is, they are given prominence by the very fact that some person takes them in a special way (as an exemplar). Thus we find that there is a Mongol saying about *üliger*, which is itself an *üliger*:

If you follow sayings (*üg*) you [only] become clever
If you follow an exemplar (*üliger*) you become wise[6]

Üg dagaval uhaantai bolno
Üliger dagaval tsetsen bolno
                              (Erdene-Ochir 1991: 47)

The *üliger* is thus the combination of the ideal represented by the teacher and his/her words or deeds, or more exactly those crystalline moments of the teacher's actions that have been 'listened to' by the disciple and made to be exemplary in the context of some particular ethical decision. From the teacher's point of view, these are his or her *surgaal*, the items of all his or her myriad sayings and doings that are the ones to be learnt. But although purposive teachings are not unknown in Mongolia, particularly in the context of Buddhist teacher–disciple relations,[7] very often the teacher does not know which really are his *surgaal*, as they appear almost as a by-product of his enlightened or spiritually gifted passage through life.[8] And so, although the *surgaal* or *üliger* appear from the teacher, it is the disciple, by actively paying attention, who provides the agency that transforms the words/act from merely having happened to something that is an exemplar.

Thus my Mongolian friend, the one who fell in love, stressed to me that Chingghis Khaan, taken as a historical personage, was not an exemplar to him. But in the circumstance of the difficult decision about his marriage, the particular principle of Chingghis's strategic affinal alliances became exemplary to him, since this provided a way to envision his own best self if he took the decision to marry. It was not that he deluded himself that he was like the great Emperor, or that he thought his marriage would actually make much difference in the tense ethnic situation in Inner Mongolia, but rather that acting according to this exemplar would make him a better, wiser human being, and would be a step to leading a more far-sighted life. This, I think, can only be understood as evidence for a sense of self as a fundamental form of thought and action.

2 Let me now move from the point that I have been making here, about the essential variability of exemplars and subjects, and the involvement of a sense of self, to a related issue. Among the things that distinguish a morality of exemplars from a morality that appears in a code is that there is no requirement that exemplars be consistent with one another or that they be coherent with regard to society in general. Because moral exemplars are unique to their subjects, they do not get tangled up in the characteristic arguments of European moral philosophy relating to consequentialism and moralities as total systems. Ever since Aristotle, many European philosophies, from those of the utilitarians to the social contract theorists, have proposed that there is an attainable ethics of harmony, whereby it would be possible for humans to resolve the contradictions between pure thought, practical wisdom and public life. However, other philosophers, with whom my argument would tend to agree, have argued that such a harmony, encompassing not only the different aspects of individual ethics but also the benign accommodation of individuals in society, is impossible. For example, Condorcet was opposed to public instruction in morality,

giving children 'principles of conduct', because he did not agree
with the idea that it was possible, or even desirable, for any public
authority to sum up the happiness of individuals as the greatest
utility of society (Rothschild 1994). Stuart Hampshire (1983) has
argued, in a sustained attack on the Aristotelian position, that we
need to recognize that human language and culture *reinforce*
differences in behaviour, and furthermore that people do this in a
self-conscious and willed way.

> There is no set of natural dispositions which is by itself sufficient
> to form a normal and natural character and to which children
> could be introduced. They have to learn our ways, or to learn
> someone's foreign or archaic ways, our forms of deceit and
> normal living, our forms of justice and courage and friendship,
> or someone's alien forms.
>
> (Hampshire 1983: 149)

Not only is the reinforcement of differentiated moral ideals
inevitable, but it involves a sacrifice of dispositions greatly admired
elsewhere. People are aware of this as they grow up and embark on a
way of life, and they know that every established way of life has its
cost in the absence or repression of others. To give a simple example,
by becoming a prudent and successful farmer one cannot have the
qualities of split-second resolution of a fighter pilot, but this does
not prevent one from knowing about them, or even admiring them.
It is exactly this quality of moralities, that they sustain 'ways of life'
– ways that are different from one another and may be in conflict
with one another – that the ethics of exemplars embodies.

The Mongolians' stories include a huge number of what we might
call 'negative exemplars', that is *üliger*-by-mockery. These stories
have a typical protagonist who takes a wrong step and turns
everything upside down (Dorjlham 1991). In other words, he is a
human who has not learnt 'our way of life' (*yos*). A typical example
is the traveller who came and stayed and stayed, and thoughtlessly
ate and drank until the household ran bare, and never gave anything
to the hosts in return. It is interesting that these wrong actions are
not really possible kinds of action in a Mongolian context, nor do
they usually take the form of mockery of alien ways of life (the
cheating foreign trader, etc.). Rather the typical protagonists are
often called 'mad ones' (*soliot*), that is, human beings who are one
of us, but who exist as it were in a natural state, without having
developed the particular characteristics of mind and conscience

cultivated in the Mongolian way of life. Thus the negative exemplar is not a story that simply says 'You should not behave like this', but rather it requires the listener actively to fill in mentally the social virtues that the mad one never acquired.

The relationship that I have described is between a thoughtful and 'specialized' subject and the exemplars chosen to develop and extend these very qualities. Its moral foundation is a sense of personal self-worth. However, it is the case that political leaders in Asia have used this very ethical formation to their own ends. But rather than develop those aspects that might lead to a 'politics of difference', they emphasized the hierarchical conforming aspect, to attempt to turn people to mass discipleship.[9] So in the Maoist period in China, and to a lesser extent in the Stalinist one in Mongolia, we can see the hijacking by the Party of the very structure I have described. Mao himself was not to be emulated, but he, as the great teacher, presented to the masses 'from his own life' many quasi-invented models of moral qualities.

A friend from Inner Mongolia remembered that when his school class went out to build roads in the early 1970s, they marched in step carrying a little white flag, on which were printed the words, 'Learn from Comrade Lei Feng!' Lei Feng was one of Mao's favourite models. He was a poor soldier who devoted himself to the people far beyond the call of military duty. He helped old people free of charge, took patients to hospital, etc., and in the course of all this serving of the people he died. Recalling this, my friend also remembered the 'Two Little Sisters of the Mongolian Grassland'. This is a famous story of two little girls who, when their parents were away, had bravely gone out in a terrible winter snowstorm to save the commune's sheep. The exemplary model of the 'Two Little Sisters', printed in millions of illustrated booklets and even translated into English, incorporated the model of Lei Feng, because it was only 'having learned from Lei Feng' that the pair were inspired to do their selfless duty of saving the sheep. There were many other such models, like Jang Se De (the charcoal burner who died while trying to warm the leader with his fires), or Bai Tu An (a Canadian doctor who died of blood-poisoning while tending the wounded of the 8th Expeditionary Army), or Jau Yü Lu (assigned to govern a remote backward region, who devoted himself to raising its standard although he himself had an incurable disease). The important thing to note here is that there were many of these Maoist exemplars, and unlike the situation in more politically relaxed periods of Mongolian life, they were designed to blot out all previous models – that is, to take over the moral landscape.

In Inner Mongolia, despite all the thought reform of the Cultural Revolution, the Maoist attempt was not to be successful. Interestingly, it was not only the political pressure that people resented. They also came to turn against the endlessly repeated Maoist version of socialist morality, that is, exemplars representing personal sacrifice for the sake of society-wide advantage. The exemplars came to be used mainly to mock people: 'So you think you are a Lei Feng, eh?' Nor did the people chosen by the Party as living exemplars (hard-working farmers, etc.) take kindly to their elevation, since the intimidation and fear of the situation violated the essentially voluntative quality of the native model. A saying of those days was:

A human being is afraid of being famous
A pig is afraid of being fat

Above all, everyone resented the brainless simplicity of these models. Now, although China is still ruled by a communist government, Mao's models have more or less zero currency. Nevertheless, the exemplary mode itself still seems to retain strong social currency in Inner Mongolia (this is not to exclude the possibility of the emergence of dissent, undercutting the role of the teacher, and the replacement of 'vertical' with 'horizontal' references for ideals, nor even, in the future, a swing to a more rule-based morality). However, as things are, the most bitter covert battles are now fought over historical and mythical figures who might serve as new and alternative exemplars to those of high socialist times. This is why the ideological battle of today is waged to a large extent in terms of obscure Mongolian bandits, Chinese princesses dredged up from the past, or the enigmatic sayings of early manuscripts.

3 I turn in the final part of this paper to the relation of the disciple to the content of the exemplar. The Maoist models, with their simple-minded messages, are uncharacteristic as far as Mongolia goes. The discourse of Mongolian exemplars tends to be highly wrought, focused and difficult to understand. Such exemplars require pondering by the disciple. In fact, they have no single meaning, but are given meaning in the context of the specific

aspirations of the subject in his or her predicament. I am afraid that it is impossible to provide an adequate feel for this in a written paper (and this is where the ethnography of moralities in this case perhaps must fail) because the evanescent and notional character of the exemplar means that it is manifest only in the casting of one's actions in a *subjectively* new qualitative and intentional light.

However, to quarry a little at the edges of this, let me try to give an example. The thirteenth-century account of the life of Chingghis Khan, *The Secret History of the Mongols*, is a favourite source of exemplary incidents, but it is notoriously difficult even for Mongols to understand. Now the Mongolian scholar Jagchid, who fled the country at the time of the communist take-over and presently lives in Taiwan, and who has adopted something of a *bagshi* role in relation to the preserving of the traditions of his fellow Mongols, published an article (Jagchid 1988) in which he attempted to draw out the moral lessons of the *Secret History*. Among others he cited a saying that was used even in the *Secret History* itself as an exemplar: 'When a bird is chased by a sparrow-hawk and flies into the bush, the bush will save it' (*Secret History*: par. 85). In the *Secret History* the context was that the saying was used by some boys to persuade their father that, despite the danger to himself, he should save Chingghis, who at that time was fleeing from his enemies, the Taichi'ud. Jagchid points out that the adage was used again, a century or so later, in the Chinese history of the Mongol Dynasty, the *Yüan Shih*, about Huo-tu [Khodu], a warrior who was at that point fleeing from Chingghis Khaan. Huo-tu, exhausted, arrived at the tent of one I-na-ssu. Chingghis sent an envoy to I-na-ssu with the message, 'Why do you hide a deer ... stuck with my arrow?', and I-na-ssu replied, 'A bush can still help save the life of a bird that has escaped from the sparrow-hawk. Am I not better than leaves and wood?' and he gave protection to Huo-tu, upon which Chingghis immediately attacked him. Jagchid explains to his readers that what these incidents, with the same exemplary saying repeated over generations, reveal is an ethic of altruism not unknown to the nomadic peoples. We can note that it was Jagchid as *bagshi* who made this particular interpretation; in itself the saying is mysterious and metaphorical, and has a potential for being understood in some rather different ways. An Inner Mongolian colleague of mine, for whom this saying was important in the aftermath of Tienanmen, said, 'This means that if someone is helpless, you must help them.' However, another said, 'There are two birds, a weak one and a

strong one; this saying is about establishing justice between them.'
Finally, there was another interpretation: 'The important idea here
is to do with the bush; we are humans and we must not be put to
shame by nature.'

One can see that such an opaque exemplar could give rise not
only to alternative readings but to successive understandings, as a
person holding it dear turned it in the harsh light of the events of
real life. I do not want to give too strong an impression of the extent
to which exemplars inspire people to *take decisions* (I know few such
cases explained to me in this way, and perhaps it is almost
impossible from outside to weigh reasons for decisions which are
entangled for people themselves). Certainly, personal exemplars
cannot be seen as free-floating, beyond significant power relations,
or unaffected by the systematic, non-contingent arena of production and reproductive social relations (cf. Smith 1994). However,
what they seem to offer is not only alternative conceptions of how
one ought to conduct oneself, but a discursive space for deliberation
about ideals. This enables people to transform themselves and
gradually to commit themselves to certain ethnic modes of being.
Investigating exemplars also gives grounds to the people involved,
and to us as anthropologists, for the questioning of the apparent
givenness of social rules, and ideas like *habitus*.

To conclude: this paper has argued that the Mongolians' construction of morality places greater weight on the 'practices of the self'
than on the issues raised by following rules. One of the most
fundamental ways of cultivating the self is through the discourse of
exemplars. The qualities of the Mongolian exemplar that I have
pointed to here make it different from the 'cultural schemas'
proposed by anthropologists to explain the motivation of action. In
one prominent tradition of cognitive anthropology, although the
schemas themselves are culturally specific, the subject of such
motivating schemas is assumed to be a universal person and self
(Quinn 1992: 194). This paper has suggested that certainly 'the
person', and for all I know 'the self' too, must be understood as
culturally formed in the context of ethics, even if we also recognize
some strata of universality underlying the notion of human ideals.
In their open-endedness, diversity and embeddedness in dyadic
relationships the exemplars examined here also seem unlike the
'cultural schemas' of Sherry Ortner (1989), where the emphasis is on
the structural and implicitly constraining nature of cultural models

repeated in history. Finally, it is clear that the Mongolian recourse to exemplars should not be likened to the later European use of proverbs and maxims. During the nineteenth and particularly in the twentieth century the use of proverbs came to be despised as 'sententious', 'commonplace' and 'hackneyed', that is, as incompatible with the Romantic understanding of the self (Obelkevich 1987). The Mongolian morality of exemplars, to the contrary, is perhaps the location *par excellence* where individuality may be explored and the sense of the self's moral being enhanced. As the example of the failed Maoist models showed, the exemplary relation is historically contingent, but in the end has been quite resistant to overt ideological pressures. Despite the emphasis that I have placed on specificity and historical contingency in this study, perhaps the best concluding remark is that of Rodney Needham (1985: xii), who boldly presents exemplars as 'characteristic features of thought and imagination to which men of any period are inclined'. He wrote of them (Needham 1985: 2) that they present us with 'the imaginative provocation offered by a poetic interpretation'.

ACKNOWLEDGEMENTS

I am very grateful to Uradyn Erden Bulag for his thoughtful discussions of the issues raised in this paper, as well as to James Laidlaw, Roberts Kilis and Signe Howell for helpful comments on the first draft.

NOTES

1 By 'forms of subjectivation' Foucault refers to the way in which individuals constitute themselves as subjects of moral conduct, i.e. 'the models proposed for setting up and developing relationships with the self, for self-reflection, self-knowledge, self-examination, for the decipherment of the self by oneself, for the transformations that one seeks to accomplish with oneself as object' (Foucault 1987: 29).

2 Hence Taylor puts to one side Wittgenstein's more challenging and enigmatic additional remark, 'When I obey a rule, I do not choose, I obey the rule *blindly*' (Wittgenstein 1973: 219) and he emphasizes Wittgenstein's general insistence that following rules is a *social* practice.

3 However, since the chosen models are often exemplars of different moral qualities, they do not necessarily form an encompassing sequence, from the general to the particular, such as that described by Roy D'Andrade for cultural schemas to guide action (D'Andrade 1992: 30).

4   In a monastery young lamas are allocated teachers when they arrive. But they do not have to stay with these teachers and are free to choose the monk to whom they will devote themselves. The result is that many senior lamas have no disciples at all, while others who are more revered may have hundreds (Arjiya Khutagt, Kumbum Monastery, personal communication to U.E. Bulag).

5   A detailed ethnographic example of similar dyadic relations among Jains in India was beautifully described by Carrithers (1992).

6   *Uhaan* (clever) refers to intelligence and reasoning, while *tsetsen* (wise) refers to a quality of sageness or prudence.

7   A sacred text or exhortation that the teacher has authorized for use by a disciple is known formally by the Tibetan term *lung*. The Kanjurwa Khutukhtu has written interestingly (Hyer and Jagchid 1983: 9) that the *lung* gives the disciple(s) a special mandate to fulfill the exhortation (read the prayer, perform the ritual), but that among lay persons this term came to be used for a telling off or scolding, or alternatively as a dry, indoctrinating and boring lecture. This suggests that a one-sided teacher-to-disciple formalization of the exemplar is inimical to its continued viability, and that the initiative of the disciple is essential.

8   The Diluv Hutagt (Lattimore and Isono 1982: 142–143) explained movingly that a previous incarnation of the Narvanchin Hutagt was possibly superior to his present incarnation, even though he was a drinker and a profligate. The earlier incarnation, for all his worldly life, had a miraculous healing touch and worked wonders, 'so we are made aware that here are mysterious things'.

9   The phrase 'politics of difference' here refers more specifically to Charles Taylor's argument in *The Ethics of Authenticity* (Taylor 1992a) and *Multiculturalism and 'The Politics of Recognition'* (Taylor 1992b). Taylor is concerned here with ideals and the practices that are meant to conform to them, and he argues against various sceptical positions suggesting that ideals cannot be subject to reason. 'Authenticity', being true to one's own individual identity in one's own unique way, has validity as an ideal. Taylor argues beyond the liberal view that the character of the just state can be seen in its impartiality to these different conceptions of what constitutes the most worthwhile, fully human life. He suggests that a new 'politics of difference' is required on the grounds that, as it is the demands of politically marginalized groups, rather than individuals, that are at issue now, the individualist construction of liberal political theory is inappropriate. Furthermore, the liberal model belongs to a philosophical tradition which is blind to ineliminable culturally embodied differences. Taylor suggests that this can be remedied by a politics of 'equal recognition', i.e. positive recognition of what makes people different, rather than what makes them the same. See Nick Smith (1994) for a perceptive critique of this position. The Mongolian use of exemplars is somewhat different from the recent Western 'culture of authenticity', since it is not a question of *new* modes of self-fulfilment but of 'self-cultivation' in the direction of historically held virtues. The importance of the teacher, who is normally of a previous generation, pulls the ideals in a retrospective direction, although we cannot exclude

that even archaic exemplars, such as those taken from the thirteenth-century *Secret History of the Mongols*, might not come to be signs for a new consciousness; nor can we conclude that Mongolian exemplars will not inspire groups as well as individuals.

REFERENCES

Carrithers, Michael (1992) *Why Human Beings Have Cultures: Explaining Anthropology and Human Diversity*, Oxford: Oxford University Press.

D'Andrade, Roy (1992)'Schemas and motivation', in Roy D'Andrade and Claudia Strauss (eds) *Human Motives and Cultural Models*, Cambridge: Cambridge University Press.

Dorjlham, T. (1991) *Mongolyn Manibadarayn Huuch*, Ulaanbaatar: Mongol Uranzohiol Hevleliin Gazar.

Elvin, Mark (1985)'Between Earth and Heaven: conceptions of the self in China', in M. Carrithers, S. Collins and S. Lukes (eds) *The Category of the Person*, Cambridge: Cambridge University Press.

Erdene-Ochir, G. (1991) *Hüneer hün hiih mongol uhaany survalj*, Ulaanbaatar: Bolovsrolyn Yaamny Surah bichig, Hüühdiin nom hevleliin gazar.

Foucault, Michel (1987) *The History of Sexuality, Volume Two: The Use of Pleasure*, trans. R. Hurley, London: Penguin.

Gaadamba, M. and Tserensodnom, D. (eds) (1967) *Mongol Ardyn Aman Zohiolyn Deezh Bichig*, Ulaanbaatar: Shinzhleh Uhaany Akademiin Hevlel.

Hampshire, Stuart (1983) *Morality and Conflict*, Oxford: Blackwell.

Humphrey, Caroline (1992)'The moral authority of the past in post-socialist Mongolia', *Religion, State and Society* 20 (2–3), London.

Hyer, Paul and Jagchid, Sechin (1983) *A Mongolian Living Buddha: Biography of the Kanjurwa Khutugktu*, Albany: State University of New York Press.

Jagchid, Sechin (1988)'Traditional Mongolian attitudes and values as seen in the *Secret History of the Mongols* and the *Altan Tobchi*', in *Essays in Mongolian Studies*, Provo, Utah: Brigham Young University Press.

Lattimore, Owen and Isono, Fukiko (1982) *The Diluv Khutagt: Memoires and Autobiography of a Mongol Buddhist Reincarnation in Religion and Revolution*, Wiesbaden: Harrassowitz.

Mauss, Marcel (1985 [1938])'A category of the human mind: the notion of person; the notion of self', in M. Carrithers, S. Collins and S. Lukes (eds) *The Category of the Person*, Cambridge: Cambridge University Press.

Needham, Rodney (1985) *Exemplars*, Berkeley: University of California Press.

Obelkevich, James (1987)'Proverbs and social history', in Peter Burke and Roy Porter (eds) *The Social History of Language*, Cambridge: Cambridge University Press.

Okada, Hidehiro (1993)'Chinggis Khan's instructions to his kin in Blo-bzang-bstan-'dzin's *Altan Tobchi*', *International Symposium of Mongol Culture*, Taipei.

Ortner, Shery (1989) *High Religion*, Princeton: Princeton University Press.

Quinn, Naomi (1992)'The motivational force of self-understanding: evidence from wives' inner conflicts', in Roy D'Andrade and Claudia Strauss (eds) *Human Motives and Cultural Models*, Cambridge: Cambridge University Press.

Rashidondog, S. and Veit, V. (trans. and eds) (1975) *Petitions of Grievances Submitted by the People*, Wiesbaden: Otto Harrassowitz.

Rothschild, Emma (1994)'Condorcet and the conflict of values', discussion paper for the Centre for History and Economics, King's College, Cambridge.

Shirendev, B. (1989) *Dalain Davalgaanar* (Through the Ocean Waves), Ulaanbaatar: Ulsyn Nomyn Hevlel.

Smith, Nick (1994)'Charles Taylor, strong hermeneutics and the politics of difference', *Radical Philosophy*, 68: 19–27.

Taylor, Charles (1992a) *The Ethics of Authenticity*, London: Harvard University Press.

——(1992b) *Multiculturalism and 'The Politics of Recognition'*, Princeton: Princeton University Press.

——(1993)'To follow a rule ... ', in Craig Calhoun, Edward LiPuma and Moishe Postone (eds) *Bourdieu: Critical Perspectives*, Cambridge: Polity Press.

Williams, Bernard (1993) *Morality: An Introduction to Ethics*, Cambridge: Cambridge University Press.

Wittgenstein, Ludwig (1973) *Philosophical Investigations*, trans. G. E. M. Anscombe, Oxford: Blackwell.

Chapter 2

'I lied, I farted, I stole … '
Dignity and morality in African discourses on personhood

Anita Jacobson-Widding

When I first began to do fieldwork among the Shona-speaking Manyika of Zimbabwe about ten years ago, I tried to find a word that would correspond to the English concept 'morality'. I explained what I meant by asking my informants to describe the norms for good behaviour toward other people. The answer was unanimous. The word for this was *tsika*. But when I asked my bilingual informants to translate *tsika* into English, they said that it was 'good manners'. And whenever I asked somebody to define *tsika*, they would say: '*Tsika* is the proper way to greet people', or '*Tsika* is to show respect'.

This does not merely illustrate the relativity of morality, but rather the difficulties involved when we try to turn one of our own culture-specific abstractions into a subject of investigation in a society where people do not even have a word for that concept. How can we elaborate methods for the ethnography of moralities in other cultures, when the concept of morality does not exist?

The problems connected with the ethnography of abstract, English concepts in cultures where there are no corresponding lexica have recently been discussed with reference to psychological concepts like 'the Self', 'mind', 'emotion', 'society' and other favourite subjects within cultural psychology or psychological anthropology (Lutz 1988: 84, Kondo 1990, Spiro 1993, Hill and Mannheim 1992, Russell 1991, Wierzbicka 1993). Wierzbicka has suggested a method to resolve these problems by recommending the employment of 'cultural scripts', that is to use 'simple sentences or short sequences of sentences that attempt to capture a society's cultural norms "from a native's point of view" and, at the same time, to express these norms in terms of universal human concepts' (Wierzbicka 1993: 220 f.). The kind of words that we should focus on for 'cultural scripts' should be 'universal human concepts', for which there are lexica in all languages, she holds. And, insofar as there is no universal word for the notion about which we want to have cultural scripts, we should rephrase our concept. Thus, for instance, the concept of 'mind' may be rephrased as 'how to think', or 'thinking', the concept of Self may be rephrased as 'person', and so on. This might work for concepts like 'mind', 'self' or 'emotion'. But what do we do with a concept like 'morality', which is culturally biased already at the level of definition? We may, of course, define morality in a value-free way, if we just state that morality concerns the norms for good behaviour in any given society. However, we would then miss the ethical implications of morality, and its reference to what Williams calls 'human well-being' (Williams 1993: 88).

My own definition of morality would run something like this: 'Morality concerns the norms for good behaviour, insofar as this behaviour affects the well-being of any other person than the actor him- or herself'. By this definition I have not gone into any particular cultural rules for behaviour. Yet I have presented a definition that depends heavily on my own culture, with its egalitarian, Protestant ethos, and its concern with individual responsibility, conscience and guilt. By introducing the *other* as an object, I have assumed that the actor has an individual responsibility for what he or she does to other people, and by specifying 'the other' as *any* other person, I have assumed that all people are equal, regardless of what social category they belong to.

If moral judgements concern the things I do to other people, rather than what I do to myself, this implies that a morally wrong act is supposed to be connected with feelings of guilt rather than with feelings of shame. Although guilt and shame have often been confounded, I think that most people in my own culture would connect the feeling of guilt with transgression of norms concerning other people's well-being, whereas they would rather connect the feeling of shame with a failure to conform to a social ideal. Alexander called these feelings 'inferiority feelings' (Alexander 1938, 1948), while Erikson describes them as an impulse 'to bury one's face, to sink into the ground' (Erikson 1963: 252). In distinguishing between shame and guilt, Piers and Singer hold that guilt inhibits and condemns transgression, while shame demands achievement of a positive goal (Piers and Singer 1971). They underline that shame arises out of a tension between the ego and the ego ideal, while they define guilt as a tension between the ego and the super-ego (ibid.: 23).

Leaving the psychoanalytical jargon aside, I think we may say that the notion of guilt presupposes a notion of *conscience*, that is an inner sense of individual responsibility for what one does to other people. This notion, in turn, presupposes the idea of the individual as a single, moral unit, with an autonomous psychic structure. Such a view of the person is, according to Geertz, 'a rather peculiar idea within the context of world cultures' (Geertz 1984, cf. Shweder and Bourne 1984). Instead, socio-centric conceptions of personhood seem to dominate in non-Western cultures (Marsella 1985: 209; Kirkpatrick and White 1985: 11; Shweder and Bourne 1984; Dumont 1970: 4, 1986: 25; Forssen 1979; Parin, Morgenthaler and Parin-Matthey 1980).

Hence, if we want to use cultural scripts as a way to approach the ethnography of moralities in a comparative cultural perspective, it seems as if we would have to focus on scripts about guilt and shame, or maybe dignity, while contextualizing such scripts with respect to the culturally constructed notions of personhood. I would like to take one case in point. It concerns the Fulani of West Africa, who are said to refer to the following proverb as one of their corner-stones of conduct: 'Three things are indignities for a respectable person: I have lied, I have farted, I have stolen – these are indignities for a respectable person.'

This proverb raises a series of questions. First, does it deal with shame or guilt? Does it have to do with morality, dignity or the social order? Second, one might wonder about the wording of the proverb. The wording is such that what is condemned is to *say* 'I have lied, I have farted, I have stolen', rather than the act as such. Does this mean that it is worse to admit a mistake than to commit it?

We will get an answer to these questions if we read the interpretation of the proverb provided by Paul Riesman, in his posthumously published book *First Find Your Child a Good Mother* (Riesman 1992), where this proverb is quoted. According to the author's explanation, all the three acts mentioned are considered to show a lack of self-control. 'To lie' means to say anything that is incorrect, even if unintentionally. It is 'to make mistakes'. Hence lying is interpreted as a sign that you are not able to control yourself. This puts lying on a par with farting. About farting, the author explains that it 'appears again and again in proverbs, sayings

and everyday comments as a particularly shameful thing for a Pullo
.... Finally, what makes theft shameful is not its undeniable threat
to society, but the fact that the thief fails the test of mastery on two
counts: first, he is poor, which implies that he has failed to manage
his own life circumstances .... Second, the thief fails to control his
own appetite, for in most cases what is stolen is food, and in any
case whenever a person uses a good for his own benefit Fulani say
that he has "eaten it" ' (ibid.: 24).

Hence, this proverb deals with shame rather than guilt, and with
dignity rather than 'morality', or the social order. Against the
overall background of the importance of avoiding shame, it goes
without saying that it is worse to admit these mistakes than to
commit them.

This all seems to be far from any notion of morality where ethics
is involved, if by this we mean that one should be concerned with
the well-being of the 'Other'. It seems as if it is only the well-being
of the 'Self' that is at stake. But if we dive deeper into the Fulani
ethnography (Riesman 1977, 1984), we will find that the Fulanis'
concern about self-mastery is a matter of recognition of the social
value of both the Self and the Other.

Self-mastery is, among the Fulani, not a virtue in itself, 'in the
abstract'. It is the core value of what the Fulani themselves call
pulaako, which means 'Fulaniness'. This implies that self-mastery
refers to how the Fulani define themselves in relation to other
people. The 'other' is anyone representing the non-Fulani agricul-
turalists, who live close to the Fulani, and who are considered to
belong to another hierarchical category, that of slaves. In order to
distinguish themselves from those who represent a different
hierarchical category, the Fulani have to show self-mastery
whenever they interact with them. However, this behaviour
conforms to the social ideal of any encounter between people
representing different hierarchical categories, even among the
Fulani themselves. To show self-mastery is thus a way of recognizing
the relative positions of people who interact, rather than to
recognize their respective individual identities. It is a way to express
social personhood, and to show what it is to be a person among
other persons.

The concept of social personhood, which was elaborated by
Fortes (1987), goes back to Marcel Mauss's famous distinction
between 'la personne' and 'le moi' (Mauss 1939). Drawing upon
both these authors, I would like to define the social person as 'the

abstract personality', or 'la personne morale', to whom other people assign certain rights and obligations. This 'person' is in some societies considered to be just a representative of a particular social category, and it is in this capacity, rather than in his or her capacity as an individual, that he or she is assigned a particular social value, and particular rights and duties. In this kind of society, of which the Fulani are an example, we thus find that the individual and the social person may be two entirely different things (cf. La Fontaine 1985). The individual has to be concealed by the social person. In some other societies, however (i.e. our own), the social person is considered to be identical with the individual. That is, it is in his or her capacity of being an individual human being that a person has certain rights and obligations, which are the same as for any other individual. Here we thus find that individual and social personhood are conflated. Individual identity is not supposed to be concealed.

The Fulani proverb may thus be interpreted as a cultural script about social personhood. It talks about the priority of collective personhood over individual personhood. Being a cultural script about personhood, this proverb may also tell us something about 'the ethical presuppositions informing and creating ... values and social relations', which is how 'morality' was defined for the purpose of the EASA conference in Oslo, in June 1994.

HIERARCHICAL SYSTEMS AND DOMINANT MODELS

To say that the Fulani proverb is an expression of standardized ideas about 'collective' personhood may be one way of seeing their insistence on the avoidance of shame. However, we may also formulate this kind of social personhood in terms of social categories. As already mentioned, the emphasis on body control in personal encounters also applies between the Fulbe 'masters' themselves, provided that it is a matter of face-to-face interaction between individuals belonging to different hierarchical categories in the kinship system. What is worth noting is that the overall hierarchical principle governing social relationships in general is referred to by a simplistic, dominant model – the one contrasting 'masters' with 'slaves'. However, this explicit model covers a whole series of relationships between different kinds of social categories. It is when individuals representing these social categories interact that their relative social personhood gets activated, while their individual selves are supposed to be concealed.

We may recognize corresponding patterns of 'categorical' social personhood among most African peoples, in particular among those who apply a classificatory kinship terminology. A classificatory kinship terminology implies, among other things, that no relative is a unique person – not even the most significant others surrounding the child in the elementary family. A child's mother is not recognized as a unique person, nor is the father – nor the child itself, for that matter. They all represent broad social categories rather than themselves. The logic implied in such a kinship system is that the rules for behaviour between social categories tend to prevail over the possibilities for individual negotiations in the interaction between the Self and his or her significant Others. Already from the age of 5 or 6, the identity of a person tends to become a function of the relative position that he or she occupies in any particular social context. Consequently, the recognition of his or her categorical position in relation to any partner of interaction will prevail over his or her identity as an individual. In accordance with this, the terms of address will seldom be those of individual names. They will rather identify an individual by reference to the social category that he or she represents in relation to the speaker.

Although such a social system would imply a continuous flexibility regarding what relative position any individual occupies when interacting with other people, it is conceptually built upon the idea of categorical definitions of relative identity. The complex patterns of social personhood that will result in such a system of relationships are generally simplified by reference to a dominant folk model of hierarchy. This model may be that of master/slave, or that of king/subject. But very often the model is constituted by the male/female metaphor.

The Shona-speaking Manyika of Zimbabwe provide an example of this. Like the other Shona groups, the Manyika apply patrilineal descent, Omaha kinship terminology and a very strict concern for hierarchical distinctions and body control in all kin relations except for those between joking partners. The Manyika observe an even more marked concern for avoidance between representatives of different hierarchical categories than the other Shona groups. This is constantly repeated in their discourse about correct behaviour, and summarized in the code of *tsika* (good manners, showing respect, 'morality').

The *tsika* code is extended to apply between neighbours and strangers, and turns all public encounters into extremely formal events. But no matter how widely the Manyika apply the idea of hierarchical distance between representatives of separate social categories, they tend to refer to hierarchy by a single, simplistic model. This model is constituted by the male/female dichotomy: the relationship between heaven and earth, mountains and valleys, high and low, superior and inferior. A case in point is the cultural script constituted by the myth of royalty in Manicaland. Every adult man would be ready to tell this myth about the first chief Mutasa. This is the version told to me by the current chief Mutasa himself:

> This country was inhabited by people who were very primitive. They did not even know about the fire. Their chief was Muponda. One day, a hunter arrived with four assistants. His name was Mutasa. He wanted to hunt on Muponda's land, and suggested that they would hunt together. So they did. After they had finished the hunt and caught an antelope, Mutasa made a fire. They roasted the meat, and Mutasa said to Muponda: 'You may decide what part of the animal you want.' Muponda then chose the back. Mutasa said: 'Oh, you want the back. Very well, in my country, that is the part of the animal that is for the wife. Thus you are the wife and I am the husband. This means that I have the right to command you. I am your superior.' Muponda had to accept this, since Mutasa was the one who had caught the animal, and made the meat edible by lighting the fire. This is how Mutasa became the king here, while Muponda became a sub-chief under him. But Mutasa gave him his daughter as a wife, to compensate for his loss of superiority.

Like many other myths about culture heroes, the story about Mutasa and Muponda lends itself to several interpretations. Nevertheless, the overt message is pretty clear: the husband has the authority over the wife, the king over his subject, the father-in-law over his son-in-law. The manifest model of the superior's right to command the inferior is the husband/wife relationship. Correspondingly, we find that this model is stereotypically repeated when people are asked to define the personhood of men and women in general terms. Both men and women will insist on the superiority of the husband and the inferiority of the wife – that is, as far as the matter is discussed in terms of general principles, or whenever it is touched upon in a public setting, when people representing different social categories are present. The 'perfect man' will be (a) a husband who is 'above' (*pamusoro*, on top of) the wife; (b) a father (*baba*) who has not only shown himself to be potent, but who also has adult dependants (married sons living in the father's homestead, and married daughters that have brought him sons-in-law). Correspondingly, the 'perfect woman' is defined as (a) a wife who is 'underneath' (*pasi*, on the floor, on the ground) in relation to her husband; (b) a mother (*mai*) who has not only given birth but also shown that she can teach her children *tsika* (good manners).

However, the husband's dominance over the wife is not the only message of the myth about Mutasa and Muponda. There is also a message about how the superior person should show respect for the inferior person. Mutasa gives Muponda a gift to compensate for his loss of superiority. Even if a gift may establish a hierarchical relationship (cf. Mauss 1969, Lévi-Strauss 1947), there are some other dimensions involved as well. As Mauss already pointed out, the giving of a gift is a recognition of a social relationship. We may take this one step further by saying that the recognition of a social relationship is also a recognition of the social personhood of the Other. At the same time, it marks the social superiority of the Self. To give somebody an especially valuable gift (such as a daughter) would then be a recognition of the other person's social value. The superior's gift to the inferior becomes a recognition of the dignity of both, as relative social persons.

As we shall see further on, the Manyika regard the recognition of an inferior person's social personhood as equally important as the recognition of someone's superiority. To recognize a person's dignity is not only a matter of paying respect upwards. The code of *tsika* (good manners, 'morality') implies that you treat everybody else in accordance with the position that he or she occupies in relation to yourself.

The cultural script constituted by the myth about Mutasa and Muponda may thus serve as a guide to Manyika conceptions of social personhood. First, it defines hierarchy as the corner-stone of social personhood. Second, it points to the importance of paying respect to the inferior party in a relationship. Third, it uses a gender idiom borrowed from the elementary family as the dominant model of hierarchy.

Being a cultural script that is publicly circulated, the Mutasa myth may be regarded as a 'text', in the sense that its qualities correspond to those that Ricoeur has defined as typical for the written text as opposed to the spoken discourse, or 'talk'. When Ricoeur defines 'text' in relation to 'talk', he emphasizes several aspects of the written discourse that might just as well be applied for the manifest message that is conferred by a cultural script. Such a message often represents the 'dominant structure' of a society. The aspects of the text that may be relevant here are: first, 'the fixation of the meaning'; second, 'its dissociation from the mental intention of the author'; third, 'the display of non-ostensive references'; and, finally, 'the universal aim of its addresses' (Ricoeur 1979, cf. Jacobson-Widding 1990, 1991).

These characteristics of the written discourse generally apply to many oral expressions of cultural values as well. In particular, they apply to standardized discourse about personhood and morality, if such a discourse is performed publicly, or as the answer to a question that has been phrased in general terms, such as 'Do all human beings have equal value?', or 'How should a husband relate to a wife?' The answer will then be phrased in equally general terms, and present the 'truth' as a matter of principle. This kind of truth generally represents what might be called 'the dominant structure' of a given society's culturally standardized values. Such a discourse has all the characteristics that Ricoeur ascribes to the written text.

However, as everybody knows, there are other dimensions of cultural practice than the reiteration of standard texts. Behind the façade of dominant structures we may always discern some more or less 'muted structures', to borrow a concept from Edwin Ardener (1989). According to Ardener, the muted structures 'are "there" but cannot be realized in the language of the dominant structure' (Ardener 1989: 130).

Ardener holds that 'the muted structures' are those that are represented by certain domineered, muted groups in a given society. Especially, he points to the muted groups constituted by women. However, I think that the concept of 'muted structures' may be widened so as to encompass any inarticulate pattern of cultural values and relationships that 'cannot be realized in the language of the dominant structure'. Such inarticulate structures may form part and parcel of the conceptions of the world held by any group or person in a society, whether they belong to a dominant group or a muted group, and regardless of whether they subscribe to the society's official ideology or not.

We generally find that 'muted structures' in the wider sense coexist with 'dominant structures' in the minds and acts of the very same people. What is important to keep in mind, however, is that these different structures are expressed, and acted out, in different kinds of situation. Further, they are expressed in completely different kinds of discourse, or different 'genres'. The ethnographer's problem will thus be the one of defining the kind of context and genre that pertain to what kind of structure.

This is where we might get some help from Ricoeur's definition of what he calls 'the spoken discourse', or 'talk'. When contrasting talk with text, Ricoeur notes that talk is a 'fleeting event'. In this kind of discourse, it is more difficult to determine the meaning, or to carry over an interpretation that is valid from one discourse event to the next. The meaning rather depends on *the subjective involvement of the speaker*. Further, spoken discourse is *part of a dialogue*, which refers to a situation that is *common to its interlocutors*. Finally, the spoken discourse is *ostensive*, that is, it demonstrates the meaning by *referring to concrete events* (Ricoeur 1979: 77).

All these characteristics of 'talk' may be applied to the discourse genres where muted structures may be revealed. If the ethnographer makes sure that the context is informal enough to permit a dialogue, rather than an interview, and if he or she manages to discuss a particular matter in such a way that the two interlocutors get subjectively involved, some muted structures may be revealed. Further, you should make sure to create a dialogue that refers to a situation that is 'common to its interlocutors', and refers to 'concrete events'.

In order to create such a dialogue, the ethnographer must thus invest his or her own subjective feelings in connection to particular events that concern him- or herself and the informant as well. This kind of reflexive ethnography may even involve the ethnographer in plain gossiping. In the end, this 'method' may reveal not only some muted structures in the informants' world-view, but also some muted structures at the back of one's own mind.

I will give an example of how my own involvement in some particular events in a Manyika village challenged my own notions of morality, and thus gave me a reason to get additional insights to Manyika conceptions of morality, by a method that does not deserve a more sophisticated label than that of 'private gossiping', inspired by my own 'moral' reaction to an incident that I found humiliating.

THE MAKING OF BIG MEN

My example is from a Manyika village in the eastern highlands of
Zimbabwe, where I stayed for nine months in 1991–1992. The
village is situated right on the border between so-called commercial
land and tribal trust land, in the mountain area of Nyanga District.
Manyika people from the surrounding areas began to settle down
here in the 1920s, after they had been chased away from land that
was by then being turned into commercial farm land. By 1990 the
village had grown into a size of about a thousand people, who lived
in about sixty scattered homesteads.

Most people in this village consider themselves quite 'modern', in
comparison with those living in neighbouring villages. Their
headman invited missionaries to begin their modernizing work
already in the 1930s. Today, all children go to school, and about 70
per cent of the adult population belong to the local Methodist
church. In 1990, the headman declared that from now on, his village
would not contribute millet to the annual rain ceremonies arranged
by the sacred chief of the area, since he wanted his village to be
regarded as 'modern'. To be 'modern' is considered to be equivalent
with conforming to European and Christian manners. Hence
everyone who wants to be considered modern has to join the
Methodist church, take part in its various clubs and committees,
and preferably one should also try to have a European wedding,
even if one had a customary marriage ceremony fifteen or twenty
years ago.

Despite this emphasis on 'modernity' as the main source of
achieving a new social value as a person, everybody holds that the
most important virtue in life is to observe *tsika*. As I mentioned in
the beginning of this paper, the Manyika translate *tsika* as 'good
manners', or 'how to show respect'. But they also say that *tsika* is
the word corresponding to 'morality', 'custom' and 'culture'. But
above all, they define *tsika* in terms of respect.

To know how to show other people respect in the proper way is
essential for anyone who wants to be regarded as a 'good person'.
You will show your respect, first, by presenting yourself face-to-face,
while avoiding eye contact. Second, you must know how to present
a message, a gift or an expression of gratitude. Third, you must
observe the correct body posture. But most of all, respect is a matter
of greeting. It is by the way you greet another person that you will
acknowledge his or her social identity, and your own as well.

If you are a man greeting a woman, you should sit on a bench, keep your back straight and your neck stiff, while clapping your own flat hands in a steady rhythm. If you are a woman greeting a man, you must place yourself on the floor, then curb your back and your neck, and form your hands into the shape of a round pot, while clapping them quietly. If two women meet, they will not curb their backs as much as when they meet a man, but when a man meets another man, he will observe an even more stiff, erect posture than when greeting a woman. He will avoid the other man's gaze, and keep his body and speech under strict control.

This strict self-control is especially marked by a man in an inferior position, whenever he meets a 'big' man, who is referred to as *baba* (father). To be a *baba* is more than just being the father of a child. A real *baba* is a man who takes part in the *dare* (men's council), and who is the boss of a homestead with numerous dependants. In order to be highly respected as a *baba* by the other men he should have several adult sons who have built their own houses in his homestead. Such a man is greeted like a king by his stiff and reserved inferiors. However, the 'king' himself may observe a more subtle body posture, and show generosity with a smile or a gift to his inferior.

What you respect is thus the other person's social personhood, while you mark your own as well. A properly performed greeting ceremony will thus be a confirmation of the relationship between two different kinds of social identities. With the exception of certain egalitarian relationships between particular kinship categories, virtually all social relationships tend to be conceived as hierarchical, at least as far as kinship is concerned.

The hierarchical distinctions are particularly marked between men and women, especially in public contexts. The symbolism of above/underneath also imbues the spatial organization, the architecture and the placement of male and female tools. However, when people comment on this symbolism, they refer to it in terms of husband/wife, rather than male/female. Hence, the social identities that pertain to family and kin have been used to construct the dominant models of social relationships. The father/son relationship and the husband/wife relationship are the most obvious examples. We may thus regard the kin-based distinction of separate categories as a dominant model of social order, revealing a 'dominant structure', where the main distinction is that between husband and wife.

But beneath the surface of this dominant structure, we may also perceive some 'muted' hierarchical structures. The muted structures consist of inarticulate rankings between people whose 'official' relationship does not quite fit into the hierarchical pattern of the dominant structure. Such relationships may develop between more or less important *baba*, or between more or less important women. Some men are considered more important than other men by virtue of rather subtle criteria, such as the authority with which they speak in the men's meeting place, the *dare*, or the number of adult sons who have shown their loyalty to their father by building a hut in his homestead. The women have their own tacit ranking lists, and their own criteria for social importance. Today, when many of the young or middle-aged husbands are away at work in town, their wives have found new avenues to negotiate their hierarchical relations. Whereas social respectability used to be based on 'perfect wifehood', many women will now further their social value by taking active part in the modernization process, either by becoming economic entre-preneurs, or by showing themselves as active Christians, or preferably both. But all the way through the new expressions of their relative social value, they continue to confirm the very corner-stone of the social order, that is the primordial importance of hierarchical distinctions between different categories of people. To demonstrate these distinctions is to observe *tsika*.

Against this background of how social personhood is negotiated and confirmed in a markedly hierarchical society, I will now proceed to report on the interaction between some Manyika villagers and a European farmer, who settled down in close vicinity to the village border about ten years ago.

The farmer was generally referred to as Mr George. The land he bought in the mid-1980s had not been occupied by any white settler before him, although it had been classified as commercial land about fifty years ago. In order to mark the boundaries of his land, Mr George wanted to put up a fence. But since he found that one of the village homesteads was situated about 200 yards inside the boundary of his land, he asked the *baba* of that homestead to move. The *baba* was Mr Julius Maswera, who had to move further down the hill, in order to let Mr George put up his fence.

This was, as far as I could see, the only 'immoral' act that Mr George had done to any of the villagers. All the other things he did in relation to the villagers would be considered utterly praiseworthy according to European standards. In his own terms, he 'worked for

God'. After having been 'miraculously saved by God', when the guerrillas burned down his former farm during the civil war, Mr George had decided to settle down in a new place, close to the tribal trust land, in order to 'work for God'. When he built up his new farm, he started right away to discuss development projects with the local party representatives. Then he did one thing after the other. He fixed boreholes for drinking water for the villagers, provided pipelines for irrigation and distributed tons of seed potatoes to those villagers who were willing to learn how to grow potatoes for cash sales. And every time that there was a funeral or a wedding in the local Methodist church, Mr George would send several hundred litres of milk from his own dairy farm to be distributed among the guests.

Personally, I was not very fond of Mr George. He was not a 'friendly' kind of person, who smiles and looks into your eyes. He never stopped to have a little chat if I happened to meet him on a path, or if I went to his farm to buy milk. As a matter of fact, he never talked, unless he had a chance to quote the Bible in order to prove something to me. He seemed to have devoted his life to 'the work of God' to the extent that there was no room for a friendly chat with other people. I thus found him pretty rude, particularly after I had not been allowed to rent the little cabin that he had built for tourists, or rather for a special kind of visitor: those who work for God. I had asked him to let me rent the cabin during the periods that it was not occupied by somebody else. I explained that I wanted to make notes there in the evenings, since there was electric light in the house. But he refused by saying, 'This cabin is for those who work for God'.

The first time that I heard about Mr George's fence was when Mr Julius Maswera's daughter Betty showed it to me, while we were walking on a path close to the fence on our way to her father. 'There,' she said, and pointed up to the slope on the other side of the fence,

> there you can see our old homestead, although it is falling apart by now. That is the homestead that my father built when he was young. And all around you can see the terraces that we used for planting our maize and millet, and the fruit trees that my father planted. But we had to move, because Mr George came and said that the land belonged to him. Then he put up that fence, and we are not allowed to pass it, not even to pick the fruits from our

own fruit trees. Yet Mr George cannot use that land for anything himself. It is too steep for his tractor.

We both agreed that this was a very bad thing to do, and Betty complained about all the work that she herself and the other members of the family now had to do in order to create a new home, to make new terraces, new fields and new fruit plantations and to find a new well. We then continued to walk, until we reached Betty's and her father's new homestead some 800 yards further downhill. Mr Maswera's new homestead was still under construction. He needed to build several cooking huts, sleeping quarters and granaries for his big family, which consisted of two wives, several daughters-in-law (with absent husbands), several divorced daughters and about a dozen grandchildren. Mr Maswera himself was a man in his early seventies, but still full of vitality and a real *baba*'s male pride.

As we arrived in his new homestead, I sat down to talk to Mr Maswera, whom I knew quite well. He belonged to the minority of people in this village who did not bother about 'modernity', and he was not in the least impressed with European ways of living. His relation to the church was rather hostile. He continued to brew beer for his ancestors as he had always done, and tried to stick to all the traditional virtues connected with *tsika*, male superiority, and the pride of *baba*-hood.

After having exchanged the customary greetings with Mr Maswera, I tried to approach the issue of the fence – but by observing as much *tsika* as I was able to do. I understood that the subject must be a delicate one, since *tsika* implies that you must avoid talking about anything that might stir up a person's emotions, especially when they are connected with a defeat. So what I said was something like: 'Can you tell me how a man constructs his homestead, and how he chooses the proper place for it?' Mr Maswera was happy to explain that every man tries to find a place high up on a hill, in order to avoid other men building 'on the top of himself'.

— That is how your own homestead was built, I said.
— Yes, it was.
— And now you have had to move further down, I continued.

Mr Maswera did not answer. I understood that I had touched upon something that I was not supposed to do. I had insinuated that he had been humiliated in his male pride. After a while, I began to talk about my own impressions of Mr George. I told Mr Maswera about the incident with Mr George's cottage, and said that I did not like his fundamentalist attitude. And then I said something about his unfriendly behaviour, and that I thought that he was a rather rude person. I concluded by saying, 'He is not really a good person, in spite of all those pipelines and seed potatoes that he has given away.' Now, Mr Maswera suddenly made his back straight and stiff, just like any man does when he greets a big man.

— What you say is not true, he objected. Mr George is a very good man.
— How can you say that? You don't like all that church work and charity. And on top of everything, he asked you to move your homestead.

But Mr Maswera insisted.

— Mr George is a very good man, he said.
— Why?
— Because he makes other people grow.
— How do you mean, grow? He just makes them grow potatoes.
— No, what I mean is *kukudza*, to make other men become big. He is not like the other Europeans, who just bump in and give you orders, while chatting and staring at you – if they even bother to come and see you themselves. Mr George comes to see the person with whom he is dealing. He came to see me, and to greet me, when I was told that I had to move. And he did it in a proper way. He makes other men grow.

Here was thus the man to whom Mr George had done more harm than anybody else, as far as I could see, and who, in addition, did not have any appreciation whatsoever for Mr George's development work and Christian charity. Yet he regarded Mr George as a good man, for the simple reason that he had shown him the kind of respect he thought he deserved as a man, a father, a *baba*. I began to see some of the moral implications of the concept of *tsika*, 'good manners'. And I began to see why the English word 'morality' was translated into a word that meant 'good manners', and which people defined in terms of proper greeting.

THE MAKING OF GIFTS

Mr George had thus conformed to Manyika standards of morality by making Mr Maswera 'big', or by respecting his social personhood as a *baba*. But how was Mr George considered by the other people in the village? Some time later I took the opportunity to figure out their attitudes. It was soon after Mr George had offered the men in the village council another development project, or 'gift'. The 'councillor' (local party representative), who was a young man without much authority in the village, tried his best to persuade the older men to accept Mr George's generous gift. But the old men seemed to be reluctant, without being able to present any substantial reasons for not accepting Mr George's offer. The women, however, were all for it. And they presented very reasonable arguments for accepting the offer, because it would further the economic development of the village.

After the big meeting, when this issue had been discussed, I decided to talk to Charity, who was my hostess during most of the time that I stayed in the village. Charity, who was one of the most eager 'modernists' in the village, had shown a lot of entrepreneurship in the last couple of years. She was one of those who had learned to cultivate potatoes, and how to sell them; she was becoming a big businesswoman by trading used clothes; and she was often also spokesperson for the other women, whenever there was a meeting concerning development or other forms of modernization. She was equally ambitious and successful in other domains of the modern sector. Thus, for instance, she was the secretary of the local school committee, and the leader of the women's club affiliated to the Methodist church. She was also a member of the church choir, although she had no voice at all, and she was always ready to mark her presence whenever there was something socially important happening in the modern sector. By the age of 35 she had recently crowned her social career by having an expensive church wedding – about fifteen years after she was married to her husband according to customary rules.

By having a 'European' church wedding, with 200 invited guests and a bridal train of ten people, whose outfits she had paid for, Charity had shown everybody in the village that she and her husband were to be considered important people – in spite of the fact that her husband was never around in the village. He worked as a butcher in Nyanga, and it was his wife who took care of all the arrangements for the wedding.

Now, this socially successful lady, who had used economic entrepreneurship coupled with Christian standards to further her position, had much to say about Mr George's offer to the village. According to her, it would be right to accept this offer, because it would further the development of agriculture in the village.

— And since it is the women who take care of the agriculture nowadays, when most young men work in town, the women are grateful to receive such a gift. But, of course, these big men who were sitting there in the *dare* [village council] were not eager to accept Mr George's offer. First, they don't have much to do with the agriculture nowadays, and they are getting old, and don't understand the modern things. But in addition, they would feel humiliated by accepting Mr George's offer.
— Why would they feel humiliated?
— Because it is a gift. A gift to the women. And a man does not like to accept a gift, anyway. Especially not if he considers himself to be a big *baba*. And that is what all these old men do. If they accepted a gift from Mr George it would turn them into women. It is only women who are paid respect with gifts.

This explanation repeats the message contained in the cultural script about Chief Mutasa and Chief Muponda. As mentioned before, one of the points made in the myth is that the superior must compensate the inferior for his loss of superiority. If the superior respects the inferior's dignity, his compensation should consist in a major gift. This is how Mr George's gift had been interpreted by Charity, and by the other women. The big men of the *dare* could not accept the gift, however, since they did not want to consider themselves inferior in relation to Mr George. But the women were happy to accept it, since this was a sign of respect for their dignity as social inferiors. It was a recognition of their social personhood, in accordance with the code of *tsika*.

However, Charity herself did not seem to be the kind of person to accept an inferior position. What was her personal view of Mr George? Was it affected by the fact that they both were devoted Christians? Or by the fact that they both were eager 'modernizers'? Further, considering the fact that this woman herself had chosen to be called Charity as an adult, she would probably appreciate

Mr George's charity work, and consider him 'a good person' – wouldn't she?

— It is true that he has done much for the village. But he has no *tsika*. For instance, whenever he offers something to the village, he will send the message with the councillor, rather than presenting it himself to the big men in the *dare*. Thus, he does not show them respect. As you know, the councillor has an inferior position in this village. The reason that the big men chose him was that nobody would listen to him. He is just a young man, and he has no *tsika*, so all the big men thought that he would be the best man to represent the socialist party here. Then there would never be any general support for the propositions delivered from the government. So, Mr George should instead come himself, when he has a message for the *dare*.

— But he is a good person, isn't he?

'Well, maybe,' Charity said, in an evasive way. Then she suddenly caught fire.

— But he never turns up. Did you see him at my wedding, for instance? No, he did not come, although I had sent him one of those invitation cards that I had printed in Harare. And did he give me any gift? No. He just let someone deliver all that milk to be distributed to everyone, because he thinks it is better for people to drink milk instead of Fanta and Coca-Cola. But what is a wedding without Fanta? He could have bought that instead. But worst of all, he did not send a gift for me. You saw and heard it yourself, right after the wedding ceremony. When all the gifts were displayed outside the church, and Mr Tafadswa showed them one by one to all the people, and announced the givers' names, you did not hear Mr George's name. So all the people knew that Mr George had not sent me any gift. Being a European, he should have given something worth at least 200 dollars. And that would have added considerably to the financial result of the wedding. As you know, the values of all the gifts are carefully counted by the man who announces them, and people will then go around and spread the news, and compare with the wedding results of other people who have been married recently. So I did not make as much as Venentia did, six months before. Yet, my wedding was bigger, and who is Venentia, after all? She is not even a member of the women's club.

Charity was quite upset when she talked about Mr George's missing wedding gift. It was obvious that she did not subscribe to Mr Maswera's opinion about Mr George – that he is a good person because he makes other people 'grow'. First, by not turning up at the wedding, he had ignored her. Second, by failing to send her a wedding gift, he had failed to recognize her dignity as a woman. This was as if Chief Mutasa would have failed to recognize Chief Muponda's dignity as a social person of inferior status by offering him the greatest of all gifts – a daughter. In doing so, he had recognized his own and Muponda's social personhood – those of a great superior and a great inferior. Mr George had not even recognized Charity as an inferior person. He had not recognized her at all. Thereby, he had missed the code underlying the Manyika concept of *tsika*.

The code implied in *tsika* is concerned with the obligation to respect other people in their capacity as social persons, rather than in their capacity as individuals. It is a code concerned with hierarchically arranged social categories, and with the necessity to mark the distinctions between different kinds of people. If you do not mark these distinctions, you will not only upset the social order. Above all, you will humiliate people, and deprive them of their sense of dignity.

The sense of dignity that people have in this Manyika village is mainly dependent upon the cultural construction of personhood. Your dignity is connected to your identity as a husband, wife, *baba*, *mai* (mother), father-in-law, son-in-law, and so on. The social categories implied in the kinship system defines you as a superior, inferior or – in certain connections – as an equal. In order to behave properly, you must know your own social position in relation to the person with whom you are interacting. But whoever is superior or inferior in this interaction, anyone's dignity depends upon the recognition of one's social personhood.

However, in a changing world, where new, inarticulate criteria develop for the assessment of social personhood, it may be difficult to identify who is who, especially if you are a foreigner, like Mr George. There is no explicit 'script' to tell you that Charity is important because she is 'modern', or that the councillor is unimportant for some obscure reason. In such situations, there is no other way to find out about the muted structures of 'who is who' than to make a careful observation of how the new identities are negotiated in interaction on the ground. Such observations may need some additional gossiping, or confidential person-centred information, in direct connection to concrete events.

But no matter how much the pattern of social relationships may have changed, and become open to negotiation in everyday praxis, the Manyika still seem to stick to a basic message of their 'cultural text'. This message is that people are not equal individuals, but deserve a special treatment depending upon what category they recognize as the source of their social value. The culturally shared expression of such a recognition is still a reliance on *tsika*, which is basically a code for *dignity* – your own dignity, and other people's dignity as well. What is 'morally good' is thus to recognize the relative dignities of the social persons who engage in interaction.

Having come so far in my conclusions, I begin to realize that there is perhaps not such a great difference between my own conception of morality and that of Mr Maswera, or that of Charity. We all tend to consider the recognition of the dignity of the social person as a fundamental presupposition informing moral behaviour. The main difference between us is the fact that we tend to define the social person differently. Whereas Mr Maswera and Charity define the social person in terms of what social category an individual is embodying, I myself define a social person as an individual. And since I regard *any* individual as a social person in his or her own right, I also believe that everybody's social value, rights and obligations should be equal. That is my own culturally derived construction of personhood, and it was that conception of myself and of my own dignity that Mr George had failed to recognize when I asked him if I could rent his cabin. What made me feel humiliated was the way he turned my request down. He did it by saying that the only people who would have the right to rent his cabin were those 'who worked for God', whether they were missionaries or not. That was what had upset my sense of dignity, which was based on my expectation to be treated as an equal human being by another European. Was *I* not just as good as those who work for God? Didn't *I* have the same right as they had to rent a tourist cabin? Was *my* social value based on religious confession rather than on my being an individual in my own right?

My negative reaction to Mr George's behaviour was thus based on the premises of personhood and dignity that underpin the conceptions of morality in my own culture. These premises are stated in the first article of our most famous cultural script about morality, which is the Declaration of Human Rights. This is how it goes: 'All human beings are born free and equal in dignity and rights. They are endowed with reason and conscience and should act towards one another in a spirit of brotherhood.'

Hence, no matter how much I try to negotiate my own relationship to other people in a creative interaction in real life, I seem to be stuck in the stereotypic notion of personhood that my own culture has constructed. So, after all, I think that even if we try to implement existentialist, interactionist or postmodernist approaches to the ethnography of morality, we have to take account what we can learn from the cultural 'text' as well. Even if we believe that we are creating the world by the fleeting events of interaction and lived experience, we are very much products of our cultural texts. This becomes obvious when we realize to what extent people's perceptions of morality depend upon their conception of personhood, and of the dignity of the Self and the Other.

CONCLUSIONS

In this paper, I have focused on the concept of social personhood in order to approach the issue of morality. I have emphasized the difference between the conceptions of moral values in societies that apply different criteria for social personhood. A main distinction has been made between societies where social personhood is supposed to coincide with individual personhood, on the one hand, and societies where social personhood is conceived in terms of social categories, on the other.

In the former kind of society, i.e. that of Sweden, and those of other countries in Europe, the individual person is supposed to be a 'single, moral unit, with an autonomous psychic structure', as Geertz puts it. This implies that every person is supposed to be equipped with conscience, and a potential for guilt feelings. It is this view of personhood that informs the moral judgements in societies where individuality and social personhood are conflated. Central to these judgements is the notion of individual responsibility, and with this notion also the one of guilt.

By contrast, I have pointed to some African societies where social personhood is defined by reference to fixed social categories, which are supposed to be hierarchically related. In these societies, two interacting individuals of different social categories will represent their respective categories rather than themselves. Hence they will conceal whatever is defined as an expression of 'inner', individual selfhood, and conform to the ideal connected with their social role. Strict self-control and formality become part of this ideal in any public encounter. However, when this ideal cannot be maintained, there is scope for *shame*, rather than *guilt*, since shame arises out of a tension between the ego and the ego ideal, whereas guilt arises out of a tension between the ego and the super-ego (Piers and Singer 1971: 23). Correspondingly, in this kind of society, the notion of shame looms large as a moral correlate, whereas there is generally no word for 'guilt'.

As a method to approach the conceptions of social personhood, I have tried to combine the use of 'cultural scripts' with informal conversations designed so as to reveal the 'muted structures' of values lurking behind the façade of the 'dominant structure' of social personhood and morality. Among the Manyika, it showed that the idea of distinction between social categories is officially articulated in terms of the husband's superiority over the wife. This is the dominant model found in cultural scripts and public symbolism. Correspondingly, the Fulani use the master/slave dichotomy as a dominant model of the distinction between hierarchically related categories of people.

However, the dominant folk model of how distinct categories are related subsumes a whole series of social relationships, which are supposed to conform to the same principle. In the cultural script about Manyika royalty, one of these other relationships is mentioned – the one between father-in-law and son-in-law – supposedly in order to point to the superior's obligations to the inferior. In actual practice, virtually all hierarchical relationships seem to be conceived in accordance with the examples provided by the cultural script about royalty. The dominant model of hierarchy does not only mark the relationship between separate categories of kin. It is also extended to relationships between more or less important neighbours, between villagers and European settlers, between unrelated men, and between unrelated women – even in a situation of economic change and 'modernization'. Although the muted structures may not be articulated in the language of the dominant structures, the basic principle of hierarchy and distinctions between separate social categories seem to inform conceptions of personhood and dignity even in the modern sector.

The reasons for this immutability are not easy to define. However, I have hinted at the possible importance of the kinship system, with special reference to the kinship terminology. Since, in any society, the kinship terminology is basic to the identification of the Self in relation to the Other, since it is by kin terms that children learn how to relate to their most significant Others, there is reason to believe that the kinship terminology is conducive to their conception of themselves, and to the formation of ideas about social personhood.

Among the implications of classificatory kinship terminology like that of the Omaha system of the Manyika, there is at least one factor that probably affects the way that children develop some basic conceptions of the Self/Other relationship. This is the fact that already at the age of 5 or 6 they learn that their most significant others are not unique individuals. There is not only one 'mother' and one 'father'. They are just representatives of broad social categories of kin. This is not merely a matter of terminology. You are supposed to behave to 'father' and 'mother' in accordance with the rules that are valid for their respective categories. This will leave less scope for individual negotiations about behaviour between unique persons than in a family with, for instance, an Eskimo kinship terminology.

Correspondingly, children themselves are treated as the representative of a kinship category, already from an early age. They are never addressed by their personal names, except when they are rebuked, or ordered about. Whenever they are praised, a kin term is used. Their value as people will depend upon how well they perform their social role. Hence they will not only learn to identify themselves and most people who are close to them by reference to social categories, but they will also learn that their value as people is intimately connected to how they perform their social role. The ego ideal will be more valued than the ego. The individuality will be concealed in interaction with people representing other social categories. And when a tension between the ego ideal and the ego arises, there will be a heavy feeling of shame.

If all this is learned at an early age in a predominantly kinship-based society, it may be assumed that the principles by which one has learned to identify personhood will be applied in wider social contexts later in life. These extended applications of the categorical definition of social personhood may not form part of the explicit, dominant structure. The Manyika are a case in point.

REFERENCES

Alexander, F. (1938) 'Remarks about the relation of inferiority feelings to guilt feelings', *International Journal of Psycho-Analysis* 19: 41.

——(1948) *Fundamentals of Psychoanalysis*, New York: Norton & Co.

Ardener, E. (1989) *The Voice of Prophecy*, Oxford: Basil Blackwell.

Dumont, L. (1970) *Homo Hierarchicus*, London: Weidenfeld & Nicholson.

——(1986) *Essays on Individualism*, Chicago: University of Chicago Press.

Erikson, E. (1963) *Childhood and Society*, New York. Norton & Co.

Forssen, A. (1979) *Roots of Traditional Personality Development among the Zaramo in Coastal Tanzania*, Helsinki and Uppsala: Scandinavian Institute of African Studies.

Fortes, M. (1987) 'On the concept of the person among the Tallensi', in M. Fortes, *Religion, Morality and Person* (ed. J. Goody), Cambridge: Cambridge University Press.

Geertz, C. (1984) 'From the native's point of view', in R.A. Shweder and R.A. LeVine (eds), *Culture Theory*, Cambridge: Cambridge University Press.

Hill, J. and Mannheim, B. (1992) 'Language and world view', *Annual Review of Anthropology* 21: 381–406.

Jacobson-Widding, A. (1990) 'The shadow as an expression of individuality in Congolese conceptions of personhood', in M. Jackson and I. Karp (eds), *Personhood and Agency*, Washington: Smithsonian Institution Press, and Stockholm: Almqvist & Wiksell International.

——(1991) 'The encounter in the water-mirror', in A. Jacobson-Widding (ed.), *Body and Space: Symbolic Models of Unity and Division in African Cosmology and Experience*, Stockholm: Almqvist & Wiksell International.

Kirkpatrick, J. and White, M. (1985) 'Exploring Ethnopsychologies', in M. White & J. Kirkpatrick (eds), *Person, Self and Experience: Exploring Pacific Ethnopsychologies*, Berkeley: University of California Press.

Kondo, D. (1990) *Crafting Selves: Power, Gender and Discourses of Identity in a Japanese Workplace*, Chicago: University of Chicago Press.

La Fontaine, J. (1985) 'Person and individual: some anthropological reflections', in M. Carrithers, S. Collins and S. Lukes (eds), *The Category of the Person*, Cambridge: Cambridge University Press.

Lévi-Strauss, C. (1947) *Les structures élémentaires de parenté*, Paris: Mouton.

Lutz, C. (1988) *Unnatural Emotions: Everyday Sentiments on a Micronesian Atoll*, Chicago: University of Chicago Press.

Marsella, A. (1985) 'Culture, self and mental disorder', in A. Marsella, G. De Vos and F. Hsu (eds), *Culture and Self: Asian and American Perspectives*, New York and London: Tavistock.

Mauss, M. (1939) 'Une catégorie de l'esprit humaine: la notion de la personne, celle de "moi" ', *Journal of the Royal Anthropological Institute* 68: 263–282.

——(1969 [1925]) *The Gift*, London: Cohen & West.

Parin, P., Morgenthaler, F. and Parin-Matthey, G. (1980) *Fear Thy Neighbour as Thyself*, Chicago: Chicago University Press.

Piers, G. and Singer, M. (1971) *Shame and Guilt: A Psychoanalytic and a Cultural Study*, New York: Norton & Co.

Ricoeur, P. (1979) 'The model of the text: meaningful action considered as text', in P. Rabinow and W. Sullivan (eds), *Interpretive Social Science*, Berkeley: University of California Press.

Riesman, P. (1977) *Freedom in Fulani Social Life*, Chicago: Chicago University Press.

——(1984) 'On the irrelevance of child rearing methods for the formation of personality', *Culture, Medicine and Psychiatry* 7: 123–129.

—— (1992) *First Find Your Child a Good Mother: The Construction of Self in Two African Communities*, New Brunswick, N.J.: Rutgers University Press.

Russell, J. (1991) 'Culture and the categorization of emotions', *Psychological Bulletin* 110: 226–250.

Shweder, R.A. and Bourne, E. (1984) 'Does the concept of the person vary cross-culturally?', in R.A. Shweder and R.A. LeVine (eds), *Culture Theory*, Cambridge: Cambridge University Press.

Spiro, M. (1993) 'Is the Western concept of self "peculiar within the context of world cultures"?', *Ethos* 21: 107–153.

Wierzbicka, A. (1993) 'A conceptual basis for cultural psychology', *Ethos* 21: 205–231.

Williams, B. (1993) *Morality: An Introduction to Ethics*, Cambridge: Cambridge University Press.

Chapter 3

The morality of locality
On the absolutism of landownership in an English village

Nigel Rapport

INTRODUCTION

'Morality' was a term I seldom heard in Wanet. In the village pub,
however, Kevin (a drinking partner) did once ask me whether I had
'any morals'; because, if not, I might join him over the summer
taking easy money off gullible tourists by cheating them at darts.
Kevin was half-joking, but I am still instructed by the exchange. For
in this chapter I explore the 'morality' of relations between local
people in Wanet – a village and valley in rural northwest England[1] –
and those regarded as outsiders: I disinter indigenous views of
'morality' by examining local attitudes towards outsiders.

Moral judgements in Wanet, I argue, often pertain to locality.
Indeed, morality might be glossed as the rights conferred upon
people by their local belonging, in particular their ownership of
local land – their priority on the land. What is 'moral' in Wanet is
for local people to defend their landownership against outsiders.
Here, as Archetti puts it (this volume), is a locally 'concrete'
discourse wherein (as with Argentinian football) moral issues are
voiced.[2]

My argument for this turns on a tone of voice, a tone of
righteous indignation when outsiders are seen to breach or threaten
boundaries of local land. And in the bulk of the paper it is this tone
of voice that I seek to convey.[3] In reported speech, I recount local
discourses as they pertain to landownership and the encroachment
of outsiders. In this way I attempt to embed 'moral' notions in
Wanet in their natural contexts of expression.

However, my ethnography appears in three separate sections. I
argue that there are multiple and conflicting discourses pertaining
to local landownership against outsiders. What 'local' and what

'outsider' refers to is variable and contradictory; what is adjudged moral is contingent. Hence, in the different sections of my reportage, 'local' and 'outsider' are contextualized first as they refer to the dale of Wanet, then to two neighbouring families in Wanet, and finally to one individual in Wanet. This discursive range is not meant to be exhaustive; rather to demonstrate diversity. Similarly, the range does not signify social–structural segmentation; the discourses do not neatly nest one within another, nor pertain to the determination of social–institutional contexts: moral discourses of land in Wanet do not cohere into one universe of meaning and value in this way. Rather, the discourses are used simultaneously, consciously, strategically, by individual speakers fulfilling their own complex understandings of moral propriety and engaging in their own acts of moralizing.

Notwithstanding this diversity, there is a sense in which these discourses do overlap, for they share a common symbolic form. All posit a mutual exclusivity between 'local' and 'outsider', and all claim an absolute right to defend 'local' borders against 'outsider' trespass. Here is an exclusionary model of land access which symbolically denies the other, the outsider, any local rights or validity, which would properly banish the other, and always leave the land with a single local proprietor. Furthermore, the discourses all speak of increasing encroachment. Thus, each weds a sense of desperation to that of righteous indignation regarding what local measures should now be taken to deal with outsiders' immorality.

Following the three different ethnographic sections below, then, the chapter concludes with a section that analyses this formal similarity concerning the morality of landownership in Wanet. The symbolic form, I argue, is a synthesizing phenomenon by which individuals in Wanet can come together and face the outside world. Their common moral absolutism is a symbolic means of individuals in Wanet continuing to distinguish themselves from an outside world (the city, Britain, 'Europe') increasingly distinguished by, and insisting upon a universalization of, moral relativism (I borrow Boon's [1982] notions of the 'Tribal' and the 'Scribal' to characterize this dialectic between outsider relativism and local absolutism in Wanet). Local discourses speak of the morality of stasis and the immorality of those who move into others' homes, therefore (and use this symbolic absolutism to justify social exclusion), while outsider discourses are seen to posit a morality of movement: to advocate mutual accommodation of locals and outsiders on home land.

In short, morality in this chapter translates as a sense of self-righteousness, as I interpret it, among individual informants in Wanet. By presenting a number of different discourses, all of which concern the land, and describing both their meaningful differences and their formal similarities, I sketch links between morality and local identity. Diverse, even contradictory 'localities', it seems, can be synthesized alike by moral discourses of a singular form.[4]

An explicatory word on 'discourse'. I understand discourses to be habitual speech acts and the regular behaviours that accompany them.[5] The discourses that I offer below as my main ethnographic material represent my notebook accounts of the words that I routinely heard spoken/behaved in Wanet. Here are local words combined and presented – 'contextualized' – in such a way as to convey my understanding of the complete 'behavioral' sense that the speech acts entailed.

WANET: FARMING LOCALS VERSUS OFFCOMER COTTAGERS

Wanet is a dale of some 650 people situated in a very scenic part of Cumbria, northwest England. In the first discourse I recount, Wanet is locally portrayed as if a single farming community. Here is how I heard of the moral battle of 'Wanet': a dale seeking to defend itself, its land and its way of life against the ownership, control and undue influence of outsiders or (more denigratingly) 'offcomers' – uninvited recent-comers from off-aways.[6]

Wanet's first inhabitants were Norsemen. They settled in dispersed farmsteads on the fell-sides in order to rear their livestock, and their isolated farms are here still. They gave Wanet its Old Norse language too: 'dale' (valley), 'fell' (hill), 'beck' (river), 'garth' (yard) and 'laith' (barn). Only after the Norsemen did the influx of Angles begin. And it was they who first gathered cottages together into hamlets and villages on the flatter bottom-land.

The tension between Norseman and Angle still resonates in Wanet. Today, it is that between the farmers (of sheep and dairy cattle), in their dispersed farmsteads on the fell slopes, and the cottagers, living alongside the roads and in villages and hamlets on the valley bottom: farmers versus tradesmen and shopkeepers, the retired and the recently arrived; local working inhabitants versus cosmopolitan newcomers and those who cater for them.

In recent years, indeed, Wanet has seen an influx of such newcomers. Of the 650 people who now live in Wanet, almost 200 were not born here (nor even in the surrounding dales) but have moved in from more or less distant towns and cities. For the dale is beautiful, pastoral. And so these people buy up property in Wanet, causing prices to rise and housing to become scarce. Some of this purchasing is for holiday homes, some for retirement homes, some for homes in which to escape the urban rat-race and make a fresh start (as artist, architect, teacher, shopkeeper, smallholder), and some for convenient commuting to work (computing, manufacturing) down the motorway.

In fact, there is a lot of bickering over land and houses in Wanet now. The natives quarrel with the newcomers, people jostle for space. Needing more land to make their farms viable, even the farmers compete with each other for any spare fields; small farms are bought up by larger ones. And outsiders, investing in lumber afforestation, or just fancying a few unspoilt rural acres, often bid in the auctions for land too – as well as for the old farmhouse. Bidding higher for their house or land than locals, they can be seen to spoil local chances of acquiring that anticipated home for marriage or retirement.

Meanwhile, from spring to autumn, tourists visit in their hordes. On a long, hot weekend, they can easily outnumber Wanet residents. They trek and camp here; or they stay in caravans or the pubs or youth hostel or they bed-and-breakfast here. However, it is a moot point the extent to which tourism (and offcomer residency) leads to more jobs for local people. Urban visitors and tastes are usually catered for by other offcomers, while there is a sad shortage of local jobs. In the past, Wanet found wage employment for a population of nearly 2,000, centring around pastoral hill-farming but with a full accompaniment of labourers, artisans and traders.[7] Nowadays, farming may remain the single most popular occupation, but it is mechanized, capital-intensive farming which involves far fewer family units and fewer extra-familial labourers. So those local people without access to sufficient land must earn or at least supplement their living as builders and joiners (on expanding local farms, or refurbishing houses and shops and pubs and restaurants of newcomer owners), as cleaners, cooks and shop assistants; or else by driving outside Wanet each day to jobs as quarrymen and mechanics, as council employees, factory hands and salespeople.

There is even competition nowadays over organizing the dale. Locals sense that offcomers are running *their* parish council and church committee, their holiday committee and youth club committee, their charity commission and school governors' board. Local women feel robbed of their Women's Institute and Mothers' Union, of their meals-on-wheels and playgroup, their Christian Aid committee, their Sunday school and their whist drives.

In sum, it is easy to feel preyed upon in Wanet, and to resent it. Locals feel that in the past the dale was private and thriving, but now it is as if there were a conspiracy by the country's economists and politicians, by the immigrants, by the lazy and morally loose working classes, all trailing out of the cities to invade Wanet and cause its demise. And all orchestrated by the government, by the county and district councils, in particular by the National Park (its Park committees, wardens and walkie-talkie-wielding patrolmen, footpaths, car parks and public lavatories, all assisting more outsiders to 'enjoy local scenery');[8] while local people, born and bred in Wanet, hardly need to be shown by outsiders how to use and preserve their dale, hardly need refurbishment grants or development restrictions in order to 'enjoy' their land!

Finally, when Wanet locals are forced to try any available avenue to make do – offering bed-and-breakfast, or a caravan site, or shop sales, converting an old barn into a holiday cottage – their efforts still appear thwarted. Building grants go to outsiders while permission is denied to locals – their plans deemed inessential for 'normal life' or 'not fitting the existing scene'! Likewise, locals are denied access to those financial measures (marginal production subsidies, set-aside grants and so on) which the machinations of Whitehall and Brussels now make vital for farming survival. In short, outside governmental bodies set up extra bureaucratic hurdles or else operate double standards which favour outsiders, whereas the traditional struggle to farm Wanet land was hard enough . . .

The above discourse is an enunciation of how, while Wanet village hosts more offcomers than ever before (with 'village' and cottage threatening wholly to separate from 'valley' and farmhouse), it is the family farm that remains the dominant local symbol. However much population figures might speak of native depopulation and suggest a transformation of the dale of Wanet from a place of work to a place of recreation and 'escape', it is farming and farmland (farmhouses, farmyards, farm animals and farmers themselves) that, none the less, retain most symbolic significance in connection with a local (traditional, Wanet) 'way of life'.

However, 'local' does not always translate so easily as 'farmer'. In other circumstances, other discourses, local rights to land and local self-righteous indignation at the flouting of those rights by 'outsiders', are understood in different terms, as we next see.

INSIDE WANET: THE HARVEYS VERSUS THE WHITEHOUSES

The Harveys and the Whitehouses are two local Wanet families with long-standing antecedents in the dale. Next-door neighbours in Wanet village, they see each other, talk about each other and evaluate each other's behaviour a great deal; each family figures prominently in the discourse of the other. And yet those discourses remain very different. For while pertinent elements may be formally shared, their significance – the meanings of those elements, how they are understood, categorized, evaluated – is very different. Just as the previous ethnographic section told of insiders to Wanet giving very different meanings to 'Wanet land', to 'the National Park', to 'holiday-home owners', to 'hill-farming' and to 'a local way of life' from those used by outsiders to Wanet, so this section tells of insiders to the Whitehouse family and insiders to the Harveys giving very different meanings to 'Vaila bungalow', to 'Cedar High Farm', to 'Florence's wedding' and to 'Doris's campers', from those given by outsiders. More precisely, each family is seen wishing to defend itself against the other's misuse of its land. Moreover (as in the previous section too), there is no question of compromising with any outsider. For the 'locals' – those living on and in a particular land – know they are absolutely right in their desire to benefit from and enjoy what is rightfully theirs.

The Whitehouses – Eric, Eira and grown-up daughter Florence – live at Vaila, a 1950s pebble-dash bungalow on the edge of Wanet village (built when Eric and Eira married). Eric and Eira are retired now, and elderly, but the family hardware store ('Whitehouse Hardware') is still run by daughter Florence. Trading has been slow these past few years, however, with people driving outside Wanet for most of their provisions, and only the post office, grocer's and tourist shops remaining viable. But the Whitehouses are not too worried because Florence is soon to marry, and then the store can be sold off; residential-cum-commercial premises on the main street of the village should be much sought after.

Florence is to marry Bob Thomas and move onto the Thomases' farm to live; Bob's parents have already moved out of the farmhouse to a bungalow built nearby. What will also be convenient is that the Thomases' farmhouse is less than half-a-mile from Vaila, and Florence and her parents will be able to keep in close touch. There is even a footpath across the fells (albeit uphill), so in dry weather they will be able to enjoy a scenic walk in the fresh air at the same time.

The footpath between Vaila and the Thomases' farm crosses Cedar High Farm, home to Fred and Doris Harvey, their teenage daughter Karen and youngsters Jessica and Craig. Cedar High does not have the land that the Thomases' farm does, situated as it is between the Thomases' and many of the outer buildings of Wanet village, nor is there much room for expansion. But Fred and Doris are in the process of developing their business, buying and renting land around the dale as it becomes available; looking up the hill at the farm David Thomas and his son are running beside them, Fred and Doris see something to aim at.

Looking out of the windows of their eighteenth-century farmhouse, nevertheless, it is Vaila that the Harveys are more aware of, because the two buildings are immediately adjacent. Furthermore, since Vaila is built on a north–south orientation and Cedar High farmhouse on an east–west, two-way vision is barely obstructed.

Florence really finds this lack of privacy annoying, and she knows that her parents do too. Wherever you happen to be in Vaila you can hear the yelping of the Harveys' farm dogs and pups – carrying on as though they were not being fed! Then there is the stale odour wafting from the Harveys' calf hulls: hardly pleasant for entertaining visitors in the back garden. And should you go into the front garden instead, you invariably face the stares of a family of campers whose tent Doris has permitted to be pitched immediately adjacent to the wall. Or else you are accosted by the disdain of Fred Harvey and his workmen brushing cow-muck off themselves (with dirty brooms) before going into Cedar High farmhouse.

Then there is the question of footpaths on Cedar High Farm land. Far from making it clear where the paths begin and how they proceed, the Harveys seem to have gone out of their way to make things confusing. Certainly, traversing Cedar High Farm from Vaila to the Thomases' Farm is more like negotiating a rabbit warren. It seems to Florence that unless the Harveys are either shamed or bullied into doing things properly they just will not make the effort.

But then the Harveys always have had little concern over getting along with their neighbours, or displaying good manners. When Fred and Doris first married and the farm began to take shape, old David Thomas would offer his help all the time – even during haytime when he had his own place to keep in order. But what did Fred do in return? Block up the Thomases' sewage outlet by illegally tipping rubbish into the beck! And when David sent the river authority officials around to complain, Fred claimed that he was only returning the compliment after David had done the same! Of course the river authority did not listen because David's tipping had merely been soil, done with permission and well out of harm's way. Since then, however, the Harveys have been as malicious as possible – when not simply pretending that Florence's fiancé and his family do not exist.

When Florence becomes a Thomas she realizes that she will be stepping into this minefield. But, just maybe, the marriage will cause a change. After all, she is inviting the Harveys' daughter Karen to be a bridesmaid at the wedding. Indeed, she treats Karen as something of a protégée. When Florence began teaching Sunday school, Karen was one of her first pupils, and ever since she has been a regular caller at the shop or Vaila. They sit and watch TV together, or Florence takes her out for a drive, always sympathetic as Karen complains about how her parents treat her as a little girl. Besides being a spiritual and educational occasion, Florence hopes that her wedding will be a day that Karen can really relish: a day to show her parents that she could soon be a bride herself.

But then you never quite know how Doris and Fred Harvey will react. Since the chapel door opens onto Cedar High Farm lane, right beside the Harveys' camping field, Florence asked Doris if, on the Saturday in question, she could make sure that there were no tents nearby which could spoil the wedding photographs. And Florence thought that as their daughter was being honoured by acting as bridesmaid – even though not a relative, and despite the strained relations between the families – Fred and Doris would gladly and immediately assent. But obtaining a promise took repeated pestering. And as for Karen's bridesmaid's dress – Doris looked enough put out when Florence asked her to make Karen a simple underskirt! It is as if Doris did not care about her daughter's independence, her spiritual development, even her pride in her appearance. All Florence does get from Doris are snide remarks about the rigours of being a farm wife and of keeping household jobs (baking, cleaning, washing, ironing) strictly to schedule; and laughter when Doris has to repeat to Florence some garbled instructions about wallpapering.

None the less, when she moves into Thomas farmhouse, Doris will be her closest female neighbour and it would be nice to be able to ask her for occasional wifely advice, compare notes on lambing successes maybe, and invite her around for a get-together (over morning coffee or afternoon tea). What is more, if Florence maintains the business that she recently began in mail-order cosmetics, then she could still deliver to Cedar High Farm and stop for a quick chat. Meanwhile, looking down from her kitchen window she will be able to see Fred on the land, and check his way of doing things and his schedule against her Bob's. She must not rush things, of course, or appear nosy or a spy for the Thomases, but hopefully relations will improve ...

Fred and Doris Harvey find their neighbours, the Whitehouses, typical of the two-faced sort that increasingly Wanet seems home to: all friendly, kind and helpful one minute, then snobbish and stand-offish the next. They have become like city property tycoons, trying to crowd them out on Cedar High Farm and make life intolerable. Back when Fred and Doris were courting, Eric and Eira were perfect neighbours; they even used to send Doris flowers. Then as soon as she and Fred married, had kids, and started making something out of Cedar High Farm, the trouble began.

For example, with ducks and calves in the front garden and reams of nappies to dry, Doris had Fred put up a washing line in the back. But the Whitehouses decided that they were not having it. So Eric took a photo of the line full of nappies and then Eira asked customers who came into Whitehouse Hardware how they would like to live next door to that sight! As if it were Vaila and not Cedar High farmhouse which had been there since the 1700s. Traditionally there was privacy and space in Wanet, and certainly on Cedar High. Now you find the likes of the Whitehouses suffocating you on your own land; sometimes, even when lying in bed, Doris and Fred hear Eric and Eira standing in Vaila driveway criticizing them in front of guests. Whoever heard of siting a cottage a few feet away from a neighbour's farmhouse, and with a contrasting orientation!

Eric and Eira are now ageing, but unfortunately their spitefulness seems to have been inherited by their daughter, Florence. Now that she is grown up, Doris and Fred try to act neighbourly towards her and give no offence. But how does Florence respond? By coming round to complain when Fred's lambs wander up Vaila's driveway (through the open gate) and eat some flowers; also by reporting the number of campers that Doris and Fred site in their fields to the National Park officers (when her shop benefits as much as anything from a village full of tourists).

The trouble is that Florence is still very immature. Eric and Eira never taught her how adults behave; instead of having her learn how to cook or clean or otherwise pay her way in the family enterprise, she was spoilt. Nor is Florence's current friendship with Karen such a good idea either; for here Karen is, squandering time and money in Florence's company, picking up all kinds of wasteful notions, instead of doing her farm chores or schoolwork. And all this wedding and bridesmaid business is just the latest joke in the affair! First, as you might expect with Florence's immaturity, the wedding is going ahead one moment but then is called off the next – and now, finally on again. Then, on such doubtful foundations, Florence expects Karen to spend money on some ridiculous bridesmaid's shoes which she will only use once. And since Karen does not yet support herself, this means a drain on the Harvey family resources; for what return? Florence just has no appreciation of familial give-and-take and here she is encouraging the same in Karen.

It might have been different if Florence had invited Fred and Doris to the wedding as well. But no. Flouting the principles of neighbourliness, the Whitehouses have chosen to add insult to injury – even inviting a load of offcomers to what will no doubt be a flashy, city-like affair. There was talk, also, of tying a rope across Cedar High Farm lane in order to direct guests into the chapel and cut off the farm completely! As if the Harveys were just too lowly to be met; as if the lane did not belong to Cedar High Farm and they could not prosecute misuse of it if they so chose!

The joke is that Florence claims to be so religious and charitable. And yet that time when a Sunday school group got stranded in Wanet by snow, Florence would not allow them to spend the night on chapel premises, or even join in with a local service. It needed Fred and Doris to offer to put them up in a couple of old caravans.

And now all this meanness over wedding arrangements and invitations. Once again the Harveys will probably end up doing the nice and proper thing: sending her a wedding card, moving the campers and hoping the weather stays fine.

But what sort of farmer's wife will Florence make? Will she have the stamina to work through her 'off days', and gain Bob's respect? Won't she find that after her spoilt upbringing and lazy hours in the shop, farming the land is just too much for her? She already heads for the doctor's at every little ailment. Florence will be spending her time baking little pastries, inviting folks to 'pop up' for coffee, and there will be Bob, wasting away for want of his meat and potatoes – unless the Thomases end up drowning her in the milk-tank first!

Whatever happens, Florence will soon be part of the Thomas set-up: looking down on them from their farmhouse kitchen, prying into Cedar High news, wishing them ill. (She and Young Bob will not be strong enough to stand up to Old Man Thomas's cursing and temper.) Maybe the best plan would be a new line of conifers to spoil her view ...

Not only does the above tell of differences of opinion between the Harveys and the Whitehouses on all manner of day-to-day matters to do with their adjacent land holdings, but also of attitudes absolutely opposed and exclusionary. The Whitehouses complain of being overlooked by Cedar High Farm campers, and the Harveys by Vaila guests; each feels their rights to privacy on their land and to the absolute absence of the sight, sound and smell of others crossing their boundaries, to have been infringed. Each is affronted by the other's denial of their right to space and the attempt to crowd them out. The propriety, as each sees it, is of exclusive access to the land that they occupy, and of the absolute right of expansion. The actuality is of outsiders somehow claiming mutual rights. And the hope of each is that this present tension might in future be resolved in their favour.

However, it should not be understood that each family and its members always or necessarily adopts a single or consistent moral position *vis-à-vis* what lies outside it, as the following section demonstrates.

INSIDE DORIS HARVEY: THE VILLAGER VERSUS THE BITTER WOMAN VERSUS THE ENGLISHWOMAN

In this third discursive section, Doris Harvey's views as a local individual are focused upon: her wish to defend her land, and her rightful claims to it, from a number of would-be usurpers. Again, the rights and the threats are of an absolute kind, and Doris works towards an absolute freedom from threat and vindication of her rights in future. What is seen here, however, is a diversity of attitude even within Doris. Just as Wanet farmers and offcomers, and the Harveys and the Whitehouses, cannot agree on the terms of their differences, other than the fact that they centre around Wanet farmland, so Doris Harvey herself expresses a number of attitudes to her land and a number of definitions of its outsiders (foreign immigrants in England, townies country-wide, government officials and petty bureaucrats world-wide, and all manner of cheating, competitive, lazy and fickle neighbours in Wanet), each of which is exclusive and of an absolute kind.

I recount three discourses from Doris, which, for the sake of clarity, I label: Doris as a villager; Doris as a bitter woman; Doris as an Englishwoman.

Doris as a villager

Doris knows that she belongs to a traditional way of life in Wanet which, in the past, could be perfect; old-fashioned perhaps (in the eyes of outsiders), but to those who grew up in it, the best. It was also hard, and bred hard people, but then they were suited to Wanet's cold and damp climate, and had learnt to live on its sodden fells. They could foretell when the dale was to be cut off by snow; when a morning moon meant late evening light; how best to exploit the dry-stone walling that marched straight up the fells, and the barns that lay just below the allotments; how to speak Wanet language and repeat local sayings and customs.

Work was hard in the past but there was always enough of it; and afterwards you would meet fellow villagers in church – each family in its own pew – or informally at homes or in the pub. Everyone took part in local events, like galas and house auctions, and kept abreast of local news by reading it up in the parish magazine or the local newspaper. Everyone prospered on the local diet of eggs, bacon, butter and bread.

Maybe the best thing about the traditional way of life in Wanet was that relations between villagers were so friendly and sure. You knew all about all the members of your family, keeping in close contact even as they moved round the dale from farm to farm; and you were certain to see them all together on Wanet Fair Day. And in those days, families were so alike too: 'Apples fell never far from the tree', as they used to say. That is why Doris is ambitious: like all Thwaites. And you could see all the same features in other families too. So John Beck walled as badly as his father; while Jane Dyson put on weight like her mother; and her Fred was a staunch Liberal like the Harveys all were. There were no gypsies in Wanet then, just local families who lived near one another and knew all about everyone's histories and plans, secrets and quirks. Villagers trusted each other.

Over the past ten years, however, Doris has found that all this has changed. There has been an invasion of offcomers in Wanet; even though they have a different mentality, with no real place here and no local names. Townies come to Wanet bringing their foreign habits and outsider ways of life with them. They are from a different, poorer breeding stock, suited to the cities maybe, but here making them seem feeble and lazy, alcoholic, poor-sighted and time-wasting; they are ignorant of Wanet weather, animals, farming and land. They have no respect for Wanet traditions, but they will not be taught, and seem intent on making Wanet just like the places they left. They steal local words and mispronounce them, or else replace them with ones of their own; just like they steal Wanet land and ruin it for farming. The church now flounders under offcomer pomp. The shops are dirty and shopkeepers argumentative and impolite. The pubs are full of weird-looking strangers, while publicans charge more, overheat the premises for their sickly clientele and close early. The school is staffed by offcomer teachers, uninterested in local ways. It turns out weak, disobedient children who are more likely to riot in the streets than survive working the land. Even adults, Wanet born and bred, are getting contaminated and becoming tired and soft. They prefer TV to work, and act as if they were better than their neighbours – quarrelling with them, hiding their real feelings, finally getting at them through offcomer solicitors. Some locals even end up thinking that they are too good for Wanet and leave the village altogether.

The only solution to the offcomer invasion, Doris believes, is to sit it out. Eventually they must realize that they were not bred for

Wanet land, and their intelligence has evolved to suit elsewhere. In the meantime Doris would like nothing to do with them: avoid outsiders completely, do them no favours, tease them and be hostile as necessary, meanwhile keeping on with the traditional Wanet way of life. She might pity offcomers their lot but nothing condones their trailing away from their homes onto other people's land ...

Doris as a bitter woman

Doris is bitter. For the world is a dump, where misfortune always seems to befall the undeserving at which other people are then happy to gloat.

Doris has not had an easy life. She began with nothing and worked hard for all she has. She started out helping run her parents-in-law's small farm of 21 acres, 17 sheep and 25 cows (7 on milk) with her husband Richard (and little more than £200 cash between them), and after five years or so of hard graft things began to pick up. Then, suddenly, Richard died. For a year Doris was crazy with grief: all of Wanet seemed concerned. Finally, gradually, Doris picked up the pieces, and began to make a go of Cedar High Farm herself. She mucked out, hay timed and looked forward to springtime on the land. But her neighbours soon changed their tune. Horribly fickle, they disliked it as she tried to get ahead, make a little money and improve herself. They preferred to pity her than envy her, and soon began standing in her way.

Then Doris met Fred Harvey, and in him found someone equally fired by a will to make Cedar High Farm work; and it proved a good partnership. After just two years, the farm was keeping them both and Fred could give up his previous job as a joiner. Now they own most of 60 acres, 100 sheep, 80 cows (40 on milk). Money is still hard to come by, and they work very hard, but slowly they are proving themselves. Doris can now feel proud at having achieved something out of nothing. She has done it for Richard, and to show other folks that she can succeed despite their hindrance and without their charity. And Doris swears that they will not backslide, and that, for example, Fred will never again have to leave their land and go out to work. The farm is her and Fred's joint project and it will see them both through.

Of course, this has made Doris no more popular. Indeed, the more she and Fred have prospered, the more jealous and opposed her neighbours have become: the more eager to ruin them, scrounge, steal, take over the farm and return her to her unhappy, grievous state. One neighbour is happy to rob them of a cheap £50 lease that they desperately wanted for pasture; another tries to outbid them for a hay meadow they are already renting; a third anonymously reports them to the National Park inspectorate and stirs up trouble. When they employ another neighbour as a farm labourer, it turns out to be merely a ploy to get on to their land, so that he can saunter around it as if he owned it, and boast afterwards that their success is due to the help and work of others.

But by now Doris knows that this is normal fare. And yet, with each other, Doris feels that she and Fred can carry on. This is her land and she will never give up an inch of it. Cedar High farmland, and the farmhouse, and their bed together: these are the boundaries of her and Fred's sanctuary, and she will do whatever is necessary to defend her home and show herself to be no easy prey ...

Doris as an Englishwoman

Doris knows that national differences reflect natural ones. Thus each of the world's nations possesses a different breeding stock, as well as a different way of life. Each nationality is naturally suited to its own nation and land, with its own habits, abilities, personal names, temperaments, problems and solutions. Fred, her husband, can tell her about these things because in his Navy days he had to travel the world. But Doris is not in fact all that interested. What happens outside England is not really relevant, and rarely comprehensible; and the more distant and weird the nation, the truer this becomes. But that's only natural. Each nationality is happiest dealing with its own kind in its own nation. Doris is at home with English situations and among fellow Englishmen, then, and it would be a joke to suggest that she could be happier elsewhere than the England for which she was bred.

What is unnatural is the mixing of nationalities. Habits meet that do not suit one another. And this has been the case since the recent, sad invasion of non-English into England. With bad consequences: Jews becoming property sharks and bleeding English tenants; blacks making ghettos, getting fat living off the dole, breeding fast and ruining the English economy. Not to mention the Chinese, Arabs and curry-eaters, and all manner of other 'tribes'. And English children being scared by meeting foreigners all round the place.

What is even worse is that mixing leads to the unnatural act of interbreeding. No species should breed with another, but in England it seems to be happening more and more; so that in the worst places, like inner cities, order is being replaced by a riotous bedlam. It is frightening to imagine these mixed breeds taking over the land in the end: all Englishmen going from white to black and becoming tribes with the rest of them.

What is clear is that a successful nation is a separate nationality (no foreigner can do an English job better than an Englishman). So Englishmen should be brought home and foreigners sent away to breed with their own kind. Then the defences can be raised, and all Englishmen rally round the flag ...

AN ANALYSIS OF DISCURSIVE FORM

Up to this point, I have been describing local attitudes to the 'other', the outsider in Wanet, as these relate to an appreciation and use of local land. Animated by self-righteousness, here are various everyday discourses which would morally exclude outsiders from landownership and use, from that proper belonging in Wanet that landownership brings.

The chief characteristic of these discourses so far stressed has been their radical diversity: who the 'outsider' is to the 'local' speaker, what their character and behaviour entails, varies per discourse.[9] And yet, beside this diversity can also be placed a singularity. For the 'outsider' has always been described as fundamentally different from the 'local'; also decried as morally reprehensible or inferior; also regarded as a threat; and also seen as properly deserving expulsion (if not worse). Here are substantively different discourses being imbued by a moral imperative of the same form: here are contradictory moral treatments (of the outsider by the landed local) characterized alike by *symbolic absolutism*. Let me explore this characteristic further.

In his work of comparative ontology, *Other Tribes, Other Scribes*, James Boon reflected on the way that identity is constituted through comparison and contrast.[10] One achieves identity by saying what one is not, by 'playing the *vis-à-vis*', by reaching out to otherness and then holding it dialectically, ironically, at bay. Identities, Boon surmised, are intrinsically comparative, fundamentally beside themselves, implicitly admitting their own negativity (Boon 1982: 230–231).

Moreover, this 'nay-saying' can occur, as a procedure to identity, at a variety of symbolic levels and junctures at the same time. If cultural environments as 'wholes' reach out toward their opposites, then such environments are also internally 'auto-dislocated', so that every discourse of which they are composed, every word and behaviour, similarly inclines towards what it is not and alludes to what is absent from itself. One appreciates the identities of cultural institutions and organizations, of social groups and persons, of 'eras, -ologies and -isms', as all in continuing antithetical relationship with the elements of their own negation (ibid. 1982: 231–233). Hence: kinship relations versus market relations; classicism versus Romanticism; psychology versus sociology, Jewish versus Christian, Joseph versus Christopher.

Finally, Boon suggested, this nay-saying, this setting up of a dialectical other, can be of two types, themselves in a dialectical relationship with each other, a historical meta-dialectic. He dubbed them 'Tribal' versus 'Scribal'; also 'generalizing' versus 'centralizing' practices. The Tribal/generalized practice of nay-saying conceives of the relationship with the other as of between *mutual necessities*. Hence: sacred and profane; male and female; night and day; moiety 'a' and moiety 'b'. Moreover, there is often the further balance in Tribal practice whereby *ego* and *alter* mutually recognize their symbolic interdependence, that 'anything they are to me, I am to them'. By contrast, the Scribal/centralized practice of nay-saying conceives of this same relationship with the other as of between *mutual exclusions*. Hence: good and evil; traditional and modern; communism and capitalism; Toshiba and Compaq. Moreover, this is a competitive practice, often organized so that the winner overwhelms or destroys or coopts the loser; expanding into the latter's space, he may hope ultimately to envelop all the outside (ibid. 1982: 235–236).

An important aspect of the Tribal and Scribal is that they do not represent an evolution. Boon, to repeat, describes their relationship as dialectical. Tribal is a condition that he cites with approbation, compared with a literate, Western fetish for a cultural imperialism which denies the value of other cultures; whose Scribal nay-saying, if not checked, may one day eventuate in a 'spiceless, uniform monoculture': the expansion of the circle of Western culture to circumscribe the globe (ibid. 1982: 237). There is an absoluteness inherent in the Scribal, an intolerance of difference, a reaching out towards a contrastive other only to overcome its oppositeness, which the Tribal does not evoke. The Tribal is ready to maintain more of a steady state (of cultural circles in partial overlap), and relativize differences in a system containing all.

Furthermore, Boon's description of Tribal and Scribal as a dialectical, not an evolutionary pair also makes it clear why his discussion is pertinent to the treatment of the other and the achieving of identity in Wanet.[11] For a Scribal nay-saying distinguishes all the above ethnography. Being a local in Wanet entails an absolute exclusion of the outsider, whether 'outsider' refers to foreign immigrants, National Park wardens, retired offcomers, tourists, the Whitehouse family next door or other farmers espied from one's farmhouse windows. Here is a Scribal intolerance towards others: others defined as a threat, in competition, in occupation of land that could and perhaps should be *ego*'s, and therefore to be excluded, expropriated, expulsed. In stark contrast to this, meanwhile, can be heard outsider claims and manifestos, government policies and National Park directives which bespeak a hopeful, intended Tribalism. That is, the characteristic form of discourse expressed by offcomers, by tourists, by the retired, by administrators, officials and bureaucrats, by 'outsiders', whether within Wanet or without, is of properly making space for the other, of welcoming and accommodating otherness, of respecting the rights of *alter* to gain access to and use of *ego*'s land. If the proprieties of life are reassuringly Scribal, according to the Wanet view, then increasingly the actualities of life are Tribal as 'locals' are surrounded by people and plans that ignore those proprieties. If the past is seen as rosily Scribal then the future is threateningly Tribal: regional, national and international expectations of symbolic relativism.[12]

And this, I suggest, provides the major tension within which life in Wanet is lived today – the indignation, the animation, the measure of life, the ideal. For if the Tribal is feared as the coming, hegemonic discursive form, then the battle of life, for 'locals', is still to retain, to return to, the Scribal.[13] The tension between the two imbues much of discursive exchange in Wanet, sometimes expressed as seeming light-hearted banter, as wishful thinking, sometimes as more openly serious and worrisome deliberation.[14] Direct action is also in evidence, especially when it comes to controlling what is seen as still indisputably local.

To return to the Harveys for a moment, then, treatment by Doris and Fred of their children is instructive as illustration of the maintenance of Scribalism, of symbolic absolutism, within the family home. For the morality of education is that children are not to question: children, Doris and Fred know, should learn solely by imitation. As children grow and mature, so they can imitate and comprehend more, but by and large this is a silent process. Parents speak, parents occupy public space absolutely; children take over from them only when parents begin physically and mentally to decline. Thus the generations properly follow one another in an exclusionary manner, and interaction between them at any one time is of an absolutist kind: absolutely silent children, absolutely moral and competent parents. One is a proper public actor and thus a legitimate member of the local community (however variously defined), or one is not.

This caused great problems for me as a newcomer residing in Wanet and on Cedar High Farm.[15] Eventually, Doris and Fred came to treat me as a surrogate child, as a silent, incompetent, immature non-actor, but at first there were a number of ambiguities to be overcome. I claimed to be British, to be adult and to wish to spend an appreciable amount of time in Wanet. And yet I did not exhibit adult competency and I did not possess knowledge or appreciation of Wanet skills. Also, I would ask questions. But if I was British, I should know the same things; and I should also know not to ask. Was I therefore lying about my Britishness? Was I casting aspersions on their Britishness? And yet, Doris and Fred knew of *their* adult and British competencies with absolute certainty. Thus, in short, I could not stay in Wanet as adult and British *and* ask questions about local life. If I was a foreign adult, I should leave; if I was a British child (despite my twenty-odd years), I should keep quiet. And then Doris and Fred might kindly undertake to (make up for lost time and) act as my teachers and role models: make a big effort and bring me within their social universe. Here was an absolute choice and my first experience of that self-righteous indignation that greeted a challenge to their categorical distinctions, and which I came to characterize as a 'moral' affront.

Of course, I chose the 'local' (child-like) option. And I was fortunate; not all offcomers were given the opportunity. They might not be physically expelled but they were despised. Formal politeness might prevail in public interaction, but they were ostracized when it came to the more significant networks of gossip. Offcomers might be able to outspend locals and buy up quaint cottages along the valley bottom and in Wanet village, but as far as possible they were refused access to the farmsteads on the fells – the symbolic as well as the actual high ground, as we have seen – and selling land to them was greeted with moral opprobrium.

To recap: the 'outsider' is regarded by the 'local' in Wanet as absolutely unwanted and unnecessary; symbolically, the outsider is denied access to local sentimental space. The only relationship with otherness recognized as proper is the latter's symbolic cooptation or exclusion and extinction. Hence, Wanet Scribalism maintains itself and works towards a better future (modelled on an idyllic past) by reiterating a discourse of symbolic absolutism. The dialectical tension that Boon posits between Scribal and Tribal is accommo-dated in Wanet through the local Scribalists' believing in its temporariness. The present situation is an aberration and the future will hopefully represent a rapid return to the past, when there was only the Scribal, when *alter* knew its place, and when that place was nowhere within *ego*'s compass. One day (soon), *alter* will vanish, will be forced to go, will see the error and inferiority of its ways and leave *ego* (Doris as a farmer; Doris as English; the Harvey family; Wanet as a dale community) alone again and in sole occupancy of and control over the whole land. Meanwhile Scribalism provides a commonality to local discourses and a differentiation from outsider discourses; also a means by which that outside can be formally engaged. So that some questions can continue to be asked: are the local proprieties of life expanding or retreating? are outsiders being encouraged or forced to leave? to what extent is my land now my own, in the sole embrace of my will? The Scribal/Tribal tension represents a (meta-)discourse for the maintenance and measuring of continued discursive difference between 'local' and 'outside'.[16]

CONCLUSION

'Morality', in this chapter, has been understood in terms of a sense of righteous indignation; this I intuited among certain informants in Wanet when outsiders were seen to breach or threaten boundaries of local land. Here was a morality of locality, I suggested, which expressed itself as an absolute exclusivity of landownership.

In conclusion, I would reiterate that this link between morality and land is to be understood discursively and not social – structurally. I do not paint a Durkheimian picture. The land is not always 'moral' in this way, or necessarily a topic of indignation or dignification; likewise, there is a diversity of ways in which individuals construct circumstances of moral propriety and outrage.[17] Finally, it is only 'the friendly ambiguities of language' (Sapir 1956: 153), its formal similarities, that enables these individual acts of moralizing, these diverse speech acts, to appear to give onto (and work for) a Wanet collectivity.[18] However social and holistic the moral may appear, in actuality, it conveys a sense of order and propriety which is always particular, partial and contingent: the discursive construction of individual actors – and their anthropologists.

ACKNOWLEDGEMENTS

I am grateful to Robert Paine, Richard Werbner, Pnina Werbner, Sophia Mappa, Eduardo Archetti and Signe Howell for their helpful commentary on early drafts of this paper.

NOTES

1 See Rapport (1993, 1994a).
2 Marilyn Strathern (also this volume) argues correspondingly for an understanding of morality through gender relations. Differences between sexual alignments in Papua New Guinea can provide information concerning moral and amoral spheres of action and existence, and the causing of deliberate movement between spheres.
3 This 'moral tone' concerns what the speaker regards as desirable as well as proper (as Eduardo Archetti would similarly phrase it), what is worthwhile as well as what is right, what is emotionally as well as intellectually acceptable. (Cf. Clifford Geertz on the proclivity of 'sacred symbols' for bringing the emotional and the intellectual into accord [Geertz 1973: 126–141]).
4 Eduardo Archetti's argument (this volume) can be read similarly: Argentinian football represents a 'national imagery' in which any number of 'individualistic moralities' can meet. Using common discursive symbols, individual actors can be heard constructing a plurality of moral meanings and making a diversity of moral choices. (Cf. John Szwed on the plurality of private economic choices which get made within the commonality of public imagery in a Newfoundland parish [Szwed 1966: *passim*]).
5 See Rapport (1987: 19–22, 170ff.).
6 While not wholly polite, 'offcomer' is the local term most frequently heard to designate those regarded as newcomers to Wanet; also, 'offcomed-'uns'. Less polite designations also occur: 'long-haired Arabs', 'trailing Hebrews', 'Herdwicks' (cf. Rapport 1993: 59).

7 To wit: drapers, tailors, butchers, boot and shoe makers, carters, gardeners, gamekeepers, jewellers, clock repairers, cycle manufacturers, carriers, railwaymen, coal agents, bakers, coachmen, dressmakers and confectioners.

8 National parks were set up in Britain (by Acts of Parliament) in the 1950s, to ensure that areas of 'outstanding natural beauty' were conserved, and their recreational enjoyment by visitors promoted. Just over a fifth of England and Wales has now been accorded some form of official 'protection' for the beauty of its countryside or the rarity of its wildlife, with local councils delegating a number of their powers and responsibilities to (partially unelected) national park committees. Wanet has been under national park jurisdiction since their inception. The land is locally owned but the park is mandated to maintain the 'settled harmony' of the dale.

9 On the development of such diverse discourses, their strategic usage and contestation, see Rapport (1987, 1994b).

10 For a detailed appreciation of Boon's work, see Brady (1993: *passim*).

11 Cf. Gregory Bateson's comparable thesis on 'centripetal' and 'peripheral' processes of social organization (Bateson 1936: 277–281). Here are two dialectically opposed ways of conceptualizing the relationship between identity, dislocation, and sameness and difference. The centripetal is based on a complementarity of members' behaviour – different and so compatible – while the peripheral is based on symmetricality – the same and so alternative. In any one moment, says Bateson, there will be an 'interplay' between these two: a tension which is ultimately constitutive of a wider social picture of relationships.

12 Comparisons may be drawn with the 'moral crises' that Eduardo Archetti (this volume) outlines for Argentinian football when outside and inferior traditions of play are seen as gaining ground.

13 In a form that might accommodate itself to any of the discourses we have heard, then, are common local words such as the following:

> In the past, Wanet was a haven: no outsiders, no dictation from Westminster and Brussels, no local change, simply a secure home. This was centred on a satisfying, traditional way of life which everyone knew and shared alike; it was fitting and right. Indeed, so right was it that people from Wanet periodically left to colonize the outside, just as Englishmen left to civilize the foreigner.
>
> But now all is different. The outsider and foreigner feel that they have the right to adulterate England and Wanet, to rub shoulders on local land. In future, therefore, a halt must somehow be called. The outsider and foreigner must be shown that they do not belong in England and in Wanet, and that their way of life is inferior.

14 For instance, accompanying Kevin's schemes for cheating tourists at darts, there is jokey talk in the pub about a Wanet Liberation Army (the equivalent of the Irish Republican Army) posting sentries on the fell-tops and policing who can gain entry to the dale; because there are undoubtedly spies from outside (even Baader-Meinhof terrorists)

already infiltrating Wanet on reconnaissance missions. Similarly, there is jokey talk of the possibility of dynamiting offcomer homes in the village (just as the Welsh have done to English cottagers), and of beating up any offcomer who tells tales about Wanet to other offcomers (and so risks others discovering it) – if the offcomers do not fall ill and finally die of their own accord, from living in an environment and occupying land for which they are not congenitally suited. More seriously, there is talk of refusing to cooperate with offcomers who sit on local committees and councils so that eventually the latter must fail and collapse.

15 See Rapport (1993: 55–68).

16 Cf. Marilyn Strathern's account of the discourse of villageness in Elmdon, Essex (Strathern 1981, 1982). All residents may 'roughly agree', Strathern explains, about the saliency of a villager/stranger opposition and about the kind of person to whom the term 'Real Elmdon' might apply. But substantively, with regard to actual use of this discourse, there is only discrepancy and ambiguity (Strathern 1982: 255). In Michael Walzer's (Geertzian-sounding) terminology, here is 'thin' moral agreement, a minimal sharing of standards, which can disguise 'thick' moral argument concerning the maximal, plural applications of those standards (Walzer 1994). What a minimalist discourse of (Elmdon) villageness does provide, none the less, is a provocative image of a boundary: a means by which people can simultaneously engage with wider English society and culture – with its predominant discourse of class – and differentiate themselves from it (Strathern 1981: 34). Also cf. Anthony Cohen on 'Real Whalsay' (Cohen 1978: 453).

17 As Signe Howell puts it (Howell 1992: 124–125, 136) in regard to the comparative study of another cognitive phenomenon, time: one might *expect* a series of cognitive mapping procedures always to be taking place, and for these to manifest themselves in a diverse range of social phenomena (subsistence activities, social and political institutions, rituals and so forth) in ways which are far from straightforward.

18 Cf. George Devereux's notion of 'ego-syntonism' (Devereux 1978: 126). Also Cf. Rapport (1994c).

REFERENCES

Bateson, G. (1936) *Naven*, Cambridge: Cambridge University Press.

Boon, J. (1982) *Other Tribes, Other Scribes*, Cambridge: Cambridge University Press.

Brady, I. (1993) 'Tribal Fire and Scribal Ice', in P. Benson (ed.) *Anthropology and Literature*, Urbana: University of Illinois Press.

Cohen, A.P. (1978) ' "The same but different": the allocation of identity in Whalsay, Shetland', *Sociological Review* 26 (3).

Devereux, G. (1978) *Ethnopsychoanalysis*, Berkeley: University of California Press.

Geertz, C. (1973) *The Interpretation of Cultures*, New York: Basic.

Howell, S. (1992) 'Time past, time present, time future: contrasting temporal values in two Southeast Asian Societies', in S. Wallman (ed.) *Contemporary Futures*, London: Routledge.

Rapport, N.J. (1987) *Talking Violence: An Anthropological Interpretation of Conversation in the City*, St John's: ISER Press, Memorial University.

——(1993) *Diverse World-Views in an English Village*, Edinburgh: Edinburgh University Press.

——(1994a) *The Prose and the Passion: Anthropology, Literature and the Writing of E.M. Forster*, Manchester: Manchester University Press.

——(1994b) ' "Busted for hash": common catchwords and individual identities in a Canadian city', in V. Amit-Talai and H. Lustiger-Thaler (eds) *Urban Lives: Fragmentation and Resistance*, Toronto: McClelland & Stewart.

——(1994c) 'Trauma and ego-syntonic response: the holocaust and "the Newfoundland young yids" ', 1985, in S. Heald and A. Deluz (eds) *Anthropology and Psychoanalysis*, London: Routledge.

Sapir, E. (1956) *Culture, Language and Personality*, Berkeley: University of California Press.

Strathern, M. (1981) *Kinship at the Core*, Cambridge: Cambridge University Press.

——(1982) 'The village as an idea: constructs of villageness in Elmdon, Essex', in A. P. Cohen (ed.) *Belonging*, Manchester: Manchester University Press.

Szwed, J. (1966) *Private Cultures and Public Imagery*, St John's: ISER Press, Memorial University.

Walzer, M. (1994) *Thick and Thin: Moral Argument at Home and Abroad*, Notre Dame: University of Notre Dame Press.

Chapter 4

The moralities of Argentinian football

Eduardo P. Archetti

While talking about the importance of football in the daily life of so many *porteños* (inhabitants of the city of Buenos Aires), Carlos, one of my informants who is in his early forties, said: 'Los argentinos somos de raza futbolística' ('We Argentinians are of football breed'), and added, anticipating my answer, 'Yes, I know, women are not of the same breed, although they accompany us, they tolerate us, and there are men who do not agree with the majority of us.'[1] He continued:

> You know what I mean. We must learn to think as a united people, as a society. Argentinians are very individualistic, with little national feeling ... except when the national football team plays. Then our patriotism emerges, including many of the people who feel that football is not important. We enjoy being well represented, that the national team plays well, and we like to win. In many senses it is a demonstration of what we are.

In some ways, I thought, he was right and he expressed an argument that I had heard many times before.

Argentina was, at the end of the nineteenth century and for the first two decades into the twentieth century, integrated into the global scene of massive world commodity exchange, vast intercontinental migrations, urban consumption images and desires, sports competitions and circulation of mass cultural products. In 1916 the first South American Cup was organized and until the late 1950s Argentinian national teams largely dominated the tournament. From 1904, when Southampton played several matches in Buenos Aires and returned to England undefeated, and until the 1930s, English, Scottish, Spanish, Hungarian and Austrian teams took the boat over the Atlantic to play in Buenos Aires against the best first division teams, and, occasionally, also in Rosario, the second largest Argentinian city. At the same time Argentinian club teams played throughout South America with great success and also travelled to Europe. In 1925, Boca Juniors was the first Argentinian first division club team to play in Portugal, Spain, France, Italy, Austria and Germany, and with great success.

Euphemistically, Argentinians call the national team *la selección*, 'the selection', in the sense of the pick of the best, while the players are called *los seleccionados*, 'the selected', the chosen. One of the favourite pastimes of my informants was to imagine the all-time selection, the eternal selection (*la selección eterna, el seleccionado de todos los tiempos*), made up by players who had played the national team during different historical periods with unequalled success. Since 1928, when Argentina reached the final in the Olympic Games in Amsterdam, generations of Argentinian men have heard on the radio, read in the newspapers and sports magazines and seen on television, the presentation of their national football teams and footballers playing all over the world. The different *selecciones* have been perceived as models and mirrors of what my informant described for me: an expression of Argentinian breed and a display of national male virtues and qualities. In this paper I will concentrate on the historical, social and cultural meaning of the national team. In connection with this I will touch upon the variations of identities related to the history of the clubs and the impact that this has had on the process of producing a national imagery.

Argentinian football fans have experienced great moments of despair and disappointment as, for example, when the national team lost the Olympics, and the World Cup finals three times, but also happiness and pride when they won two World Cup finals. Argentinian football history is rich and dramatic, local and global, and is embedded in moral values and judgements and more or less articulated discourses. The complex codes of honour and shame are usually related to unexpected victories or defeats when an expected loss is transformed into a startling victory or clear superiority is turned into a humiliating defeat. My ethnographic account will reflect the type of research that I have been carrying out intermittently in the city of Buenos Aires since 1984. My focus is on the plurality of male identities and moralities as created and transformed in the popular cultures of football and the tango. The research combines a historical reconstruction, based on written and oral sources, with the predominant contemporary moral debates in which my informants are engaged.

THE FIELD OF MORALITY

Assuming that the field of morality covers a vast area of actions and evaluations, it is difficult to imagine that we can attain the totality of moral codes and ideals without directing our concern to particular concrete activities. In this direction, we study morality, what is good or evil or right and wrong, through issues in which morality, presumably, is reflected. We can analyse morality when we look at explanations of disease and misfortune, of fate, of gender relations, of marriage and family, of accepted games and so on. Actions and beliefs are key indicators not only of the moral code but also of contexts and actors. The anthropological analysis allows us to find local moral codes by examining contexts and concrete discourses (see Rapport this volume). But still, in doing so, anthropologists diverge in how to reflect the importance of society as a moral system. There is a tendency to perceive moral codes as the main support of social relations between groups and persons. It is expected that anthropologists shall provide an ethnographic account of virtues, obligations, sanctions and feelings that make possible a detailed description of social moral values and modes of achieving them (see Edel and Edel 1959: 9). I do not intend to deny the importance of such an assumption, but personally I feel that we can gain new insights if we also consider the field of morality and moral analysis as a dynamic cultural code that informs, creates and gives meaning to social relations (see Melhuus this volume).

Lukes (1981: 410–434) has pointed out that Durkheim gradually deepened his view of morality as a social and cultural phenomenon, moving away from an exclusive concentration on moral rules and their obligatory character. Durkheim did not accept that a rational definition of duty, or a utilitarian respect for sanctions, are sufficient as a basis for moral commitment. Morality requires compassion, fervour and a sense of engagement. Thus, the later Durkheim (1953: 91) emphasized both the desirability aspect and the emotive character of morality, postulating that it is through ritual practice and social effervescence that norms are internalized. If we look for those moments of effervescence, we are usually confronted with periods of creation and renewal when new ideas and new relationships emerge out of crisis and conflicts. To ask, then, what is right and wrong is not enough. We also need to focus our research on what is desirable or worthwhile for the actors. It is important to see that these are different questions, for, while perhaps everything that is desirable to do is also something that one is obliged to do, it is still not the case that *saying* that something is worthwhile or desirable is the same as saying that one is obliged to do it.

If we accept the crucial role of desire in the constitution of the emotive character of morality we need not necessarily eliminate from our analysis either the cognitive or the affective components. The cognitive component in Durkheim's consideration was related to the key role played by moral beliefs. Durkheim (1953: 77) emphasized the importance of finding moral ideals through the consultation of popular beliefs and people's reactions when such beliefs are contravened in practice. Holding true to moral judgements, the strong sense of the meaning of beliefs does not exclude an opening to examine other cognitive components like thoughts, apprehensions or imagination. Moreover, subjective affectivity in the sense of expressing pity, fear, sympathy, admiration or tenderness, constitutes the basis of the relation between the individual and the society. Feelings fuse cognitive aspects with desires and sanctioning, negative or positive, acting as moral indices (see Edel and Edel 1959: 188). Durkheim (1915: 207–208, and 1992: 112), in his study of religion as well as in the study of civic morals, provides a theory of the emotive character of morality in terms of the importance of subjective affectivity.

If we accept a perspective on morality that holds open the possibility of considering the construction of meanings as not completely given, as containing choices for the actors, our ethnographic account must deal with the type of arguments used, how discontent is expressed and accepted and how ambivalence and pluralism are tackled. This implies that there exists a division of normative ethical theories about what is intrinsically desirable into monistic and pluralistic theories. The existence of these different theories illustrates the point made by Evens (1989) that moral choices must be seen as conditioned by projects and reasons rather than by causes. This approach permits the consideration of moral choices and morality as a way by which actors construct meanings. Moral codes or fundamental values are not directly translated into behaviour; they are often mediated through moral choices.

Morality is not silent; it must be articulated in discourse. It must, to a great extent, be public since moral discourses include processes of guidance. In the everyday life of modern Western societies we are barraged with a variety of moral claims and counter-claims: the moral arguments in support of them are diverse and conflicting (see Strathern this volume). Moral choices could not exist without the possibility of relating projects and reasons to the existence of sound moral arguments. The elusive power of moral discourses is commonly related to three general properties: the claim to objectivity; the claim to universality based on relating an observed similarity of behaviour to a given context; and the concern for practicality, for action and for attitude-moulding. Beyond these claims, as Evens (1989) has argued, moral discourses constitute autonomous modes of discourses. Morality in society, no matter how carefully it is elaborated, can never become fully empirical. Actors cannot discover what they ought to do or what is desirable from a knowledge of non-moral facts alone, including the facts about human nature and conduct. As anthropologists we must try to find empirically the focus of organization of moral discourses in the analysis of the occasions and styles of moral utterances, how much generalization is used, and how arguments are patterned. Through the analysis of moral discourses in Argentinian football I attempt to depict an active and public process of understanding, evaluating and arguing about the following:

1 Male virtues.
2 The importance of traditions, roots and historical continuity.
3 The meaning of styles and ways of playing football.
4 Ideas, concerns and definitions of 'happiness' and of 'feeling happy'.

With regard to the meaning of 'happiness' and 'happy' I will particularly concentrate my analysis on the importance of connecting happiness to given feelings and emotions or, in other words, I will explore how the actors themselves relate 'important emotions' to the realization of inner desires made possible by male virtues displayed in the style of playing. A deep personal engagement in football implies a given risk: the fans always stand on the terraces with similar amounts of fear and hope. But fear and hope are not only related to the mere result of a match because to be happy is not necessarily associated with victory. Provisionally we can accept that a man is happy if he is not subject to gloom, anxiety, depression, discouragement, melancholy and, especially among fans, shame. In the ethnographic presentation it will be clear that to be happy requires positive feelings. It seems to me that we would not call a man happy if he did not frequently feel joy or enthusiasm or enjoy what he was doing or experiencing. My informants usually speak in connection with football about 'feeling happy' (*sentirse feliz*) and rarely about 'being happy' (*ser feliz*); this important distinction will become clear in the presentation of my findings.

By discussing the moralities of football I try to analyse how the historically available symbols and ideological statements are re-created in new patterns of meaning. The moral discourses of social actors create a scene in which available symbols and historical narratives, new experiences related to given situations, images and sports results, new questions, answers to these questions and judgements about the correctness of these answers are mixed together. Thus, normative discourses can be seen as general attempts to understand the nature of moral responsibilities and to persuade others that one's understandings and evaluations are 'correct'. The presentation of discourses will be guided by the theoretical arguments put forward in this section.

THE MORALITIES OF FOOTBALL

In the presentation of my ethnographic findings I will concentrate on the way that morality is constituted as a discursive practice when Argentinians reflect on the historical achievements and defeats of the national football. I will show that at moments of crisis, morality is presented and experienced in terms of moral choices. This perspective renders possible an analysis on the plurality of male identities and moralities as constructed public discourses in Argentina. I hope to be able to show that while it is crucial to get to know what is defined as good in itself, it is also crucial to determine what is perceived by the different social actors as worthwhile and desirable.

After an unforgettable match in the South American Cup between Independiente from Argentina and Olimpia from Paraguay one Wednesday night during the very cold winter of 1984, I was sitting with 29-year-old Héctor, a devoted fan of Independiente, in an old café in the main plaza of Avellaneda, an industrial neighbourhood of Buenos Aires. We had decided to escape from the crowd fighting to get into the buses going to the centre of Buenos Aires. While waiting for the cappuccino and the traditional glass of genever Bols, Héctor insisted on telling me a story which, according to him, was a beautiful synthesis of the philosophy of football as a game: the contradiction between elegance and force. He began:

When I was a child, in the 1960s, my father slowly introduced me to the history of Independiente. He would say that it is not possible to experience every situation in life at a football arena, but, he repeated again and again, that a vast amount of situations and ceremonies of life are part of the game. Thus, he always told me stories full of heroes and villains. The heroes and villains, who were always players, were transformed into victims, orators, judges, killers, jugglers, workers, bureaucrats, usurers, impostors, criminals, mercenaries, magicians and survivors. My father insisted that under the influence of the passion and the involvement of the game, different types of men coexist – expressing generosity, misery, enthusiasm, tragedy, comedy, magic and hope. He told me a very beautiful story, one that he believed represented the contradictions of football. He remembered that in the 1920s Independiente had a good team, with an excellent right insider, Lalin, a juggler, and a very effective killer, the centre-forward Seoane, *The Pig*. The episode happened in a match against Estudiantes de La Plata. During the first half Lalin kept the ball for himself, all the time, danced and dribbled with it. 'Can you picture, my son,' he asked me, 'when you play football with an orange until it softens and you see the juice? Well, Lalin transformed the ball into an orange, in each match the ball was transformed into an orange. Seoane did not like it at all. His job was to produce goals and to win. You know, to make goals is indeed the most dramatic moment of football. Lalin was postponing the moment when winners and losers are divided and joy and disappointment are experienced. Seoane did not like it. In the break, Seoane insisted on getting the ball: "Lalin, if you can give me the ball, just one cross-ball, and that is what we need, I give you my guarantee, one cross-ball, one goal." At the beginning of the second half,' my father said, doubting for a moment, 'I think it was in the second minute, Lalin sent a cross-ball, a perfect cross-ball, and Seoane, like the goal-machine he was, volleyed it into the goal. Goal, what a nice score,' my father added. 'Seoane, very happy, ran to embrace and to thank Lalin and said: "You see, if we play like this we will win, we will always win." Lalin answered laconically: "Yes, I am sure, we can always win, but if we play in this way I do not enjoy the game." '

I remembered this story and each time I met Héctor during 1984 and again in 1988, we agreed on the ambivalent meaning of joy, of happiness and of feeling happy expressed in the story told by his father. For Lalin, we imagined, to feel happy was not ultimately related to victory, which was the real meaning of football according to Seoane. For Lalin the pleasure of the game was not to inflict moral pain on the losers; in his world, there was no compelling place for efficient and determined centre-forwards. Lalin knew that in football the loser has an opaque destiny of forgetfulness. In my discussion with Héctor, he mentioned that his father used this story in order to counterpoise 'the romantic figure of the juggler to the cold and metallic role played by a killer'.

Several years later, during my stay in Buenos Aires in 1993, I understood that the story of Héctor's father was, in a way, part of an Argentinian historical narrative in which the oral sources are mixed with heterogeneous authoritative texts (see Humphrey this volume). Ricardo Lorenzo, a prestigious sports journalist and writer, referred to the event in a short article (Lorenzo 1946: 47). All the theatrical elements in Héctor's father's story are present, but the end is different. Lalin's reply to Seoane states the importance of victory: 'Yes, but I do not enjoy myself. Is football to mean just goals? How horrible!' (ibid.).

Ernesto Sábato, the great Argentinian novelist, incorporated the story into his novel *Sobre héroes y tumbas* (Sábato 1961: 86–87). The setting here is located to a bar in Parque Lezama, a neighbourhood of Buenos Aires. Some friends, drinking the traditional afternoon vermouth, exchange ideas about the negative transformations in modern football which have brought about an extreme aggressivity among the players, only interested in winning and less and less in the creation of beauty. One of them refers to the Lalin–Seoane story in order to illustrate the overriding importance of goals. In this story, the reply of Lalin is: 'Yes, but I do not amuse myself', and the narrator concludes: 'You see, if you like, here lies the problem of Argentinian football' (Sábato 1961: 87). The conflict of Argentinian football is, then, the abandonment of elegance and beauty and the consolidation of a way of feeling the game based on the cult of efficiency and results. The narrative indicates a profound and irrevocable change in which the ethos represented by Lalin can be seen only as an anachronism.

In 1986, in a long interview just before the World Cup in Mexico, Jorge Valdano, a player with Real Madrid in Spain and a striker in the Argentinian national team, remembered the story of *Sobre héroes y tumbas*. In his narrative the names of Lalin and Seoane had disappeared as main actors; nevertheless the roles that they played were retained. The setting was moved from a football stadium to a *potrero* (any irregular open space in the city of Buenos Aires used for playing football, imagined, by most Argentinian football lovers, as the areas where the 'national style of playing was modelled').[2] Interestingly enough, Seoane is transformed into 'a practical player' and Lalin into 'a crack'. At the end of the story, the practical player, after scoring, says 'You see, you passed me the ball and I scored' and the crack answers, 'Yes, I see, but I enjoyed myself much more than you.' Valdano explains: 'For Sábato, this was the problem of football, but for me this is its great secret, nothing more or less. The struggle between two kinds of apparently incompatible bodily practices, elegance and force, determine at the end the popularity of the game' (*El Gráfico* 1986, 3479: 11). Thus, according to Valdano, the main contradiction of football implies that the pre-eminence of ability over force or vice versa must be understood as a permanent feature of the contradictory character of Argentinian football. Male individual virtues are transformed into contrasting styles and moral attitudes. Lalin and Seoane represent different, contradictory and competing male styles. The competing masculinities are thought of either as problematic or enigmatic. Through the performance of football players this contradiction is transformed into a public concern. In Valdano's interpretation, masculine styles in football are multiple and of permanent character. The story illustrates how meaning is dependent on who is performing or speaking.[3] The original *juggler* in Héctor's tale was converted into a 'crack' representing virtues such as ability, dribbling, elegance and beauty, while the *killer* was seen as expressing force, efficiency, determination and practicality. Héctor always insisted that these styles were moral choices. He suggested that searching for and realizing different football styles conveys information concerning 'our and their beliefs about how we see what the world is like' ('nuestras creencias en el fútbol, y las de otros diferentes, indican cómo vemos el mundo). He told me:

You see, I feel a strong sympathy, even more, I can identify with players like Lalin, and this is not purely irrational. Even I can recognize that players like Seoane are needed, but they must never take over the game. My feelings are reasonable; I am choosing what I think is right for keeping the essence of the game. This is my truth.

Héctor gave me some 'reasons' for his moral considerations and his knowledge of football in a way that showed that he accepted a possible disagreement. He added: 'I know very well what I prefer and I know what kind of players and games and styles will affect my basic attitudes.'

I discussed the relationship between ability and force in relation to male moral choices and the Argentinian style of playing with many of my informants. Juancho, in his late forties, introduced a dicothomy based on *serio* ('serious') and *alegre* ('joyful'), which I also later found when reading the sports magazine *El Gráfico* of the 1920s and 1930s, but he rejected its validity for understanding the history of Argentinian football.[4] He argued:

You see, many people believe that Argentinian football, as represented by the national team, has moved like a pendulum between seriousness to joyfulness. Joyful football has been identified with creativity, imagination, dribbling, doing things in an unexpected way, and serious football exactly the opposite, like total tedium (*el tedio total*). I do not agree. For me, being serious means to play with engagement, with discipline and with a real will to achieve victory. To play well always implies creativity and imagination. It is possible to be serious and to play well. You see, in Argentina, seriousness has been identified with the cult of force and masculine courage, with the myth of the Uruguayan Indian grip (*la garra charrúa*). Courage will never replace imagination. The Uruguayans defeated us in two finals, at the Olympic final of 1928 and in the World Cup of 1930, because, we were told by many, they were more macho than us. You see this way of explaining these two dramatic defeats confirmed the myth of the ability of Argentinian players and their lack of strength.

Juancho refers to the traumatic defeats accepting, in a way, the myth of the generosity of Argentinian football as opposed to the systematic use of tactical considerations that could guarantee a victory. The history of the final at the Olympics in Amsterdam in 1928 when the Uruguayans defeated, in the second match, the Argentinian team 2 to 1 was repeated in 1930. The written accounts tell us that in the final of the World Cup in 1930 which was played in Montevideo, the capital city of Uruguay, the Argentinians controlled the match due to their technical superiority and were leading by 2 to 1 in the first half. What was supposed to be an easy victory was transformed into a nightmare in the second half. The Uruguayans 'humiliated' the Argentinians, winning by 4 to 2. Bayer, in his history of Argentinian football which was used as the basis of a script of a popular movie in 1990 and seen by millions and millions of Argentinians including Héctor, Juancho and Tomás, writes on the two defeats:

> The River Plate [an expression that included Buenos Aires and Montevideo, the two cities of River Plate] placed the two finalists in Amsterdam. And again the Uruguayan Indian grip [*la garra charrúa*] wins. Two to one. Indisputable triumph. The Argentinians play well but the Uruguayans show more personality; they are not intimidated, they stand up [*mejor parados*]. In order to get some consolation, the Buenos Aires newspapers write: 'The River Plate football [*el fútbol rioplatense*] has won.' Argentinians must wait two years for vindication .... For the final of the (first) World Cup thousands and thousand of Argentinians take the boat to Montevideo .... In Buenos Aires thousands and thousands listen to the radio transmission in front of the newspaper buildings of Critica y La Prensa .... In the stadium, a real climate of war predominates. The Uruguayans must not win, as they did in Amsterdam. The Argentinians would like to be rid of the complex of paternity. Luis Monti, the Argentinian centre-half, has received thousands of threatening letters telling him that if the Argentinians win, he will be killed. The Uruguayan supporters knew Monti very well: he is a great player but fragile and unstable. In spite of the tremendous pressure, Argentina leads 2 to 1 at the end of the first half. Forty-five more minutes and Argentina will be World Champion. The Uruguayans do not surrender but, on the contrary, play with more stamina. Using violence in a couple of situations and insulting Monti when the referee cannot see them, is enough. Monti crumbles .... The Argentinians show signs of physical weakness and the defence is a strainer. The Uruguayans score three times and that is that.

They became the first World Champions in football. Argentinian will continue to be their sons.

(Bayer 1990: 34–35)

As in the story about Lalin and Seoane, we can see that victory in decisive situations is intimately associated with the deployment of some male virtues: courage, physical strength, tactical rational planning and moral endurance. In addition, these virtues are seen by Bayer as constitutive of paternity and the relations of father and son. Before the match, equality was recognized and accepted, but the defeat transformed Argentinians into sons and Uruguayans into fathers. Bayer (1990: 35) contrasts the figure of Argentinian Monti, 'good player but fragile and unstable', with the great Uruguayan 'heroes': Nasazzi, a man of great energy; Fernández, a centre-half covering all the ground with his physical strength; Scarone, the technical player; and Gestido a 'real male' who always stands up. The fragility of Monti was perceived by the press and the fans as the main reason for the Argentinian defeat. Monti was called 'double breadth'. His nickname was an indication of his impressive physical figure. A very strong athlete, a technical but rather aggressive player, even violent, his style of playing contributed to the public recognition of 'The Cyclone' as the *nom de guerre* of his club San Lorenzo de Almagro.

The defeat of 1930 was so traumatic that Argentina sent a third-class team of the amateur league to the World Cup in 1934, disguised as a protest against the purchase of its players by European clubs, and refused to participate again until 1958. Juancho told me:

I will not deny our fascination with technical ability and the cult of dribbling. This is our tradition, what we usually call *la nuestra*, but it has always been under threat. You see, you can have a nice style of playing, fantastic individual players, players with success in great international club teams, but you need victories, international victories by the national team. Without victories, I mean important victories, you cannot have a tradition in football. To get a tradition you have to be known. Others have to accept your way of feeling the game; other teams have to respect you and even be afraid of playing against you. A tradition in football is related to a certain aesthetics and to criteria for defining a correct style. It is again *la nuestra*. We failed in the two finals of 1928 and 1930 and we decided not to expose ourselves, we decided not to take risks. We sent hundreds and hundreds of individual players to Europe, to South America. In a way we exported quality. I will give you an example: in the winning Italian team of the World Cup in 1934, there were four Argentinian players, almost half of the team. Well ... it was much more than half because they were one insider, the centre-half and the two wings. We stayed in South America; we won the South American tournament many times and we defined ourselves as 'the best in the world'. For many, many years it was enough to win over Uruguay and Brazil. But we knew that the power, the international recognition and the consolidation of a tradition really happens in the World Cup. My father always said that winning the South American tournament was like playing in the patio of a house, the patio of a house in a *barrio* [neighbourhood], while playing in the World Cup was like playing in the shop-window of an important department store in Florida street, in the centre of Buenos Aires.

I insisted on discussing why Argentinians, including the players, football authorities and, of course, 'aficionados', perceived themselves, despite the evidence to the contrary, as belonging to a 'football tradition' that was 'the best in the world'. Juancho, without hesitating, answered me in the following way:

You must remember that Argentina had problems in being identified by others as an important nation. Football made it possible for us to be recognized as something in the world [*por el fútbol nos han reconocido como algo en el mundo*]. An authentic masculine passion was developed, and, for many men, the majority of men, football becomes a part of what I will call an internalized national identity including the sense of football. We thought: well, at least, we play good football and we export football players .... Because of this the defeats and the failures are especially painful for us. When the national team is defeated in very important matches it affects me and many, many others like me. Sometimes I ask myself, why is this so important to me? Perhaps it is childish, but in each defeat there is more than football. It is our prestige and self-esteem that is at stake. You see, each time we lost an important match, we asked ourselves why. How was it possible? And we hope that it will never occur again, never again. The failures showed our fragility and our weakness. At the time, when the football authorities, supported by the government, especially under the government of Perón, decided not to take part in the World Cup, not only were we exporting players, but the best club teams dominated in South America and played with brilliance in Europe during their tours. We were 'the best'. We truly believed that the best football in the world was played every Sunday in Argentina, but we were never really convinced that we were invincible. The myth of invincibility was a creation of the Uruguayans after they won the World Cup in 1950, defeating Brazil in the finals in the Mecca of football: the Maracaná stadium in Rio de Janeiro. You see, we had not participated in the World Cup after 1930, and when we decided to participate again in 1958 we had created an image of ourselves that we were the best . . . . Too many expectations, great, great expectations . . . we were defeated in the qualifying matches by Czechoslovakia. This, we had never imagined. We always considered England, Italy and Germany as the great powers – but Czechoslovakia? Never, unthinkable . . . . Well we were defeated by the devastating score of 6 to 1. What a shame. You must understand that this was the end of the world. The crisis of our tradition. A moral crisis. Since then, for many, many years we could not distinguish right from wrong.

Juancho is touching upon one of the dark chapters, perhaps the darkest, in the history of Argentinian football: the débâcle with Czechoslovakia in the World Cup of 1958. Juancho is not exaggerating. In their recently published dictionary on Argentinian football, Fontanarrosa and Sanz (1994: 17) define Argentina as 'the country where until 1958 everyone believed that they had invented football'. Juancho is telling us that through the world of football, Argentinians created a powerful imagery, producing a collective memory based on selected images and stories referring to a beautiful style of playing. He also talks about this style as *la nuestra* which literally means 'ours' – but implying 'our way of playing', and the defeat is seen as provoking 'the crisis of our tradition'. His narrative on the importance of 'a national tradition' is a description of the constitution of identity in opposition to difference, and inside against outside, assuming the superiority of the inside (*la nuestra*) as a preparation to resist the possible invasion of other forms, other styles of playing football. Thus the sudden superiority of the outside, of outsiders, needs an explanation, especially when it is perceived as a 'moral crisis', as the crisis of 'our tradition'. At this stage it is important to keep in mind that for Juancho the sign of crisis is associated with a state of confusion: Argentinians could not distinguish 'right from wrong'.

Juancho expanded his arguments on the Argentinian tradition and the style of *la nuestra* in the following way:

> Our style, *la nuestra*, is related to the football played in the *potrero*, a small field where twenty play against twenty. There, if you get the ball you must keep it, you must hide it, you must treat it with love, you must protect it, you must flatten it; you must not give it away because if this happens you will never get it back. *La nuestra* is the cult of dribbling ... the ball should be kept on the ground, never in the air. Our style is neither English nor Brazilian. They like to have the ball in the air: the English like to get into the penalty zone as quick as possible and the Brazilians are known for performing the ballet they are used to. *La nuestra* is not natural, is not atavistic, it is the product of two historic circumstances: the ideology of the *potrero* and the development over time of a certain taste [*el desarrollo de un cierto gusto*].

I asked him whether – accepting *la nuestra* as historic and related to given circumstances – changes were possible. Juancho replied:

> Of course. This happened after our defeat in Sweden in 1958. We imported what we called 'the European tradition' [*la tradición europea*], a kind of football based on physical strength and planning, collective planning with no possibility of being ourselves. No more freedom, no more creativity. The most important aspect of football was not to play but to win. We got confused and we did not get good results in the following World Cups. We must never forget our roots.

As I mentioned in the introduction, Durkheim insisted on the importance of taking into account moments of crisis for the analysis of moralities. Juancho is explicitly relating the crisis of a tradition to a moment of effervescence in the history of Argentinian football. He also accepts the possibility of another football morality based on other principles. He is not essentialist, he is just traditionalist in the sense that tradition provides roots, continuity and identity. He gives a historical morally derived interpretation in the sense that choosing what is right or wrong is open. Thus, styles of playing as means of producing and/or reproducing identities can be seen as possibilities, as moral choices. He recognizes the coexistence of *la nuestra* with a style called *la tradición europea*. *La tradición europea* remains as an alternative. Thus, for Juancho, a certain football practice is a moral selection (see Evens 1993: 111–113). In his analysis, the Argentinian style, *la nuestra*, is fragile and its reproduction uncertain. He insists on *la nuestra* being an authentic style, as a social product of a collective practice in the *potrero* and as the consequence of the existence of a certain *taste*, as something that, perhaps, for many Argentinians, is not fully conscious (see Evens 1993: 111). Obviously, the same could be said of others choosing *la tradición europea*.

Juancho is not alone. He presents a socially accepted narrative of the events. Bayer writes:

> The greatest shame of Argentinian football: Czechoslovakia's victory 6 to 1 .... The front pages of the newspapers expressed disappointment and anger: 'Even crippled, they [the Europeans] run more than the Argentinian players', 'The Argentinian football remained in the past; it exists in pre-history.' And as a reaction against the justificatory arguments of the players, a newspaper wrote: 'You must not cry as women for what you did not defend as men.' Openly, many newspapers accused the Argentinian players of lack of maleness. When they arrived at the airport of Buenos Aires they were received by a shower of coins and insults. Hundreds of fans waited with the intention of attacking them. By order of the political authorities, the tax officers confiscated all the gifts that the players had bought for their families during their stay in Europe .... Silvio Marzolini [an international player] analyses the episode: 'The World Cup in Sweden was a total failure for Argentina but it marked an important change in our football because we were obliged to acknowledge the importance of physical preparation and the need for a careful analysis and respect of the rivals.'
>
> (Bayer 1990: 85–88)

Bayer adds:

> The 1960s provoked a total mess in Argentinian football. They tried to change it, to modernize it, imitating the Brazilians .... But the result was the formula of 'every player back, every player a defender'. Defence gained priority to the detriment of offensive football.
>
> (Bayer 1990: 89)

Lázaro, in an interesting essay on the ethical and political language in Argentinian football, also comments the events of 1958:

> we were prepared to show to the entire world our daring stamp, our childlike tenderness, our innocent wiliness, and we were quite sure that when they saw us they would love us. We thought to sow in the sons of school discipline, in the sad kids of the cold European countries, the joy of *el potrero* and the feast of abundance. In this spirit our players, the coach and the happy and optimistic journalists, guardians of the purity of the doctrine [*la nuestra*] and the doctrine of purity, left Argentina .... The disaster in Sweden is the origin of the maelstrom of Argentinian thought. More than a maelstrom it will be a whirlwind. The old chain of virtues that distinguished the Argentinian creole [*el criollo*] will break into halves. One half will softly whisper about the 'past times' when it was a great pleasure to watch Argentinians play football. The other half will always find arguments for demanding a radical change of mentality. This bifocal ethic will sweep across the world of football transforming it into a fertile field for ethical and political debates.
>
> (Lázaro 1993: 31)[5]

With Juancho as well as with Lázaro some common key arguments are at work: the importance of *el potrero*; the style of *la nuestra* as an expression of innocence, creativity, tenderness, the picaresque, virtues related to childhood; the acceptance of the quality of football as an innocent game will vanish if maturity, speculation, planning, replace the childish spirit that every man has inside; the concern for the purity of a doctrine (*la nuestra*); and the relevance of keeping a tradition in order to avoid intellectual and moral confusion. *El potrero* as a perceived space of freedom is related to childhood (Archetti 1995). We can say that football, like other games, is opposed to work, duties and family obligations. It is interesting to note that in Argentina many of the great players are defined as *pibes* (young boys).[6] They also agree, joining Bayer, on the historical impact of the débâcle in Sweden because, since then, two moralities have coexisted in Argentinian football.

It is interesting to notice that in this narrative the image of a 'child' (without a father) is seen as very positive, as a potent image of freedom and creativity, while being a 'son' (with a father) is defined as negative, as an indication of subordination and control. Creativity in Argentinian football has often been related to players being imagined as 'children' who will never reach maturity. As I pointed out before, these narratives confront us with a plurality of male identities and moralities as created and transformed in the popular culture of football.

In my second conversation, Juancho continued to elaborate on this problematical issue:

After this great defeat in Sweden, Argentinians believed that the solution was to copy Europeans ... to import physical strength and discipline and to combine it with Argentinian technical ability. As a result of these ideas, the Argentinian virtues were perceived by many people as negative. All of a sudden, the most important value was to win. The moral was to achieve good results without examining the means used to obtain them. This developed into a kind of cynicism. The world of football, professional football, was dominated by cynical people: coaches, players, authorities, the public .... During the 1960s, and up until the World Cup of 1974, it was terrible ... many people will not agree with me but the defeat in the World Cup of 1974, 4 to 0 by Holland, this marvellous Dutch team under the leadership of Cruyff, was more important than the defeat 6 to 1 by Czechoslovakia in 1958. We tried and tried to play like the Europeans but we lost and lost and, at the same time, we continued to export talented, skilful players to the best European clubs. It was terrible, we were without moral strength until Menotti was appointed coach of the national team at the end of 1974. With him we entered into a period ... well, I am not afraid of perhaps exaggerating, we enter ... a period of moral regeneration. Menotti insisted on playing *la nuestra*, our style, while accepting that in order to beat Europeans what was needed was to equal them physically. How to explain this better? ... Yes, I have got it: once the equality in physical power [*poder físico*] had been achieved, the difference is obtained through the use of talent, technical control of the ball, dribbling .... I always say that with Menotti we remarried our past, our tradition .... You see, this marriage was successful. With him as coach we won the two World Cups of 1978: first, with the senior players in Buenos Aires and later with the junior players in Tokyo.

Juancho is right: Menotti presented himself as a kind of crusader and his victories transformed him into a successful prophet, a very influential and powerful prophet. He summarized his success as coach of the national teams in the following way:

> It was necessary to find a path pooling together all our efforts in search of one identity. I thought that this was the secret: we had lost our identity, we lived running behind the 'last word' in football, trying to catch the last system or recipe that lay behind the last success, and in this way we forgot what was our idiosyncrasy.
>
> (Menotti 1980: 15)

And more recently he has added:

> Who will put in doubt the existence of an Argentinian football style? An authentic national football exists, in the same way as an Argentinian way of life exists, and it was modelled since the origins of our nationality with passion, with sacrifice, with patience and with rebelliousness .... Once I heard somebody say that 'there is no national football because the football is universal'. I would say that man is universal, but that the best way to reach universality in any activity is 'to paint one's own village'. And the Argentinian football players who left the country, from Julio Libonatti to Diego Maradona, became well known because they painted the village with the magic of the Argentinian dribbling, which is bantering, different, with a hallmark of identity. I dare to say that I could recognize in any pitch of the entire world an Argentinian player .... In our past the way of playing was intimately related to our sentiments .... This made possible the survival of a line, of a style, modelling *la nuestra*. It was the acceptance of the good taste that was not only present in football but also in the way of clothing, in the music, in the dance, in the customs .... Football must also be measured with aesthetic criteria .... Happily, the aesthetics and the good taste of Argentinians are unchanged, and they believe more and more in our style, in *la nuestra*.
>
> (Menotti 1994a: 51)[7]

On the day of the victory in the finals against Holland, Menotti coined a phrase that has since become installed in the collective memory of Argentinian football lovers: 'our victory is a tribute to the old and glorious Argentinian football' (Bayer 1990: 133).

The crucial defeats are not only seen as an act of treason. Tomás, in his late forties, always insisted on pointing out the fact that these kinds of defeat are critical because they bring about unhappiness. He says:

> In 1974 the defeat by Holland was a moment of shame for us. As football fans we felt unhappy. You see, we could feel happy with a great victory, but a victory is not enough. A victory is not a guarantee that I am happy. My friends, I am quite sure, will agree with me. It is important to gain a victory with style, with superb football. A victory obtained just through fighting, without class, no ... I will not feel happy.

Tomás expanded this idea:

> You see, I go with my friends to the ground to admire the talent and to be moved emotionally. I am moved by the beauty of a particular player or by the beauty of a game ... the emotion you feel at this moment is what I call feeling happy ... it is just a moment in a football game, but it can last for hours, days, you can talk with your friends, you can communicate this feeling to others, and then it is transformed into memory. I always thought that if we were able to have thousands, well hundreds, of these moments we could be better persons. I know very well indeed that football is not everything in my life or in the life of the most engaged supporters or in the life of my friends. I also know that to be happy, well in a more permanent way, does not depend on football. Football simply permits you to feel happy.

Tomás also accepted that his way of conceiving happiness was not unique:

> In Argentina we are divided ... Menotti always insists on the importance of beauty. Do you understand? I would say that he is on the left of Argentinian football. Bilardo [the other successful Argentinian coach, winner of the 1986 World Cup in Mexico] never uses this argument. For Bilardo, happiness can only be obtained through victory. For Menotti a defeat – if played well [*una derrota en buena ley*] – will not necessarily bring about unhappiness. You see, you have before you the two confronting worlds in the Argentinian football of today [*tenés enfrente los dos mundos del fútbol actual argentino*].[8]

It is easy to see that in our conversations Tomás presented consistently non-controversial assumptions related to the importance of conative–emotional dispositions for the analysis of morality in football. He insisted on the importance for a football lover to allow himself to become emotionally aroused by various types of situation experienced on a football stadium (for example, being ready to feel shame or indignation if beauty was lacking, or becoming happy when it was manifested). I believe that he is a convinced relativist: he accepted the existence of different values, exemplified by the ethical worlds of Menotti and Bilardo, and also the fact that these differences are fundamental for achieving a proper understanding of Argentinian football history. He contended that these disagreements could not be eliminated, their being important for maintaining ethical diversity. He said to me several times: 'it is important for Argentinians to agree on the issues that divide us' ('es importante para los argentinos estar de acuerdo en lo que nos divide'). He made an important distinction between 'being happy' and 'feeling happy'. He explicitly denied that football will bring about a well-balanced psychological state in which one's total life pattern and general circumstances permitting 'being happy' are matched. For him, 'feeling happy' at the terraces was related to certain emotions. Happiness in this way is associated to a species of joy in regard to one's partial situation. Tomás accepted that, in this sense, football can function as a compensation for one's negative total situation, but 'this is not my case', he frequently told me.

CONCLUSION

I have presented an ethnographic account of the moralities of Argentinian football which, although incomplete, allows me to make certain interpretative suggestions. The presentation of findings followed the four empirical fields mentioned earlier:

1 Male virtues.
2 The importance of traditions, roots and historical continuity.
3 The meaning of styles and ways of playing football.
4 Ideas, concerns and definitions of 'happiness' and of 'feeling happy'.

Since it is difficult to reach the totality of moral codes and ideals in a composite nation state such as contemporary Argentina, the selection of particular concrete fields and contexts that may be treated as privileged arenas for study is very useful. Many possible topics have not been taken into account, particularly those pertaining to the field of rules and sanctions governing the game (see Nilsson 1993). My main aim has been to show that the analysis of moralities needs to combine the aspect of desire and the emotive character of male morality in a concrete ritual practice. Football is such a privileged arena in a country like Argentina.

My informants were at different stages of their life cycle, a fact that made possible the historical perspective that I was interested in dealing with. The youngest was 35 years old and the oldest 58 years old. The majority belonged to the Argentinian middle class and some of them were well educated. But I also had lengthy dialogues with fans belonging to lower classes, service workers and unskilled state employees. Usually, young people are less concerned with the past, or with history in general, and they perceive the future as relatively open and are, in most cases, full of hope. Mature people, on the contrary, having lived through a variety of historical events, can easily identify patterns and can reflect on discontinuities. They can retrieve from their memory actors and contexts that can provoke careful moral reflections. The narratives of Argentinian football are presented by my informants in a *prototypical* form using common discursive symbols and producing a plurality of moral meanings (see Rapport this volume). The actors themselves, through their narratives, bring time and history into the fabric of their lives and vivid experiences. Johnson argues that a central task for any moral theory must be to understand how actors narratively construct their lives and how their deliberations are framed by those narratives (Johnson 1993: 152). In my paper the focus is on the moral discourses and concerns of mature football 'aficionados'. From this perspective the moments of effervescence which make possible critical moral reflections will be different for different social actors representing different generations. To my informants 1930, 1958 and 1974 were key years; the years of shame and humiliation for Argentinian national football – and as a consequence, for male Argentinians' national self-esteem. For the young supporters the year of 1993 has been, and, I am quite sure, will be in the future, a year of shame and confusion. In October 1993, in a qualifying match for the World Cup in 1994 Colombia defeated Argentina 5 to 0 in Buenos Aires. Juancho expressed what many Argentinians felt when he said:

> In the future, even for us old people, the defeat by Colombia will be seen as perhaps more important than the other setbacks. You see, Argentinians taught Colombians to play football, they were,

for years and years, our sons, they respected and admired us, and now they humiliate us. I feel bad not only because of the five goals, but mostly because they play our way, they play *la nuestra*, and we play nothing.[9]

The story of Lalin and Seoane as well as the confrontations on the meaning of different male virtues, styles of playing and ways of achieving happiness illustrate the 'painful coexistence', as one informant put it to me, of contrasting moralities in Argentinian football. Social actors are exposed to contradictions and paradoxes in the construction of moral meaning. Thus identity, *la nuestra*, can be seen as atavistic or as a product of choice. Tomás, with his relativistic position, accepting and tolerating contradictory moral standpoints, is a clear example of the very dynamics of moral choice.

Finally, I hope that my ethnographic account of moral choices permits these to be viewed as the result of individual preferences which are not taken in any kind of social vacuum. The history, or better, histories of Argentinian football have been written about in popular books and are continuously written·every day and every week, in journals and sports magazines. Moreover, in a regular fashion the visual history is displayed on television or can be bought from the extremely large collection of videos existing on the Argentinian market. My main argument in this paper has been the following: the present moral discourses of social actors are embedded in history, the actors use history and their own life stories or, better perhaps, they construct historical representations of football and themselves as supporters in order to find meaning and to argue about what is correct and what is wrong or what are the ways of feeling happy. I believe that by using the voices of my informants extensively this argument has been made clear. My paper can be seen as an example of the imaginative synthesizing power of moral narratives.

ACKNOWLEDGEMENTS

I would like to thank Signe Howell and Marit Melhuus for their critical comments.

NOTES

1 Carlos meant by *raza* (literally race) something that is related to a common past, to a collective memory and to a history from which you, as an Argentinian male, cannot escape. Thus the word *raza* 'implies a historically bounded human condition' and is, in this sense, perhaps subject to change. Carlos could totally agree with an Irish supporter summarizing what he felt during the match that Ireland won 1 to 0 over England in 1988: 'It was extraordinary – eight hundred years of race memory packed into ninety minutes of soccer' (Hem 1994: 173).

2 In Argentina, the mythological origin of the way of playing is usually related to this concrete urban space, *el potrero*. The word is, however, of rural origin, indicating a space where wild horses graze. Thus *el potrero* is associated with wildness, freedom, creativity and fantasy. The word *baldío* was sometimes used with the meaning of *potrero* (see *El Gráfico* 1928, 480: 11 and 1933, 716: 4).

3 Cornwall and Lindisfarne have consistently argued the importance of producing ethnographic accounts that take us beyond the image of a single category of 'men'. They write: 'The many different images and behaviours contained in the notion of masculinity are not always coherent: they may be competing, contradictory and mutually un-determining' (Cornwall and Lindisfarne 1993: 12).

4 The dichotomy *serio* (serious) and *alegre* (joyful) was related to the style of different first division teams (see *El Gráfico* 1949, 1549: 8–12). We can see that the Lalin–Seoane contradiction is reproduced at the collective level creating contradictory styles. If we accept this historical reconstruction which was also related to the 'taste' of the supporters, Argentinian football, since its beginning, was divided into different club identities and styles (see *El Gráfico* 1931, 636: 13). Thus *El Gráfico* was obliged to find in the 'joyful style' the expression of the Argentinian style, of *la nuestra*. In the essentialist perspective of *El Gráfico* the 'national style' is one, it must be a product of a superior and more authentic tradition.

5 Behind the pseudonym 'Lázaro' hides a prestigious Argentinian professional philosopher educated at La Sorbonne.

6 For example, Diego Maradona is called *el pibe de oro* (the golden young boy). To be a *pibe* is related to freshness, authenticity of feelings and extreme creativity. In Argentina, a football aficionado usually expects to see 'real football' when it is played by the *pibes* and the *fútbol-pibe* is opposed to 'normal football' (see *El Clarín Deportivo*, 2 May 1994: 4). The calculating and conservative style of playing is always associated with maturity, to losing freshness (*perder la frescura*).

7 Dante Panzeri, a brilliant writer and sports journalist of *El Gráfico*, defended in the 1950s and 1960s the Argentinian style, *la nuestra*, against the imposition of European systems and tactical discipline. For Panzeri the essence of football beauty was expressed in the unexpected, in the improvising and creative capacity of individual players. He believed that 'systems' kill fantasy. His concise definition of *la nuestra*, as a matter of 'Argentinian taste', is, for me, the best: 'our taste regarding good football

implies a way of playing with short passes, low balls, penetrating, subtle, from the backs to the strikers' (*El Gráfico*1958, 2020: 39).

8 Menotti has elaborated on the meaning of 'happiness' in football (see Menotti 1993, 1994b). He has constantly repeated the formula: 'Football was always a beautiful pretext for being happy' ('el fútbol fue siempre una hermosa excusa para ser feliz').

9 Since the 1930s Colombia has been a 'land of mission' for Argentinian coaches and players. This was more evident in the late 1940s when the most important cracks of the Argentinian professional league emigrated *en masse* to Colombia after a long strike for better wages (see Pedernera 1993: 72–76). In 1941, Fernando Paternoster, a mythological centre-back of Racing Club and the national team who played in the World Cup finals of 1930, emphasized the importance of Argentinian football as a model and an ideal for Colombian youth (*El Gráfico* 1941, 1123: 9, see also Giordano 1955: 533).

REFERENCES

Archetti, E. P. (1995) 'Estilos y virtudes masculinas en *El Gráfico*: la creación del imaginario del fútbol argentino', *Desarrollo Económico* 35, 139: 419–442.

Bayer, O. (1990) *Fútbol argentino*, Buenos Aires: Editorial Sudamericana.

Cornwall, A. and Lindisfarne, N. (1993) 'Dislocating masculinity: gender, power and anthropology', in A. Cornwall and N. Lindisfarne (eds), *Dislocating Masculinity: Comparative Ethnographies*, London: Routledge.

Durkheim, E. (1915) *The Elementary Forms of the Religious Life*, London: George Allen & Unwin.

——(1953) *Sociology and Philosophy*, Glencoe, Ill.: Free Press.

——(1992) *Professional Ethics and Civic Morals*, London: Routledge.

Edel, M. and Edel, A. (1959) *Anthropology and Ethics*, Springfield, Ill.: Charles C. Thomas Publisher.

Evens, T. M. S. (1989) 'Two concepts of "society as a moral system"': Evans-Pritchard's heterodoxy', *Man* (n.s.) 17: 205–218.

——(1993) 'Rationality, hierarchy and practice: contradiction as choice', *Social Anthropology*, 1 (1B): 101–118.

Fontanarrosa and Sanz (1994) *El pequeño diccionario ilustrado: el fútbol argentino*, Buenos Aires: Clarín-Agruilar.

Giordano, H. (1955) 'El éxodo de los jugadores argentinos a Colombia', in *Historia del fútbol argentino*, vol. III, Buenos Aires: Editorial Eiffel.

Hem, H. S. (1994) 'Dubliners: an anthropologist's account', unpublished M.Phil. thesis, Department of Social Anthropology, University of Oslo.

Johnson, M. (1993) *Moral Imagination*, Chicago: University of Chicago Press.

Lázaro (1993) 'Doctrina del fútbol', *La Caja*, 3: 30–31.

Lorenzo, R. (1946) *25 años en el deporte*, Buenos Aires: Editorial Atlántida.

Lukes, S. (1981) *Emile Durkheim*, Middlesex: Penguin.

Menotti, C. L. (1980) *Fútbol: juego, deporte y profesión*, Buenos Aires: El Gráfico.
——(1993) 'Entrevista', *La Maga*, 2: 2–5.
——(1994a) 'La defensa de una escuela', *La Maga Colección*, 2: 51.
——(1994b) 'Entrevista abierta', *El toque*, 2: 2–3.
Nilsson, P. (1993) *Fotbollen och Moralen*, Stockholm: HLS Förlag.
Pedernera, A. (1993) *El fútbol que viví ... y que yo siento*, Buenos Aires: Editorial Sineret S.A.
Sábato, E. (1961) *Sobre héroes y tumbas*, Buenos Aires: Fabril.

Part II

The gendering of moralities

Chapter 5

Double standards[1]

Marilyn Strathern

'The law', says Carol Smart (1991: 155), 'does not operate according to any one set of standards.' Feminist critics in jurisprudence have taken issue with the law's claim to objectivity and neutrality: insofar as the law's claim aligns with men's rather than women's interests, men and women are differently empowered. In drawing attention to the difference that gender makes, these critics render this implicit skewing explicit.[2] But her remark carries a second connotation. The law's claim to neutrality and objectivity was only ever a claim – 'a claim to be refuted, not taken seriously'. It is not a unitary phenomenon with a single purpose; there is no single foundation nor any single outcome to the application of any one principle. 'In other words it [the law] is more complex ... than the model implied in much of the work on feminist jurisprudence would have us believe' (Smart 1991: 155).

If feminists have criticized the double standards by which men and women are privileged in relation to the power of the law, Smart suggests that the criticism deploys double standards itself – bringing the richness and diversity of knowledge about women's experience to bear on what is construed as monolithic orthodoxy. The charge is not so dissimilar from that often brought against anthropologists who pit their nuanced understandings of local knowledge against monolithic readings of Euro-American conventions. I would only add that double standards may serve political purposes. Depicting the law as operating according to its claim to neutrality affords a single position that can be attacked from another single position – feminist jurisprudence can rally round a common target. The kind of complexity to which Smart refers makes the task of social criticism much more diffuse. If this is true of the field of jurisprudence, no doubt it is also true of questions about morality.

What in retrospect interests me in this debate is the moral effect of (consciousness of) gender. Making explicit the different bases of men's and women's orientations is held to be enlightening by uncovering information that should make a difference as to how acts and events are evaluated. Sufficiency of information is in turn an element in the processes of moral reasoning to which Signe Howell refers in the Introduction to this volume. I take it as a Euro-Americanism that the moral person acts knowingly. And I take this as further implying the selective ability to sift through information, to make evaluations out of differences.

Rendering difference explicit has a place in Euro-American ways of organizing knowledge that should itself be made explicit. It is found, for instance, in the assumption that inequalities endure despite society's best efforts to overcome them, which is why asymmetries in men's and women's interests have to be brought into the open. Now that women have the vote, we have to remind ourselves of all the circumstances in which women do not 'really' have a vote on what matters. But what kind of moral force does gender difference have when nothing need be brought into the open, when the different positions of the sexes are invariably explicit and men's and women's interests already differentially evaluated?

This was a question raised by Lisette Josephides (1982) in connection with sexual antagonism in the Papua New Guinea Highlands. Where antagonism between men and women is overt, other disjunctions become masked or disguised. She points out that elaborate cultural attention to inequalities between the sexes obscures inequalities between persons of the same sex (specifically the way that unequal access to resources affects men).[3] What is also obscured in the rhetoric of divisions between male and female is the gender division that I would make as an outside observer: between same-sex and cross-sex alignments. The Highlands ethnography on which I draw shows people sifting through different types of information in a knowing way. Their judgements, and ability to prevail on other people's judgements, are crucially affected by whether they find themselves acting with others of their sex or with those of opposite sex. In turn, some of the tension that this produces is found in the means to which people resort, in extreme cases, to get others to act in *un*knowing ways.

T.M.S. Evens (this volume) ponders on mirror images and chiasmic possibilities. But where he uncovers gender (difference) as an implicate order, I deal with circumstances where the switch or transformation between perspectives comes from the deliberate creation of alternating effectiveness.[4] Men's and women's acts are both subject to gender alternation, in so far as either can act now in a same-sex and now in a cross-sex context. Differences between sexual alignments and thus moral domains are not waiting to be brought to consciousness. Rather, they are overt; each engages the person at different temporal moments, so that switching from one to the other may be knowingly engineered. The person's effectiveness, or power of action, is transformed in the process. To this doubling of standards is added another. Persons may also transform others, a process of coercion in which the moral (immoral) agent turns another into an amoral actor. The latter is made effective through being deprived of knowledge.

This ethnographic base adds a different kind of complexity to Smart's critiques. Moral reasoning in Hagen, I contend, engages a gender distinction between same-sex and cross-sex alignments. This variously impinges on relations between men and women. But either sex may also be put beyond the pale of moral judgement altogether. The result is what on the one hand we may call two moral domains (men or women acting in reference to others on a same-sex or cross-sex basis), and on the other the possibility of acting with reference to others in an amoral way.

GENDER

Table XII in *Women in Between* (M. Strathern 1995), entitled 'Females involved in poisoning', lays out information gleaned from some eighteen stories, told in 1964–1965 by both men and women, in which women were the chief suspects. The time span to which the stories refer is 1910–1950 and the women were from northern and central Melpa-speaking areas in Hagen, Papua New Guinea Highlands. Reputed targets were often men of the (agnatic) clan into which the woman had married; in fully half of these cases the intended victim was her spouse. Here is an account from a woman married into the natal clan of the female poisoner, corroborated by her husband. Penambe and Kope are high-order political groupings (tribes).

In the 1920's Oma married Penambe Wiya Muri. Muri's other three wives were jealous and subjected her to co-wife magic (*amb wølik*). A Kope man, from Penambe's major enemies, took advantage of the situation and approached her, promising to marry her himself if she poisoned her husband. Muri sickened and died; the Kope man, who was also a BWZH (sub-clan brother's wife's clan sister's husband) to Muri, had been visiting there, and was summoned to the divination that followed the death. The test indicated him guilty, but he jumped up and told the men that it was Oma who had poisoned Muri, and already she would be trying to escape. They did indeed catch her in flight and executed her, the Kope man dealing the fatal blow to save his own skin. But he was a marked man and was later killed in battle.

(M. Strathern 1995: 178–179)

We are dealing with a reconstructed chain of events, neither of the principals able to tell their own tale. The account was sympathetic to Oma as the victim of jealousy magic from her husband's other wives, and this, we infer, gave her a personal motive. However, the account shifted from her actions as administrator of the poison to the motives of the husband's enemy in prevailing upon her. The Kope man both enjoyed a distant affinal connection with the husband and was from a clan categorized as a major enemy. Whether he in turn had been prevailed upon by others we do not know; we do know that at the moment when he was accused, he instantly accused one of the women present. The error of judgement was to indicate his inside knowledge; people subsequently reasoned that he must have had designs on the women.

Let me pick out three elements in the chains of reasoning likely to have been involved. First, from all those present the desperate man pointed a finger at the deceased's wife. A wife was regarded as at once intimate enough with her husband to be able to slip unsuspected substances into his food and detached enough in terms of her own personal loyalties not to be entirely identified with him. There was nothing unusual in this: widowed spouses were often vulnerable to attack from the grief-stricken kin of the deceased, and across Melanesia (e.g. Damon and Wagner 1989) protested their innocence through onerous mourning duties. Second, in this political context, distance between husband and wife was not sufficient for the woman to be presented as acting on her own account;[5] it seems that she had to be *persuaded* to take this course of action. In being so persuaded she also became an agent acting on behalf of another person. But of course she was betrayed by the Kope man, who prevented her from ever saying what happened. Finally, there were two parallel narratives here. One was about spouses, the other about enemies. Both sexes had their enemies. The woman was harried by her jealous co-wives; the husband was the target of the enemy clan's designs and specifically of another man. These were same-sex relations. At the same time the actions depended on two crucial sets of cross-sex relations: between the woman and the husband/lover and between the men whose relationship was regarded as mediated by the woman's marriage.

MEN AND WOMEN

One could use the account of events in the 1920s as an example of double standards operating for men and for women. Set alongside contemporary events in 1964–1965, in which women appeared as scapegoats in disputes between men,[6] it exemplified the asymmetry in men's and women's ability to be effective. It was seemingly enough for the accused man to point at the woman for her to be killed. In the otherwise altered circumstances of the 1960s, post-pacification, when people were no longer fighting and suspects no longer tortured, women were often 'blamed' for men's misfortunes and judged by the general stereotype of females as the source of men's downfall. This was a largely rhetorical matter, to do with women's exclusion from the twin areas of oratory and wealth which made men politically effective. Nor did they have recourse to arms. I doubt if a woman could have made a public accusation with such instant effect. Their (public) powerlessness in turn affected people's reasonings about their motives.

What seemed double about the standards, then, was the choice between relating motives to 'personal' or to 'political' ends. The accused woman was represented as succumbing to personal motive whereas the accused man's actions were put into the context of political relations between clans. This did not mean that women never act on behalf of clans, but that stereotypical female behaviour was personal.

Well, we have been here before. Ascribing women's motivations to personal ends conceals the significance of women's experiences as opposed to men's, which is why, in the feminist arguments to which Smart refers, it was so important to politicize 'the personal' (and personalize 'the political').[7] But for their part Hagen men did not *conceal* the fact that clan politics involved primarily male actors.

Rather, they elaborated on the fundamental difference in men's and women's placements: men's clan loyalties could be unambiguously defined through an integration of personal and collective identity, even if not always acted upon, while women's were inevitably divided, prototypically between clan of origin and clan of marriage.

This openly acknowledged opposition was echoed in the Hagen contrast between men who spoke and fought in public, and women who acted in private (cf. Merlan and Rumsey 1991: 31–33). Women did not participate as principal figures on the collective occasions when men were seen to act with a single mind.[8] In fact the dogma of a 'single mind', the purposefulness by which Hageners convention-ally distinguished men's from women's potential for action, could be read as the inevitable constraint of male politics. When a male person's actions revealed a single intention, this replicated the unity of clan or sub-clan on public occasions. It was in private that a man harboured multiple thoughts and purposes, even as the clan was internally composed of diverse persons. A woman's 'many minds', on the other hand, were held to be more consistently calibrated to differences between clan of origin and clan of marriage, and to the heterogeneous relations of domestic kinship. As a consequence, while her acts, like a man's, momentarily resolved diversity of intention, the action that she was likely to take was seemingly much less predictable. Whereas men could relate their endeavours to clan ends through a rhetoric of solidarity which assumes its primacy in their minds – a man was presumed loyal unless proved otherwise – women had to demonstrate loyalty to diverse sets of cognates and affines. Stereotypically, their social identity was much less helpful a clue to their intentions. Indeed, when her actions had significant political repercussions, people might reason that the woman was an agent for men's purposes. Let us look at that poisoning accusation again.

SAME-SEX AND CROSS-SEX RELATIONS

As the story was told, the Kope man lured Oma to administer the poison by appealing to her own desires and aligning them with his. He thus held out the promise of intimacy between them, including sharing the knowledge that they had poisoned the old husband. The new conjugal union would be modelled on the old, predicated on an identification of the man's and woman's interests. In the course of this, the woman would have scored off her female enemies and the man his male ones. The cross-sex coalition between the potential spouses became the instrument through which same-sex ends were, so to speak, achieved.

The husband–wife relationship set up the sexes in a simultaneously complementary and antagonistic way. The difference between them was supposed to be joined to productive ends, a jointness constantly created against the pull of other loyalties. Indeed the pairing of men's and women's interests as conjugal partners was so overt that conjugality (cross-sex coalition) was sometimes likened to brotherhood (same-sex alliance).[9] The question here is not whether the spouses were 'really' joined, but the fact that this cross-sex alignment of interests was fundamental to the way in which the behaviour of husbands and wives was judged. The Kope man's enticement figured in the moral reasoning by which *the story-teller* made the narrative plausible.

Insofar as the aspiring husband wished to take another's place, one cross-sex alignment substituted for another. There was no change in the moral character of the (conjugal) relationships at issue. In the same way, there was no change when same-sex alignments were replicated – for instance, when a clan turned mourning for a deceased member into revenge for his death, augmenting one display of solidarity with another. But there were circumstances in which change in moral orientation not only occurred but was actively sought out. This was ordinarily accomplished by appeals to different kinds of knowledge.

Either kind of gender alignment could be thought about from the vantage point of the other; as I have suggested, the murderous couple used their cross-sex interests to achieve simultaneously same-sex ends. But if one of these vantage points had to take precedence over the other, then the moral bases on which people act must be shifted and one standard supplanted by the other. When people deliberately sought to bring about such a change, they had to change their own and others' minds; among men, in the Hagen of the 1960s, rhetoric played a significant role in this.

Appeals to the value of male collective life was openly used to transform men's thinking, so that instead of 'thinking on' their wives and domestic obligations, they would 'think on' their brothers and clan ancestors. They would be reminded of everything that they knew about past history, current alliances and reputations at stake. By the same token, what applied to men could not apply to women: assertions of clan interest could not deploy the same gender strategies. Men were unable to admonish wives and sisters, as they did their brothers, to forget about cross-sex relations in the interests of same-sex ones. Indeed the problem was precisely that they could not *appeal* to an alternative set of standards. They could invoke the identity of the clan into which a woman married or her sentiment for her home. But in gender terms a woman's cross-sex ties with her male kin were similar to those that she has with her husband, and the same moral standards applied: she was supposed to look out for the interests of both. So other strategies might come into play. Sometimes it was enough to rely on a woman's ability to switch knowingly between different cross-relationships; on other occasions men aimed to supplant her orientations with their own. How might this be done?

The putative Kope husband had sought to eliminate the first husband from the woman's thoughts in order that she would think on him, one set of interests supplanting another. However, a woman might be deflected from her conjugal orientation not only through appeals to her interests and emotions but through obliterating them. Andrew Strathern (1981: 15) recounts a case in which a clan connection was disclosed between a male victim and male poisoner. It was normally unthinkable for one clansman to poison another – the accused person must have been subjected to madness sorcery from his enemies. This kind of madness is called *wulya* and the sorcery substance *wulya wulya*. The sorcery would have put him out of his right mind for no one with his full faculties working would have done such an act. Now, similar madness was detected in cases where women were induced by their clansmen to poison their husbands. Sometimes women were said to have poisoned their husbands on behalf of their natal clan in knowing response to their brothers' appeal; but if their loyalty wavered, their minds were instead directed through sorcery administered by the brother or whoever had an interest in the husband's death. Indeed, accounts from the 1960s reported this surmise much more frequently in respect of women than of men.[10] *Wulya wulya* thus established the social source of the deed in whoever instigated the chain of events. There was no diminishing a woman's liability (she was still harshly punished), but the deed was located in the collective realm of political male action. Dislocating the woman's 'mind' from her 'person' relocated intentions in the minds of other, single-minded, actors. The sorcery both bypassed her own ability to sift through information in a knowing way and reduced political uncertainty by placing a woman's actions within the sphere of men's, as instruments for men's (same-sex) relationships.

Why, in order to serve the same-sex interests of men, must the woman 'forget' her own cross-sex interests? The reason was that a woman's cross-sex concerns are ordinarily coordinated: in promoting her husband's affairs she ought also to be promoting her brother's. This in turn depended on the brothers-in-law having interests that were mutually reinforcing. When they ceased to be so, it was, from the woman's point of view, the relational embeddedness of the one relationship in the other that had to be undone.

MORALITY

Again we seem to be on familiar ground. The feminist debates to which Smart referred turned on two approaches to women's experiences (see note 1). Focusing on women's experiences may bring to light what is needed to enable women to achieve generally agreed ends; or else, on the contrary, it may enable one to critique the ends themselves, bringing to light human potentials that men's perceptions conceal. On this second position, she quotes Carol Gilligan's classic work (1993) with American men and women. Gilligan contrasts an ethic of justice with an ethic of caring: whereas the men in her study speak of abstract and collective values ascribed in a general way to human nature, women emphasize relationality. Yet if the two resulting ethics epitomize apparent differences in men's and women's modes of moral reasoning, in this (Euro-American) culture both indicate potentials in human life. Gilligan concludes with the way that two disparate modes of experience are in the end connected:

> While an ethic of justice proceeds from the premise of equality – that everyone should be treated the same – an ethic of care rests on the premise of non-violence – that no one should be hurt .... [B]oth perspectives *converge* in the realization that just as inequality adversely affects both parties in an unequal relationship, so too violence is destructive for everyone involved.
>
> (Gilligan 1993: 174, my emphasis)

Here the relational capacities of women almost take on the aura of moral reasoning as such.[11] 'Moral problems', Gilligan says, 'are problems of human relations' (Gilligan 1993: xix). Women's orientation appears the more encompassing mode by virtue of being about the encompassing capacity of relations: the embedding of one set of relationships within others. In Gilligan's account this leads to a complex understanding of the implication of different values in one another.

In women's development, the absolute of care, defined initially as not hurting others, becomes complicated through a recognition of the need for personal integrity. This recognition gives rise to the claim for equality embodied in the concept of rights, which changes the understanding of relationships and transforms the definition of care. For men, the absolutes of truth and fairness, defined by the concepts of equality and reciprocity, are called into question by experiences that demonstrate the existence of differences between other and self. Then the awareness of multiple truths leads to a relativizing of equality in the direction of equity and gives rise to an ethic of generosity and care. For both sexes the existence of two contexts for moral decision makes judgement by definition contextually relative.

(Gilligan 1993: 166)

Despite the 'relational' orientation of women in terms of the care ethic, there is nothing in Gilligan's account to suggest that the men of whom she is speaking are any less able than women to perform the conceptual operation of relating as such.[12] Euro-American culture allows that both are capable of perceiving the relations between the ethic of care and the ethic of justice; the difference is that women are, so to speak, allocated the 'care' of relationships between persons and hence must work to make them explicit (cf. M. Strathern 1995).

What was interesting about the Hagen case was that the double standard evoked when persons switch between orientations did not turn into a difference between a world of interpersonal relationships and a world conceived abstractly, between claims in the name of experience and claims in the name of human nature. Rather, the pivot was between two sets of relationships between persons, so that one may speak of two orders of relating ('two times/types of sociality').[13] Indeed, it would be a mistake to think that because women in Hagen were more often than men put into the position of having to deal with interests represented as diverse and hetero-geneous, as in balancing the claims of natal and conjugal clans, that they were regarded as more 'relational' than men in their disposition. *It is relationships that had different standards.* Two distinct standards were found in the counterpoised moralities of 'political' and 'domestic' life – they summoned alternative modes of relating.

It will be intriguing therefore to consider Simon Harrison's (1993) model of relations from Avatip in the Sepik area of Papua New Guinea. He envisages not the double of alternating moral universes but a double in which one set of relationships has a moral dimension in a way that the other does not: the one enlarges on moral responsiveness where the other evokes amoral powers. If such amoral powers can be identified in Hagen, they lie, as we shall see, beyond *both* political and domestic relations.

MEDIATED AND UNMEDIATED RELATIONS

The two modes of relating might be characterized as mediated and unmediated. This double mobilized distinct emotional circuits. The first comprised a 'male' domain where public talk, like public gift giving, was said to inflame as well as soothe people. Hagen politics involved a constant circulation of messages between potentially independent groups seeking to balance out their fortunes. Clans might exchange aggressive or friendly actions, feelings being mediated through oratory or through transfers of wealth. Satisfaction lay in the claim to have equalled or bettered one's rivals. The second emotional circuit was predicated upon explicit dependency relations that offered an alternative basis for moral reasoning and might work without the mediation of wealth or public talk. In either case, people's capacity to respond to and to evince such emotions was taken as evidence of fully functioning 'minds'.

In the context of the first circuit, states of feeling could be blown up to collective proportions, whole clans mobilized to seek revenge through anger or allies moved to sympathy for one another. Mediation was necessary because collectivities do not have minds; there had to be an instrument to set the diverse inclinations of clan members on a common course. When by contrast these emotions were evinced in the context of dependency (through vehicles such as the giving of food or damage through the withdrawal of help), people's effect on one another was immediate; adjustments did not depend on the facilitations of wealth exchange and public talk. The relations at issue in this second circuit were those of domestic kinship – between spouses, parents and children, close kin with an interest in one another's welfare. Such influence was especially manifest between mother's brother and sister's children; as for spouses, either had the capacity to assist or injure their partner. Domestic kinship was not a 'female' domain; rather it was predicated on cross-sex relations. Ties between persons constructed through both male and female links enmeshed kin of both sexes in unequal reciprocities, dependencies and lifelong debts.

The morality of clanship rested on a replication of identities that persuaded by virtue of its replication and these identities had an abstract quality to them (loyalty to the clan was [like] loyalty to a brother). Ties of close kinship, however, were first and foremost particular; their morality was rooted in specific histories and obligations. Here loyalties were born of the interdependency of those who owed their growth and nurture to one another. The person in the context of close kin ties was involved in countless reciprocities of intimacy. These two emotional circuits underwrote two genderings of action, same-sex and cross-sex. In both spheres persons should 'think on' those to whom they look for reciprocity. But, as we already know, same-sex relations among men had collective dimensions to them not available to women (and was the locus of their domination over women; M. Strathern 1988: 336). Same-sex relations were thus replicated among men, blown up into 'group'-based activities. The counterpart in women's affairs was the exaggeration of their linking roles between such groups. If clansmen were visible in their brotherhood, and in their hostility towards enemies, they had instruments of mediation to deploy to that end. Women by contrast were visible as mediators in themselves. As a consequence, it was their relational capacities that were knowingly at issue in the mediation of clan relations

Listen to two stories of betrayal. They were recounted by the woman who told the tale of Oma and by her husband, on separate occasions in 1970, when *Women in Between* (Strathern 1994) was already in press and Table XII committed to the shape it had then. They cast a rather different light on things. The couple is on my mind because I owed them much, and never really discharged my debt. To give their names would not be politic; I call them Kokla and Kaepa. Both were recalling events from a pre-colonial past.

Kaepa told me about how he had killed an enemy. The man, Op, was from his own tribe, but from a major enemy clan within it. Major enemies were always on the lookout to do one another down, but this opportunity was instigated by an affine, Nde; a brother of Kaepa's[14] was married to Nde's sister, one of several marriages between the groups, and Kaepa referred to Nde and his agnates as *nanga wua pukli* ('my root men'), as the 'mother's brothers' or 'base' of the offspring of his own clan. Kaepa and Nde were thus aligned by an acknowledged cross-sex link, and indeed Kaepa's daughter would later marry into that clan too.

Op had killed a lineage brother of Nde's and Nde felt compelled to act on his anger. But his chances of getting near Op were remote, which was why he enlisted Kaepa to help. Op would know that Nde and his brothers were seeking revenge; by contrast, although Kaepa was also from a major enemy group, there would be no particular reason for suspecting him as an individual. None the less, Kaepa did not want to take unnecessary chances himself. He in turn enlisted the help of a cross-sex connection of his own, a cousin who had given his daughter to the victim, Op, in marriage; we are left to guess at this man's reasons but one may have been the promise that his daughter would not be harmed. At any rate, Kaepa prevailed on his cousin by appealing to the alliance between their clans (through previous marriages, 'our ancestor's mother came from there,' he said). At that time Op was spending his days in a bush dwelling, as men did either when they had gardens to prepare or were afraid of showing themselves in public. He was described as hidden for safety in the bush with his wife (making gardens is a quintessentially cross-sex activity); the problem was to lure him out into the public, political spaces where he would be exposed to other men. It was to get him to do this that Kaepa had to enlist his cousin's further help. Accordingly, Op came out of hiding and visited a ceremonial display, an archetype public event. Kaepa and his mates were waiting for him on the road home; they had with them a spear that Nde had supplied. As Op approached, Kaepa's brother (the one married into Nde's clan) seized it and killed Op on the spot; his wife was saved; she was told to get off to her natal clan as fast as she could.

This was an affair conducted entirely by men, but in pursuing their goals and persuading others to act, they engaged the loyalties of other men through appeals based as much on cross-sex grounds as same-sex ones. Each of the relationships made visible (the brother wishing to avenge his brother; the affine who could count on his 'root man') carried its own moral weight. Ties through women thus had an affect to them that might be as crucial as ties through men. In addition, however, men had the power to carry out such deeds because they had at their disposal the instruments through which their effect on others could be registered at long range – abstract tokens of public effectiveness, objects of mediation. Nde gave a spear to the killers for the moment when they were able to set upon Op. There is another long-range instrument of mediation too: wealth.

Why did Kaepa allow himself to be prevailed upon? Although the standing enmity between his and the victim's clan was public motive enough, was there a personal motive? Kaepa started out his story by telling me of the wealth that Nde had promised him. Nde showed him one pig, and said there would be ten. After the party reported back to Nde, taking a broken portion of spear with Op's blood on it, Nde's clan handed over nine domestic pigs and a wild one, along with ten pearlshell valuables. Op's widow is said to have put off her mourning attire and decorated herself for the occasion.

Women did not have the same access to such objects of mediation, as they also lack oratorical skills or unambiguous claims to clan support. But they had relationships at their disposal. That is, their influence over others could be negotiated from the vantage point of their own mediatory position (and cf. Van Baal 1975). We do not know what direct input Op's widow may have had in her husband's downfall; the story is not told that way. Kaepa's wife Kokla, however, told me a tale in which a woman turns a man's expectations of intimate cross-sex dependency to her own ends.

An Elti woman was married to a Mokei man with no other wives, and she could not understand why he beat her all the time. He may have feared her as someone from a potential enemy tribe, and refused to eat her food (lest it contain poison). She was unhappy, and her brothers took pity on her: they told her that, provided she could lure him to her natal place, they would kill him. Here is a reverse gender reading of danger and exposure: she had to entice him away from his refuge among his agnates, the safe same-sex environment of his men's house, into a position where he would be exposed to the cross-sex interests of his affines (wife's kin). She built up his trust to the point where he began to eat her food. Disarmed, he agreed to accompany her back to her place, whereupon her brothers murdered him. In the end, however, it was thought that the husband claimed her. She had returned to her natal home but before the gardens she had planted began to bear she sickened and died, and although no one knew for sure, perhaps her husband's ghost killed her.

Here the woman used the kinds of moral expectations that a

spouse will have about conjugal intimacy to override his caution. The moral rationale of her actions was given by the same token: she had been refused the intimate interdependence that she could have expected from the relationship. She thus used one particularistic and cross-sex set of relations (with her close kin) to extricate herself from another (with her uncooperative spouse). It was not really a solution, but it was morally intelligible as a form of revenge.[15] She came to a quick end, however, as people who follow only their own inclinations are said to do. Kokla told this tale without providing further reasons on the brothers' part for coming to the aid of their sister; to say that the woman had been acting out of interests of her own, as Hagen people might well say in such circumstances, was in this case my and not Kokla's gloss.

MORAL AND AMORAL

Hagen clans figured prominently in moral reasoning – they afforded one of the bases for understanding how people selected and evaluated relations, same-sex among male agnates, cross-sex between male and female. Collective values thus provided justification for some acts, and condemned others as against collective interests. If one wished to press the English contrast between 'moral' and 'immoral' behaviour, however, the latter would include not just betraying one's own clan, but also more generally going one's own way in not heeding others. What were being ignored might be obligations belonging to the alternative field of relationships, again same-sex or cross-sex, namely that constructed through particular, interpersonal ties. Judgement clearly depended on one's perspective. In either case (in either moral domain) people would assume that other aims, whether other relationships or inscrutable ends of one's own, had taken precedence.

Harrison (1993) offers a most original critique of collective ideology. His critique is addressed to the Sepik counterpart of Hagen clans, namely Avatip male cults; he argues that the politics and ritual ('religion') through which such collective bodies realized their presence in people's minds and actions should not be regarded as moral at all (and cf. Langness 1977).[16] On the contrary, they made people deaf to the kinds of understanding to which they were ordinarily open. If I extend this analysis to Hagen, it would be to observe that there were occasions when people shifted not between two moral domains but between moral and amoral states of being.

The aggression with which Avatip men once carried out raids, Harrison (1993: 111) argues, stemmed not from 'anger' (a subjective state calibrated to their relations with others) but from their 'power' (through magic that closed up their understanding and made them indiscriminately hostile to those less potent than themselves). Many political acts in Hagen could, by contrast, be attributed to an exaggerated subjectivity; anger appeared as collective anger and relations between clans were calibrated like personal relations. But there also seemed to be moments when people's acts ceased to be governed by such moral considerations. *Wulya wulya* was a way of putting someone else into this amoral state.

Now Laurence Goldman (1993: 283) offers a caution on the problems of questioning about intentions when questioning is an alien means of access. Those accounts from Kaepa and Kokla were elicited through questions. I had wanted to pursue the role of *wulya wulya*, the magical substance that I had been told could be administered to a woman to make her lose her mind (relocate her intentions in the affairs of men) so that she might be induced to poison her husband. I thought I was losing mine when, on further questioning in 1970, Kaepa declared that men would never do this to a woman, although they might get *her* to administer it to the husband. Perhaps it was a way of making me see the point: *wulya* bypasses intermediaries. I shall return to this. Kaepa's versions did, however, have the same outcome: men get too careful, suspecting every mouthful they take, especially from the hands of others than their wives. The substance might be administered by the wife herself to override his care, thus giving others opportunity to poison him. The point about food from strangers was that men had to eat when they took journeys, and *wulya* magic might be needed to get them to venture forth. This was what happened on the occasion that they killed Op.

When Kaepa was commissioned to help kill Op, he knew that, like any other homicide, Op would take precautions not to expose himself. There was no chance of influencing the wife since she and Op were hiding in the bush – they had to entice him into the open. When Kaepa enlisted the services of his cousin, Op's father-in-law, he did not rely on this man's powers of persuasion, the medium of talk; Kaepa supplied the father-in-law with *wulya* substance, and it was because the man introduced this substance into places where Op sat and slept that Op ceased to think of his own safety and ventured out to the ceremonial ground. Kaepa described his quest for the substance which took him on a long mountain journey. Here he mobilized a yet further set of cross-sex linked kin, being shown the way by a maternal kinsman and a brother-in-law (ZH) who lived in the vicinity.[17] These men eventually received part of the payment that Kaepa obtained. Kaepa thus drew on the support of an affine to procure the *wulya* substance that he was going to get an affine of the marked victim to use with lethal intent. Affines may be morally persuaded either way. Whereas a Hagen man can depend on the more or less axiomatic support of his clansmen (contrast O'Hanlon 1989), affines and cross-linked kin who are such sources of outside strength may equally well turn treacherous.

The *wulya* substance that was sent to Op was meant to make him forget that, were he to venture into the public world of male politics, then he could expect revenge from his victim's brother. As the story has it, when he left the seclusion of domesticity he met his end. And Kaepa? What on earth made him risk a perilous journey to find the substance, and enlist the aid of others to help in his dangerous venture, any of whom could have betrayed him? The wealth: the pigs and shells. And what are these? In the same way as the generalized and otherwise abstract expectations of clan morality may be embodied in specific acts of revenge, so too may the generalized and otherwise abstract value of relationships that circulate between men in exchange be embodied in gifts of wealth. Kaepa wanted the wealth. Valuables may be objects of mediation, but he found a way of getting them *that bypassed their mediating functions*. He did not have to invest wealth of his own in the relationship with Nde; he just had to kill Op. So while the pigs and shells were a medium through which he could enhance his future relationships with other men, he obtained them through immediate means: promise of wealth unencumbered by past debt (cf. A. Strathern 1979). It would bring instant power. Wanting wealth for its potential bypasses the conventions of moral/immoral behaviour: we could call the acts that ensue amoral.

And women? If it is the single-sex replication of emotional states that leads to the kind of aggrandizement of self-interest which can lodge in a desire for wealth rather than for relationships, what might be the female counterpart here? It is clear that there is no collective dimension to women's lives that has the moral force of men's engagement in politics. But, it may be suggested (M. Strathern 1988: 250, 252, after Gillison 1980; cf. Gillison 1993: 171–172), there is a same-sex equation between a woman and what she produces, and above all between her and her food. In Kokla's tale, the woman who lured her husband to his death did so by making him feel more confident, and taking food from her was a sign of this. Yet she had not relied only on her blandishments. Her brother had supplied her with *wulya* substance to confuse the husband so that he 'forgot' his caution and allowed these intimacies. Kokla cited an instance where a husband took similar measures to get rid of a lazy wife: the woman was conversely at fault for not looking after his gardens and pigs and, we may surmise, feeding him, and he so confused her through *wulya wulya* that she wandered about attached to everyone and to no one. So here, in accord with Kaepa's remarks (on other occasions she disagreed), it is the victim who is given *wulya* substance, not the intermediary. The following story of an intermediary who is also a victim comes from someone else.

In this narrative a woman was tricked into thinking that she had men's support for her own designs when she had fallen victim to theirs. Rangkel was married into an enemy group. The target of her male kin was her husband's brother, a man the height and build of one of their own men who had been killed. The woman's kin gave her substance that they said was magic to make the husband's brother think on her. Rangkel was to put it in her mouth and breathe it over the brother-in-law, and it would make him so generous that he would share delicacies or valuables with her.[18] They alleged that it was 'woman magic' (love magic that women used to make men cleave to them, including husbands and, as here, husbands' brothers who could then be expected to help support them; they would provide such men with food in return). Rangkel did not know that she had been given *wulya wulya*, and when she breathed it over the man, she was inhaling it herself as well. Her desire to seek favours from the husband's brother had become a vehicle for violence: when these same kin subsequently supplied her with poison, she was unknowingly under the influence of *wulya* and fed the poison to her friend who died. However, she had established such a position of trust among her affines that they did not suspect her, and after a while the effects of the *wulya* wore off. That did not prevent the husband's brother's ghost from eventually killing her in turn. So the marked man took food from Rangkel thinking that it would nourish when it contained the poison that would destroy, while she had breathed *wulya wulya* over him which put them both out of their minds when she thought she was enhancing their interdependency and intimacy. The dead man's revenge closed the account.

Perhaps Rangkel had also been taken by greed. There was no problem between herself and her husband, but she wanted to enlarge her influence, make more productive the relationships that she had with other men in her husband's settlement. She would gain her desire by short-circuiting the ordinary routes, in this case to relationships of trust which are slowly built up on a daily basis through interactions and transactions. The magic would bring instant influence. To this end she was able to draw on same-sex powers of her own. The food that should have nourished the man she gave under what she thought was the effect of woman magic, an *exaggeration* of her own female attributes, a replication of substances that would make her giving of substance (food) the more effective. This was, like Kaepa's seeking the mediatory objects of relationships (wealth) through non-relational means, an amoral enhancement of relationality. It was as though her actions only had ends of their own, and they ended in this tale with her end.

Other contributions to this volume comment on the extent to which anthropological accounts of morality have fallen prey to the conflation of morality with society (e.g. Howell after David Parkin). By translating as moral Hagen evaluations of actions made with reference to others on a cross-sex or same-sex basis, collective or particular, I do not just fall prey to a similar conflation: I would *emphasize* the role that an explicit relationality played in their judgements. If we designate this a sphere of morality, it encompassed both 'moral' (selecting between relationships) and 'immoral' (ignoring relationships for one's own ends) dispositions. But, rather like Caroline Humphrey's amoral rules (this volume), Hageners also envisaged an amoral relationality.

If moral reasoning involved the knowing sifting of information, then *wulya* sorcery bypassed this process. Persons might be induced to act unknowingly, and to that extent amorally. But sorcery was not the only thing that put people out of their minds; desire-greed (*kum*)[19] could do the same. In one instance (Kaepa and his brother over Op's murder), the killers were swayed by desire for wealth; in another, Rangkel was swayed by a desire for intimacy. After all, others were able to gain access to them in the first place, turning the person (Kaepa, Rangkel) into an agent acting for *them*, by playing on his or her already present desire for direct power or influence over some third party. Those who sought such influence, as well as subsequent victims of it, ceased to be open to moral judgement.

Greed-desire turned both objects of mediation (gifts) and the substance of unmediated interactions between persons (food) into powers of another kind (bribe, poison).[20] The power of these objects was that they offered the means of bypassing the ordinary, time-consuming processes by which relationships were established and cultivated. They were not immoral. On the contrary, they exaggerated certain positive values of relationality. But they rendered moral reasoning impossible. I have argued that it is appropriate in the Hagen case to understand moral reasoning as a response to the capacity for evaluating relationships – because of their commitment to different kinds of relationships people knowingly sifted through information both as a prelude to taking decisions and in judging the decisions of others – and relationships existed between persons by virtue of the way that they were mediated (by gifts, for instance) or made substantial (as through food). Yet what brought them into visible existence, the items presented as gifts or food, might, in extreme circumstances, take on a life of their own (cf. Battaglia 1994). It was as though relationality could be summoned by itself.

I have described instances that show an exaggerated desire for relationality, whether through gaining objects of mediation without entering into mediating relations, or through seeking influence via a precipitate intimacy. Perhaps it was the paradoxical disembedding of the desire for relationships from relationships themselves that made people deaf to the amities and enmities that otherwise informed moral reasoning.

NOTES

1 The material for this chapter was inspired by Paula Brown's 'Enemies and affines' (Brown 1964); a version appears in a festschrift for Paula Brown, *Work in Progress*, edited by Hal Levine and Anton Ploeg, published by Lang Verlag. It was originally given at the EASA conference panel convened by John Davis under the rubric 'Gender and morality'.

2 Smart (1991: 145) delineates two different approaches to women's 'experience' taken by feminist legal scholars. Both challenge legal orthodoxy and method, and assume that the basis for restructuring law must be women's experience. The first argues that we start with the needs and wants of women as to what is fair and just; the second

disowns theory based on abstractions such as 'fairness' and 'justice' in favour of reference back to women's experience via the small-scale and interpersonal.

3 Among several comments on this chapter of which I have taken advantage, Josephides (personal communication) asks about same-sex relations between women, such as public fights between co-wives. My placement of same-sex female relations will emerge later.

4 Rumsey (n.d.) characterizes the practice of pairing as '*the* characteristic trope of Western Highlands social life'. The argument in this present chapter proceeds by binarisms as an analytical response on my part to this trope, with its constant creation of possibilities through a doubling or divergence of procedures and outcomes (and see M. Strathern 1988: 188–189). It is, however, much simplified by the constraints of exposition; for a critique and extension of the two types of sociality to which I refer below, see especially Merlan and Rumsey (1991: 200, 203–204).

5 Women were sometimes said to take political initiative, usually out of empathy for their own brothers (an instance is recounted in M. Strathern (1994: 178); more conventionally, the male kinsmen were presented as the principal actors. However, while persons might act as agents for others, Hagen people emphasized that men and women alike ordinarily had to carry out their own actions for themselves: their will or mind must be set on their deeds (cf. Merlan and Rumsey 1991: 227).

6 This took various forms, including collusion between men to make it appear that a woman was the cause of bad relations between them; between affines, the trouble that women caused was to their potential alliance (which could be presented as based on *either* cross-sex *or* same-sex relations).

7 Politics is, of course, carried on in both public and private, and men seek simultaneous political and personal advantage for themselves. These English terms carry the unfortunate resonance of greater and lesser degrees of 'sociality'. The second part of the chapter invokes a rather different contrast between two modes of relating.

8 Argued at length elsewhere and not rehearsed again here. In two recent papers Andrew Strathern (1993, 1994) has returned to the subject of the Hagen *noman* ('mind, will, intention'). For an extensive treatment of intentionality (including commentary on the Hagen ethnography), see Goldman (1993).

9 The relationship may be played out in many ways:

> wives may be cast into the role of ally or enemy as well as helpmate. Sometimes they are kept sweet with gifts, sometimes coerced, sometimes urged to help. In their individual lives particular couples may make any of these terms dominant. In men's imagery of the female, and specifically the female as wife, all three are run together. The wife-as-enemy is classified as untrustworthy, liable to succumb to hostile impulses, as treacherous as male enemies are, to be beaten into submission; wife-as-ally can be counted upon most of the time, but must be flattered, complimented, given the generous attention

that will make her feel good; wife-as-clan-member is appealed to as a rational person who can see where long-term interests lie, who acknowledges the significance of group affairs and is bent upon common goals. All three involve notions of females as persons with orientations of their own; they differ in the degree of disjunction between husband and wife and the method of coping with this.

(M. Strathern 1981: 184)

At the time of writing (late 1970s, early 1980s) I used the language of 'personal' and 'social' interests.

10 I am grateful for Michael O'Hanlon's observations (personal communication) on similar ideas among the neighbouring Wahgi where people sometimes differentiated between men's and women's sorcery in its effects (and see note 18 below).

11 Gilligan observes:

The reinterpretation of women's experience in terms of their own [web] imagery of relationships thus clarifies that experience and also provides a nonhierarchical vision of human connection .... But the power of the images of hierarchy and web ... *signifies the embeddedness of both of these images in the cycle of human life.* These disparate visions in their tension reflect the paradoxical truths of human experience – that we know ourselves as separate only insofar as we live in connection with others, and that we experience relationship only insofar as we differentiate other from self.

(Gilligan 1993: 62–63, my emphasis)

12 A point on which she has been misunderstood. Gilligan does not offer an unqualified valorization of relationality – she repeatedly *problematizes* the cultural understandings of 'relationships' that appear to demand selfless responses (see e.g. Gilligan 1993: xiii).

13 On two times/types of sociality see M. Strathern (1988: e.g. 92–96, 280). I would refer the reader to Overing's (1985: 172, after Horton) discussion of 'personal kind' terms that classify the world according to modalities of relationship rather than the 'natural kind' terms of Western philosophy. Read's (1955) classic paper first stated the issue for the Papua New Guinea Highlands.

14 Part of the story is told by Kaepa in the first person, part attributes the actions to both him and his brother.

15 On the suicidal nature of women's retaliations see M. Strathern (1994: 281–283).

16 Harrison both derives his insight from Tuzin (1982) and differs from him:

Tuzin argues that the domestic and ritual domains of this [Arapesh] society are governed by 'two mutually abhorrent ethical doctrines' (Tuzin 1982: 352), whose irreconcilability poses an enduring moral dilemma for men. On the one hand, Tuzin argues, the spirits of the cult are the highest religious expressions of the social solidarity of the village (Tuzin 1982: 342). On the other hand, men have problems with justifying the violence against non-initiates which their religion ordains. At Avatip, there is a very similar dilemma, but it is not between irreconcilable moral codes. It lies rather in the fact that religious values and moral values are distinct. They are values of two quite different kinds.

(Harrison 1993: 119–20)

17 Kaepa said that the *wulya* substance came from a place called Kum, at the stony head of the Kum river. A similar term *kum* is used of magic of various kinds, for the stones that lie in rivers and fly up to make people sick when they have eaten too much pork, and for the greed that makes them forget the circumspectness by which they usually conduct their lives. *Kum* may be translated as witchcraft insofar as it is thought of as a mobile substance that attaches itself to people; it makes them want to consume things and in the end consumes them (see A. Strathern 1982). *Kum* is a sort of free-floating desire, nothing but itself. O'Hanlon (1989: 56–59) offers an account of *kum* as it is understood by Wahgi people; he also refers to a poison called *wulyawl*, after the name of a plant, which he related to the term for being out of one's mind (Wahgi *wulyo*). I have followed the Hagen convention of referring to the sorcery by the term for this mental state ('madness') but was also informed that there was another similar but not identical term for the substance itself.

18 The valuables would be ornaments for her personal use or items for her husband to use in exchanges in which she had an interest (e.g. with her own kin).

19 See note 17 above. Both greed and desire have too many moralistic overtones in English to stand by themselves, and neither convey the free-floating or autonomous state indicated by the Hagen term.

20 Josephides (personal communication) properly questions the apparent prioritization suggested by the positive and negative overtones of the English (as though gift were the archetype and poison its subversion). O'Hanlon (1989: 63) observes that it is social situations that turn one kind of substance into another, render 'dirt' poisonous for instance; on the indeterminacy of the objects of gift exchange, see Merlan and Rumsey (1991: 218–220).

REFERENCES

Battaglia, Debbora (1994) 'Retaining reality: some practical problems with objects as property', *Man* (n.s.) 29: 1–15.

Brown, P. (1964) 'Enemies and affines', *Ethnology* 3: 335–356.

Damon, Frederick and Wagner, Roy (eds) (1989) *Death Rituals and Life in the Societies of the Kula Ring*, de Kalb: University of Arizona Press.

Gilligan, Carol (1993 [1982]) *In a Different Voice: Psychological Theory and Women's Development*, Cambridge, Mass.: Harvard University Press.

Gillison, Gillian (1980) 'Images of nature in Gimi thought', in C. MacCormack and M. Strathern (eds) *Nature, Culture and Gender*, Cambridge: Cambridge University Press.

——(1993) *Between Culture and Fantasy: A New Guinea Highlands Mythology*, Chicago: Chicago University Press.

Goldman, Laurence (1993) *The Culture of Coincidence: Accident and Absolute Liability in Huli*, Oxford: Clarendon Press.

Harrison, Simon (1993) *The Mask of War: Violence, Ritual and the Self in Melanesia*, Manchester: Manchester University Press.

Josephides, Lisette (1982) *Suppressed and Overt Antagonism: A Study in Aspects of Power and Reciprocity among the Northern Melpa*, Research in Melanesia, Occasional Paper 2, Port Moresby: University of Papua New Guinea.

Langness, L.L. (1977 [1974]) 'Ritual, power, and male dominance in the New Guinea Highlands', in R. Fogelson and R.N. Adams (eds) *The Anthropology of Power*, New York: Academic Press.

Merlan, Francesca and Rumsey, Alan (1991) *Ku Waru: Language and Segmentary Politics in the Western Nebilyer Valley, Papua New Guinea*, Cambridge: Cambridge University Press.

O'Hanlon, Michael (1989) *Reading the Skin: Adornment, Display and Society among the Wahgi*, London: British Museum Publications.

Overing, Joanna (1985) 'Today I shall call him "Mummy": multiple worlds and classificatory confusion', in J. Overing (ed.) *Reason and Morality*, ASA Monograph 24, London: Routledge.

Read, Kenneth E. (1955) 'Morality and the concept of the person among the Gahuka-Gama', *Oceania* 25: 233–282.

Rumsey, Alan (n.d.) 'Pairing and parallelism in the New Guinea Highlands', unpublished manuscript (University of Sydney).

Smart, Carol (1991) 'Feminist jurisprudence', in P. Fitzpatrick (ed.) *Dangerous Supplements: Resistance and Renewals in Jurisprudence*, London: Pluto Press.

Strathern, Andrew (1979) 'Gender, ideology and money in Mount Hagen', *Man* 14: 530–548.

——(1981) 'Compensation: should there be a new law?', in R. Scaglion (ed.) *Homicide Compensation in Papua New Guinea*, Port Moresby: Law Reform Commission of Papua New Guinea.

——(1982) 'Witchcraft, greed, cannibalism and death: some related themes from the New Guinea Highlands', in M. Bloch and J. Parry (eds) *Death and the Regeneration of Life*, Cambridge: Cambridge University Press.

——(1993) 'Organs and emotions: the question of metaphor', *Canberra Anthropology* 16: 1–16.

——(1994) 'Keeping the body in mind', *Social Anthropology* 2: 43–53.

Strathern, Marilyn (1995 [1972]) *Women in Between: Female Roles in a Male World*, London: Academic Press, reissued by Rowman & Littlefield, Lanham, MD.

——(1981) 'Self-interest and the social good: some implications of Hagen gender imagery', in S. Ortner and H. Whitehead (eds) *Sexual Meanings: The Cultural Construction of Gender and Sexuality*, New York: Cambridge University Press.

——(1988) *The Gender of the Gift: Problems with Women and Problems with Society*, Berkeley & Los Angeles: California University Press.

——(1995) 'Needing fathers; needing society', in H. Diemberger, A.

Gingrich and J. Helbling (eds) *Die Differenz der Anderen: Beiträge zur Sozialanthropologie der Geschlechter*, Frankfurt: Suhrkamp.

Tuzin, Donald F. (1982) 'Ritual violence among the Ilahita Arapesh', in G. Herdt (ed.) *Rituals of Manhood*, Berkeley and Los Angeles: University of California Press.

Van Baal, J. (1975) *Reciprocity and the Position of Women*, Amsterdam: van Gorcum.

Chapter 6

Inside an 'exhausted community'

An essay on case-reconstructive research about peripheral and other moralities

Andre Gingrich

> For some to have honor in this sense, it is essential that not everyone have it.
>
> Charles Taylor, *The Politics of Recognition*

An 'exhausted community' (Jahoda 1991), the sociological concept that I employ in this essay, is characterized above all by social apathy.[1] Social apathy in such communities coexists with three contesting factors: resignation, despair and, to a lesser degree, the attitudes of those who have not yet become apathetic; it is related to the growing pressure from regional political forces and their dominant doctrines and to insurmountable economic processes supported by them. On the local level, it is accompanied by a series of related indicators, including an increasingly restricted margin within which local actors still try to apply alternative strategies and to participate in deviant discourses; the growing influence of local institutions loyal to the dominant regional doctrine; and a parallel, gradual abandonment of local ties to previously coexisting, alternative institutions and cosmologies. Such indicators take their toll on an individual level as well. Among the long-term unemployed in European societies, for instance, indicators of social apathy include a lowering of individual expectations and activities, disturbances in personal perceptions of time and space, and a rise in violence against oneself or family members.

In view of a certain spectrum of current anthropological debates concerning domination and resistance, I consider the exhausted community concept a differentiating and useful one. Analyses of social hierarchies too often end up in the trap of exclusive dichotomies. One group of authors tends to analyse processes of social hierarchies mainly in terms of the maintenance and reproduction of an existing order, in which the dominated are seen as contributing, in one way or another, to their own subordination. Another prefers to analyse such processes in terms of creative interaction, emphasizing the ways in which individual actors deal with domination's effects and giving its overall social impacts less consideration.

Both perspectives tend to focus on specific, narrow aspects of social hierarchies and often overlook a wide range of intermediate situations. For some long-term situations and stable social groups, neither Godelier's (1982) notion of tacit 'consentment' to dominant doctrines and systems of power nor anthropology's currently fashionable notions of resistance to and creative dealing with constellations of power provides sufficient conceptual tools. Sometimes these perspectives may in fact designate prevalent social attitudes, but at times when tacit consent ('resignation') or resisting creativity ('those who have not yet become apathetic') represent secondary or marginal factors, a one-sided research focus upon these secondary factors produces misrepresentations. For instance, exaggerating the importance of resistance and creativity for these social contexts and groups sheds more light on the anthropologist's attitude than on the situation of the groups in question. Reifying a resisting creativity then implies a naive optimism that simultaneously belittles local suffering and underestimates the strength of regional powers and doctrines.

The present paper does not describe or explain how my tribal hosts in Arabia became an 'exhausted community', nor are the overall symptoms and indicators of social apathy analysed empirically. Instead, I deal with social apathy as a given fact and seek to understand how it can interact with ethnographic fieldwork on moralities.[2] I show how a prevailing climate of social apathy presents initial challenges for ethnographic inquiry but then directs a qualitative research process towards methods that help to explore overt and covert moralities.

I begin with a brief outline of research notions useful for identifying moralities in non-secular, scriptural societies, and the Muslim world in particular, by assessing some key notions: those of honour, grace and 'the forbidden' (shame) and their relevance for the discussion of my ethnographic example. After describing the phases of interaction between my ethnographic fieldwork and the local attitudes of social apathy, sullen *laissez-faire* and cautious support, I discuss the problem of writing texts based on such ethnographic data. At that point, the elements of a processual, middle-range typology begin to emerge, contrasting competing moralities in today's Arab-Muslim world.

UNDERSTANDING MORALITIES IN MUSLIM SOCIETIES

I use the term 'morality' in the 'narrow' sense articulated by Howell (this volume); for more specific analysis of moralities in non-secularized, scriptural societies, this definition overlaps with concepts of collective moralities outlined by Weber and Habermas (Eder 1988): forms by which communities or societies establish normative ordering for individual social behaviour. To some extent, legal and moral orders coincide. Law is capable of setting positive normative, moral standards for practical behaviour, and thus informs elements of social practice. Likewise, negative standards are established by the threat of sanctions or retaliation in case of transgression.

Whether the research focuses on individuals' agency, negotiations and interactions or on the structural aspects in a social system (Rosen 1984), the legal system is not merely a formal codification independent of everyday life. Beyond its actual application, it has a return impact, as a moral order, on social practice. By opening up or restricting spheres of agency and interaction, the legal system constructs some of the moral standards of everyday social practice. Nevertheless, moralities can exceed legal systems, as when something conforms to the law but is perceived as morally repellent.

Multiple moralities inside scriptural, non-secular societies correspond to legal heterogeneity. A few of these moral and legal systems attain the more stable status of dominant, scriptural doctrines that are part of the overall, sacred cosmology. In Muslim societies, legal heterogeneity relies on at least three interrelated, variable and overlapping forms: state law, Islamic law and customary law. In some regions these three and their associated moral values have almost fully accommodated one another, merging at the expense of customary law. Elsewhere, if the legal and moral traditions of state and of Islam are sufficiently flexible, they may have penetrated each other in a more balanced way. At another extreme, they may have influenced each other only very loosely, mainly by remaining separate, as when state and Islamic legal traditions exert only superficial influence at the local levels.[3] Anthropological debate on local Muslim moralities has generally touched on only one of these possibilities: the debate on honour, shame and grace has been preoccupied with contexts of the accommodated relationship between Islamic, state and customary laws and moralities. In such contexts, state and Islamic legal traditions are deeply and profoundly intertwined with local moral and legal orders.

During the last few decades, the well-known triangle of honour, shame and grace was central to anthropological discussions of Muslim moralities. Research in southern and southeastern Europe has provided important comparative materials (Herzfeld 1980; Peristiany 1965; Peristiany and Pitt-Rivers 1992; Stewart 1994), as have studies in South and Central America (cf. Melhuus this volume). Morocco has been a major area for ethnographic inquiries and related theories on honour and shame. Authors of very different orientations, including Ernest Gellner, Clifford Geertz, Pierre Bourdieu, Raymond Jamous and Fatima Mernissy, have relied to some extent on Moroccan cases to develop or prove their concepts and theories, allowing us to evaluate them against a set of comparable and closely related ethnographic and historical cases. At the same time, the narrow geographical focus leads to a crucial shortcoming for understanding the much larger and heterodox Islamic world. Because of the almost exclusive concern with the 'accommodated' combination of state, scriptural and customary notions in many Moroccan cases, certain assumptions have gone unquestioned.

The case of the *haram* idea illustrates this Moroccan bias. *Haram* is an important concept in many local moralities of the Maghreb and elsewhere, but the debate has usually overlooked the fact that it is by no means independent of a wide spectrum of scriptural connotations. Anthropologists have shown that in the Maghreb, honour often stands for a moral category that is defended, or challenged, by oneself and others, i.e., through the efforts of adult men, usually of tribal origin or background, or from non-tribal social equivalents. In general, honour has both a basic, permanent aspect and a more flexible side. Defending and challenging individual and collective honour opens up a spectrum of strategic and tactical options that may or may not lead to open conflict.

Jamous's brilliant analysis has revealed three basic forms of violent conflict. First, fights following raids that become mock conflicts entail a restricted, ritualized and endless exchange of violence in which young men prove themselves capable of gaining honour. Second, conflicts that follow killings are initiated by adult men of honour and lead to a blow-by-blow sequence of vengeance killings. Third, conflicts between groups of tribal 'big men' and their respective clients occasionally lead to massacres (Jamous 1992). These conflicts, in turn, may or may not be settled by the intervention of outside mediation. Mediators are often holy or noble men who have greater access to grace than others, and accepting mediation frequently implies rituals that place honour under the higher value of grace. Grace is the overall value that ultimately intervenes to halt, at least temporarily, an escalation of violence.

The defence and challenge of honour itself has to do with contesting the forbidden or protected sphere, *haram*. These discourses and social practices are dominated by male actors, who control central decision-making processes at the household, village and tribal levels. It is always their honour that is at stake. Bourdieu's research (1972) has shed some light on women's distinctive roles in the network of strategic interactions, and Mernissy (1975, 1987) has elucidated their historical role in policy-making. For the Moroccan case, however, the proposition that women's moral position is confined to the *haram* sphere has remained largely unquestioned. Bonte has recently (1991) reemphasized and elaborated this for Mauritanian examples as well.

The moral location of women and children as protected appendages to men's honour represents a powerful and effective local concept. But the extent to which women, in their own segregated interactions, refer to that concept, requires more detailed exploration. Abu-Lughod's work with the Awlad Ali of north-western Egypt (1986) is the most interesting study in this regard, and implies that the female-centred idea of 'modesty' sometimes serves as a second, parallel concept for women's moral behaviour. Its basic subordination to the first concept, however, encompassing male notions of honour and status, seems to remain beyond doubt.[4] Thus, the dominant morality on many local levels in the North African, and particularly the Moroccan, context represents women as having no independent honour of their own and as being one of the most vulnerable elements of a protected sphere, usually called *haram*.

SCRIPTURALISM, HONOUR AND PERSON

One result of the Moroccan bias in anthropological research on Muslim societies is that the close association between these local *haram* concepts and the related scriptural traditions has rarely been considered. To analyse frequent instances of local occurrence without relating them to their scriptural meaning isolates one segment of a moral, legal and political system from its other elements.

Since the early centuries of Islam, mainstream Muslim jurisprudence (*fiqh*) has placed the concept of *haram* at one extreme on a scale of five moral values. Recommended and obligatory acts (*mandub* and *wajib*) constitute one end of the scale; reprehensible and prohibited acts (*makruh* and *haram*) stand on the other. In the centre stands *mubah*, that which is permissible or indifferent. *Haram* thus represents that which is prohibited. On an even higher ideological, theological and ritual level, *haram* stands for the sacrosanct districts of Mecca and Medina (Coulson 1969: 80–83). From everyday to the highest levels of cosmology, *haram* denotes the morally and legally 'forbidden' – including, as Dresch (1989: 58, 146) has pointed out, a semantic field for all that is set aside as sacrosanct. A basic consideration of scriptural notions, then, is clearly essential for an understanding of local moralities. A sharp distinction between 'high' and 'folk' Islam, as has been emphasized by Gellner, leads nowhere in cases where a superior, scriptural value of morality has been literally inscribed into local moralities. It is embodied and incorporated through local actors' social practice, in the strategies and interactions of defending or challenging male honour and the female *haram*.

For women, being part of a subordinated, protected sphere, without the capacity to stand up against men, is only one important implication of the *haram*. In fact, the notion of a protected, pious life of modesty and decency inside the *haram* represents an ideal that few women can attain. It offers the promise of not having to work outside the home, a promise associated with affluence and with being the female 'centre of the household' (Gingrich, forthcoming). In short, being protected is combined with an ideal of upward social mobility and of becoming the emotional core of the family. In this sense, the *haram* also entails a threat towards those women who do not strive to attain the ideal.

With its promises, threats and restrictions, the *haram* notion is directly linked to personhood, which, as Jacobson-Widding points out (this volume), provides an important approach to the study of moralities. *Haram* connotes quite different fields of moral agency according to faith, age, gender and status. This conceptual combination of individual, person and *haram* functions as a cultural script (cf. Jacobson-Widding this volume) in many spheres of Muslim societies. The Franco-Algerian scholar Mohammed Arkoun recently outlined the dominant Muslim doctrine of personhood:

> The 'Muslim' person develops and asserts himself or herself within dogmatic closure .... Not every individual is a person, and persons are more eminent (*afdal*) insofar as they approach the ideal of piety called for by the Qur'an and the family of the Prophet (*ashraf*). This general principle for the classification of persons and individuals is complicated by legal definitions of the status of men, women, children and slaves (up until the abolition of slavery).

Arkoun illustrates these remarks (1994: 99f.) with a graph depicting Muslims as the first category of believers, a category within which men, women, children and slaves are ranked in that hierarchical order.[5]

The dominant doctrine therefore separates 'person' from 'individual'. 'Person' is a collective concept represented by adult men of appropriate faith and status; it allocates 'their' women and children to subordinate, differentiated positions inside that realm, positions that are circumscribed by the connotations of *haram*. The dominant doctrine therefore combines a selective reading of *haram* as a collective personification of the forbidden, and as that which is 'set aside as sacrosanct', with a hierarchical sub-classification (*ashraf*, other free men, women, children, slaves). In this combined form the notion of *haram* informs social practice.

To isolate these scriptural definitions of moral values and persons from the very social relations that they inform is to misrepresent both. Moreover, it indicates an obsolete anthropological disregard for history and historical processes. The debate, after all, concerns local societies exposed to the scriptural and moral influence of Islam for several hundred, if not more than a thousand, years. During this period, a personified *haram* sphere as the subordinate appendage of male honour has become a local embodiment of the dominant doctrine.

HARAMIZATION

I classify these intrinsic, accommodated forms in which local moralities and gender relations incorporate and embody a central, scriptural category as one form of haramization. The term therefore signifies moral codes that inform gender relations in a particular way: the results are those lifestyles in Muslim societies in which women are part of the personified, sacrosanct sphere of 'their' men. While women have no honour of their own, protection of their sphere and challenges against other men constitute an essential element of men's honour. One key element in this moral code is the obligation that men not attack, or even directly approach, other women verbally or physically. Since women are considered sacrosanct, a man receives all the shame when he approaches a 'decently behaving' woman. Women in such situations may therefore avoid shame, which could be ascribed to them if they were accused of having provoked it. In the extreme case of attempted or actual rape, for example, a woman must immediately and publicly denounce the attack. Moral and legal rules concerning direct violations of *haram* may vary for women from one ethnographic case of haramization to another, but for men the moral implications are clear: shame falls on those who directly violate or destroy the *haram* sphere.

Haramization has both internal diversity and external limits. To some extent it follows the hierarchies of social stratification. Historically, urban women of higher status groups in the Arab-Muslim world were affected earlier and more profoundly by its implications (Spellberg 1994; Reif 1995: 306), and a higher economic and social status provided more opportunities for women to fulfil its obligations and obtain its rewards. Likewise, the implied threats in this moral code more frequently focused on the lower and middle strata of society, where the social and economic constraints, together with restricted access to scriptural knowledge and doctrine, provided fewer opportunities to live out haramized lifestyles. Other moralities and lifestyles persisted, or were transformed or created, among these lower and peripheral social groups. They may or may not have included codes of honour and shame, but they embodied little of the dominant doctrine and its notions of *haram* and personhood. Other segments of the lower and middle social strata (often groups related to sacred places and centres) followed Islam's call at an early stage (Gochenour 1984). By joining the community of believers as equals before God, some gradually adopted the obligations of a pious lifestyle and of scriptural notions of morality and personhood.

In addition to this unequal social distribution of haramization along vertical lines of social stratification, there are three major dimensions of horizontal differentiation. The first is denoted by the schisms that differentiate various paths of faith within Islam. These schisms may concern women's legal rights, as in the case of differing rules for inheritance and divorce between the major Sunni and Shiite legal traditions (Madelung 1979), or women's political and ritual status, as in the differences between Alevite and Sunni or Shiite practices (Gokalp 1981). Such distinctions often involve rival self-images of a superior moral understanding of haram and of the correct, pious social practice.

The second horizontal dimension of the social practice of haramization concerns its embeddedness in family relations. Tapper and Tapper (1992/1993) have demonstrated that local concepts of honour and shame are embedded in contrasting social contexts of family and kinship. Comparing data from various parts of the Muslim world, they show that structures of kinship obligations and household adherence determine control over and protection of women. *Haram* moralities, then, are situated in one of two broad family and kinship constellations. In one, more common in the Turcic-speaking regions, the male relatives of a married woman's new family are almost exclusively responsible for her after her marriage (cf. also Strasser 1995: 52). In the second, more frequent in the predominantly Arab-speaking world, a married woman is protected not only by her husband's male kin, but also by her family of origin, and both groups share responsibility for protecting overlapping spheres of the *haram*.

The third horizontal differentiation concerns the external limits of haramization. Islamization and haramization are not identical. Becoming a Muslim essentially requires accepting the basic formula of faith, and respecting and obeying the five 'pillars of Islam'. Haramization is much more specific, signifying only one among many lifestyles in the Islamic world. Many Muslim groups do not practice haramized lifestyles. The construction of a one-to-one relationship between Islamic faith and haramization is itself the result of powerful ideological activities within the broad range of Muslim diversity. This identification produces strong moral pressures, conveying the threat that those who do not practise haramized lifestyles are not true believers. Primary targets of this threat are groups of new proselytes and former modernists. A third target group comprises some of the more traditional middle, lower or peripheral segments of society which historically were less affected by haramization.

The current spread of a new kind of haramization occurs under conditions combining the moral threat of not being true believers with other kinds of pressure. Various responses to this situation exist. Some groups accept the *haram* regulations voluntarily; some do so reluctantly or pragmatically; and some perform only a minimum of duties. Still others, having tried to reject *haram* regulations for as long as possible, have today become 'exhausted'. As pressures from regional, political and moral forces increase, the overt pursuit of alternatives to *haram* regulations is abandoned, but without explicit consent. This is one explanation for the situation that prevailed in my fieldwork area.

'BALANCED' HARAMIZATION

In the early 1980s, after studies in Syria and southwestern Saudi Arabia, I chose a new fieldwork site in northwestern Yemen. Northern Yemen has been an area of rich agricultural traditions and various succeeding state polities since antiquity. In Islamic times, the Yemen's urban settlements were centres of state power, craftsmanship and a continuous scholarly tradition in theology and the sciences. Most of the population, however, inhabited rural areas along the coasts, in the southern lowlands, and in the central and northern highlands. Northern Yemen experienced two periods of somewhat feeble domination by the Ottoman empire (in the sixteenth/seventeenth, late nineteenth and early twentieth centuries), which never reached far beyond the main urban settlements and strategic routes. Both colonial encounters were terminated by Yemenite tribal and peasant movements under Imamic leadership. The Imams came from the high-status group of descendants of the Prophet (Sada) and ruled northern Yemen until the Republican revolution of 1962. In 1990 northern and southern Yemen were united into the present Republic of Yemen.

Because of this history, the highlands of northern Yemen are often stereotyped as a region of traditional royalist influence, where the Sada are particularly strong. Ethnographic and historical research, however, shows that Imamic and Sada influence in these tribal regions generally was unstable, limited and dependent on shifting alliances with various tribal groups (Dresch 1989; Gingrich 1993). Tribal interactions with Imamic state influence and scholarly Sada traditions were common in some regions and, until recently, almost non-existent in others.

This has impacted local moralities as well. In the highlands of Yemen and southwestern Arabia, moralities are transmitted in scriptural traditions preserved by educated male descendants of the Prophet and other scholars. Many chiefs' lineages of tribes and tribal sections also preserve written elements of customary law, and among these groups the *haram* is usually a socially relevant concept. The major tribal groups and some sections of rural society outside the tribal realm, however, entertain somewhat differing moral concepts. Women, children and some elderly people have a weak (*da'if*) tribal status: they usually cannot represent themselves in legal, political or other matters involving personal rights and prestige, but must be represented by men. This situation does not necessarily include gender segregation and differs to some extent from the weak status of non-tribal persons. Whereas both groups (except male tribal children) are considered permanently weak, tribal men, too, may pass through weak phases in their lives, as when they are guests in hostile tribal areas or when they ask for asylum. In these cases, the protection and representation of personified, weak spheres also constitutes a question of male honour, whereas immoral transgressions may be either shameful or forbidden – *ayb* in various degrees, or *haram*. The interplay of these two notions indicates the respective influence of two overlapping but distinctive moral and legal systems. They can be classified according to the few scholarly and the many tribal traditions in the southwestern Arabian highlands.

If many local Moroccan cases seem to represent the more intrinsic, 'accommodated' merging of scriptural and local moralities and legal systems, then the majority of cases in the southwestern Arabian highlands represent the more 'balanced' combination. The weak spheres inside these tribal highland societies display a number of parallels to prevailing scriptural moralities and *haram* notions but show almost as many differences. At the same time, the social agents and literary contents of scriptural moralities have taken over a number of moral ideas and attitudes from tribal law.

AN INQUIRY INTO EXHAUSTED NON-HARAMIZATION

Following a brief visit to the tribal regions of northwestern Yemen in the early 1980s, I reread sections of the diaries and reports of Eduard Glaser, a late nineteenth-century Austrian traveller and Orientalist (Müller and Rhodokanakis 1903; Dostal 1993). Glaser's brief mention of the area was based on reports by Yemeni travellers of higher social status, and his summary of their reports of paganism and related ritual practices shows that he was conscious of their inherent bias. Yet some parts of Glaser's summary, relating to gender self-presentation and practices, seemed partially to confirm my own impressions that social life among these groups differed in several ways from the usual highland standards.

When I returned to northwestern Yemen in the mid-1980s my principal research focused on star calendars and related questions; but even in this seemingly neutral field of inquiry I could not avoid questions of local law and moralities.

During the initial part of my stay, I lived in the village of the tribal chief's lineage. When I visited other parts of the tribal territory, I noticed that in everyday life, married tribal women and unrelated tribal men greeted one another. I was told that it would be impolite not to greet married women myself. Elsewhere, the opposite was true. Among the chief's lineage, some women kept themselves apart, while others did not. When I asked how to greet women properly, my hosts explained that those women who did not greet me or other men had been married into the chief's families from outside the tribe. Among local tribespeople, everyone was somehow related, which required open, cross-gender greeting. A male stranger such as myself should behave in the same way as the local people. The explanation seemed plausible; only later did I realize that the tribe had some 20,000 members, many of whom saw themselves as being 'related' to each other in only a very ephemeral way.

I carefully began to discuss some of Glaser's and my own information with men from the chief's lineage. My hosts laughed: yes, they knew that they had a reputation for astrology and strange rituals, and for being fierce warriors and infidels. Perhaps a tenth of it was true, but the rest was nonsense. Of course they were among the best warriors of the region, but does not every tribe say so? Their reputation for being infidels was due to the fact that they had never allowed descendants of the Prophet to live in their territory. Since the 1960s Republican revolution against the Imamate, when this tribe had supported the Republic, the Prophet's descendants (then mainly Royalists) have disliked them, and therefore urban scholars often criticized them. Yes, among other tribes the Prophet's descendants often played an important part in sacrifices and in rituals asking for rain and other blessings, or in mediating feuds. Among this tribe, however, members of the chief's lineage maintained that they had always performed these tasks themselves.

Later, after consulting other sources I confirmed this information as far as it concerned the Prophet's descendants. More importantly, I witnessed numerous instances of disputes being settled according to tribal law and listened to these legal decisions being prepared by men inside the chief's lineage without any direct participation by Sada or other legal experts.

My initial excitement and curiosity were thus transformed into a slightly disappointed but much more sober attitude. A certain amount of Glaser's information about this tribe in the 1880s appears likely to have been rumour. No trace existed of any 'cult of trees and mountains', for instance, and other allegedly pagan curiosities had most probably been presented to Glaser in a distorted way, and had certainly changed during the succeeding hundred years. A distinctive local dialect and a certain degree of tribal autonomy were the most important reports that I was able to confirm. The tight control of customary law by the chief's lineage was related to the rejection of the former royalist state, its law and its agents.

During the chief's settlement of major intratribal disputes, tribal women had sometimes stood up to defend their own cases or to serve as witnesses for other women. I had interpreted this as a local speciality of tribal law. Still, when I was invited to live in another tribal village by a woman from there who had married into the chief's village, I was surprised. Wasn't it her brother's responsibility to invite me into her village of origin? After all, hospitality was a prime element of tribal honour. Perhaps, I thought, her status as a woman married into the chief's family was higher than that of other tribal women and might allow behaviour that haramized social relations would not. Later, when I received similar invitations from women who had no direct relationship to the chief's lineage, I thought that perhaps they were competing for the prestige of hosting a friend of the chief's family, and that this competition somehow included women's participation. Perhaps they considered me a 'weak' individual, since I had no weapons and belonged to no tribe of equal ranking. Could a weak tribeswoman invite a weak, non-tribal male? My confusion about women's status was linked to questions about my own transient status: in local terms, was I a 'scholar', a 'friend of the chief's family', a 'distant tribesman', or a 'weak' individual? When I had a verbal dispute with a local astrologer, and told my new tribal hosts, they laughed and said: 'Now you know that we all consider you equal. Otherwise nobody would fight with you.' My social status was clarified.

Some days later, when a woman from another tribal section visited the household where I was staying and invited my male host and myself to her village, I began to realize that women in this tribe have the right to greet, and be greeted by, unrelated tribesmen; the right to stand up for themselves in tribal law cases and to testify as witnesses for others; and the right to cross-gender invitations. In all such cases, women are active; not 'set aside' or represented by someone else. Yet the information that I had received in the chief's village had presented honour as concerning men alone, and grace as something to which only a few men had access. My subsequent observations and interactions in other tribal villages seemed increasingly to contradict those initial statements. Women's greeting behaviour, their roles in legal procedures and as hosts indicated a differing notion of honour. When I asked women or men about the implicit evidence, however, their answers were evasive or embar- rassed.

I did receive more explicit answers from men of higher status, such as local chiefs or the few men of literary knowledge. Their standard answer was that these were 'old habits, dating back from a time when we were all illiterate; but now they are being abandoned'. The answer indicated that my questions raised the fear of being accused of immoral behaviour or of being ridiculed: obviously their typical experience with outsiders. The fact that I was a man, and of some learning, was additional reason for this reaction.

In retrospect, I had so far touched only the surface of this exhausted community's social life, which had internalized, to some degree, key elements of the official morality. It held that only men have honour, some men have privileged access to grace, women have no honour of their own. Other attitudes were inappropriate and should be verbally denied and practically abandoned. The chief lineage's men, their wives 'from outside' and a number of village men of higher status were the main local agents of the 'balanced' haramization that historically has prevailed in highland Yemen.

Among the tribal majority, and in spite of the exhausted, partial internalization, a number of visible and important social practices still openly contradicted the official version. If questioned by an outsider, these non-hegemonic, alternative practices sometimes caused embarrassment. Nevertheless, they were common enough that the tribe's paramount chief, in his role as supreme judge in customary law, had to accept and deal with them. Their range extended from everyday routine behaviour (greeting) to special but frequent occasions (hospitality), to rare decision-making processes (customary law cases), and they were regarded as part and parcel of 'that which is generally known' (*urf*), i.e. a part of customary law that is transmitted orally or, as in all these cases, by ritualized behaviour.

Some weeks passed as I continued my main inquiry on star calendars and cosmological questions of time and space. Though an outsider, I already knew much more about tribal life, dialect and internal politics. I was preparing a vaccination campaign for cattle. I had become more trustworthy, more predictable and more 'tribal' to my hosts. They knew that I observed and wrote down everything that interested me, and they trusted me. In answer to that trust, the following section is brief.

WOMEN'S HONOUR

Sudden turns in intratribal relations between neighbouring sections of my host tribe led to the outbreak of two armed disputes. Both revealed an explicit concept of women's honour, together with its component: in such situations, women's duty was to fight against tribal opponents.

The two conflicts finally were settled, but tensions persisted. The season was extremely dry, and when it still had not rained two weeks after the second peace settlement, families from my host village began to prepare a bull sacrifice to ask for rain as God's blessing and grace. My host village had not been actively involved in the two conflicts, and its members asked all groups involved to join in the preparations. Some days later the rain ceremony (*istighātha*) took place. No members of the chief's lineage were invited (in spite of earlier claims by the chief's lineage that this would never occur), although their contributions to the peace settlements were generally acknowledged. Tribal women from the villages in question, however, did participate. By both official and 'exhausted' standards, such male and female behaviour in situations of conflict and ceremony would be unacceptable. Male attacks on any weak individual are shameful and contradict the highland code of honour; women, as weak persons or as part of the *haram*, cannot stand up for themselves, either peacefully or in arms.

In the rain ritual, the absence of members of the chief's families and the active presence of tribeswomen also indicated another local understanding of God's grace. Grace seemed ritually accessible for everyone concerned, men and women alike, rather than something to which only a few distinguished men had privileged access. Here, at my host village's initiative, it reinforced peace. I could not be certain, however, if these were merely exceptional, circumstantial cases. Absence of the chief's family from the rain ritual had several possible explanations. Case-reconstructive research (cf. Flick *et al.* 1991), involving the careful, step-by-step reconstruction of earlier cases through accounts of several eye-witnesses for each, offered a methodological path of inquiry into differing local notions of honour and grace. Events had changed villagers' attitudes toward discussing such topics with me: they knew that I did not find these events 'shameful', so I did not have to search for people to answer my questions. More and more tribespeople brought up these subjects themselves during our conversations. I could thus explicitly focus on earlier, comparable instances of feuds and sacrifices in my interview strategy. Several interview subjects talked about the same group of former events, and some referred to cases that no one else knew much about. In all these interviews, feedback from the interviewees allowed me to reconstruct individual cases and then analyse them sequentially.

This phase of inquiry evolved gradually, as the course of events (armed conflicts and rain sacrifice) and my previous routine (individual interviews on other topics) permitted me to introduce the first phase of case-reconstructive research more or less spontaneously into our conversations. In time, I knew of at least fifteen fairly well-documented previous local cases and their respective sequences. Comparing these cases raised a number of questions, which I discussed with my host's middle-aged sister and their mother. During one such conversation, the old lady suggested that other women with some experience in these questions join us.

This led to the decisive and most fruitful phase of inquiry. Over a three-week period I spent four or five afternoons in what became a case-contrasting procedure. The sequentially reconstructed cases of the first phase were contrasted against each other and against hypothetical, 'what if?' cases. Previously, I had interviewed an equal number of men and women, but the collective interviews took place exclusively with groups of five to seven elderly or middle-aged women. These meetings were no secret, but the women I talked to had made clear to others that this was their private business. When I met one of the village chiefs during this period, he indicated that he was perfectly aware of the meetings – not too happy about them, obviously, but with a sullen *laissez-faire* that I later encountered within the tribal chief's family, and which still allowed some joking: 'You know, some women among our tribe always want to have their own way. What's the use of arguing with them?'

In a sense, then, these group conversations were 'protected interviews'. The method of case-reconstructive research led to identifying two different discourses on the local level: an overt, exhausted discourse advocated by village chiefs and persons with commercial interests in the wider regional markets, and another, more covert discourse pursued by elder women in phases of crisis. That this inquiry was possible at all, and that its social circumstances did not lead to any serious problem or conflict, is itself telling.

Until one or two generations ago, haramization had been virtually absent among the tribal majority. The battles and sacrifice that occurred during my presence were exceptional by present standards, but were instances of a social practice that had prevailed until recently. Women's participation in collective ceremonies and rain sacrifice rituals, as well as in defending their personal and collective tribal honour, had been central elements in a differing, peripheral and certainly anti-hegemonic morality. Local tribal morality presupposed that women who defend themselves are 'good and honourable', and it was considered the duty of women without children to do so if their village was attacked. Men who attacked women in such feuds did not behave immorally, but displayed respect for persons who could defend themselves. The 'weak' and the 'forbidden' were aspects and standards of individual behaviour, not a personified, protected sphere in which tribal women were included collectively.

While usually 'smaller' than that of men, women's honour existed in its own right and not merely as the vulnerable, protected appendage of men's honour. In armed conflicts, female honour was restricted to defensive actions and did not permit challenge to others. In terms of landownership, another asset to a tribesperson's honour, women owned less than most men. The same morality and moral demands implied an access to God's grace that did not a priori exclude women and was accessible to every tribal adult. Only the specific, legal connotation of God's 'peace', as part of His grace, was considered somewhat more accessible to the chief's lineage through their settling intratribal armed conflicts and legal disputes. The connotations of fertility, rain and abundance as other important aspects of God's grace, however, could be accessed equally by both sexes through the same kinds of prayer, ceremonies and rain sacrifice rituals.

I do not address the question of whether this is a relatively recent historical phenomenon in a tribe that has had to mobilize its internal moral, social and demographic capacities in order to resist a constantly growing outside pressure since the seventeenth century, or whether there may be earlier developments underlying this local morality as well. In the twentieth century, however, this and other tribes of northwestern Yemen and parts of neighbouring south-western Saudi Arabia represent one set of cases among many. In the tribal periphery of the predominantly Arab-speaking Muslim world, women often had the right to, and the burden of, an honour of their own. They do not belong to a sacrosanct, personified sphere, nor are they 'set aside' and given special protection.

In most, if not all, cases, these moralities of non-haramization – which differ among themselves as much as they differ from the haramized discourse – have come under an increasing pressure that has left its 'exhausted' traces. In the present case, elements of non-haramized morality (greeting, hospitality, legal rights) still consti-tute an integral part of social practice. They are embedded, however, in an overt, exhausted discourse that dominates local minds and moralities. Other elements of this non-haramized morality (armed conflicts, rituals) function as covert discourses and as practices held in reserve for cases of emergency, when the notion of independent female access to honour and grace is reactivated.

WRITING ON MORALITIES

Writing about ethnographic data with reference to moralities is itself a form of social practice, intervening in the dual context of local field inquiry and anthropological discourse. Here as elsewhere, the context of local inquiry imposes a number of ethical and political obligations to which any author must respond, and which require that publication not reinforce existing local tensions and pressures to the host group's disadvantage. I have attempted to ensure this by two means: I have decontextualized the ethnography from its more immediate local aspects of identification, focusing on some materials and excluding others; and I have recontextualized this selected and abstracted data on a comparative scale. Contrasting local ethnography with studies from other parts of the world is certainly important for anthropological discourse; it also helps to fulfil moral obligations towards one's informants. A text that begins with a lengthy theoretical debate will, it is hoped, invite only those with sincere anthropological interests to continue reading.

More specific difficulties arise from writing about this subject within the context of anthropological discourse. To a certain degree these difficulties are methodological. In any local inquiry into moralities, forms of transmitting, preserving, contesting and acting out moral norms and standards have no a priori locus of occurrence. Legal systems play an important role in standardizing moral and immoral behaviour but are not identical to social practice or moral principles. Detecting the impact of moralities on spheres of social interaction is further complicated when diverging moralities are explicitly manipulated (cf. Strathern this volume) or are covertly contesting, as here. In this case, their fragmented and dispersed form is 'partially connected' to the prevailing social climate and political condition of an exhausted community.

Writing about these fragments requires following their actual dispersal inside various aspects of society, including written texts of customary law, elements of ritualized everyday behaviour, stories preserved by elderly women and rare cases of sudden crisis. Local rituals and aspects of customary law were the main elements for transmitting this peripheral morality in reserve, under an exhausted surface, and elderly tribal women were important agents in it. I have chosen to follow here the twisted paths and puzzles of my actual inquiry, which permits me to retrace the face-to-face interplay between exhausted and deviant elements of local moralities and the dispersed, localized forms of hierarchies, institutions, discourses and practices, and to describe the interaction between anthropologist and hosts. This self-reflexive element, with its emphasis on intersubjectivity, should make possible a critical evaluation of the inquiry's conditions.

Another set of difficulties in writing about moralities is more conceptual and theoretical. Where direct, popular access to literary knowledge has a long history of being either non-existent or extremely limited, ethical presuppositions and normative standards have been transmitted through other media of complex, enduring standards. Their competitive or complimentary coexistence with the dominant literary and electronic media has to be reckoned with on any local level, as Humphrey (this volume) makes clear for Inner Asia, citing precedent examples in the genres of stories, riddles, proverbs and sayings by famous people. For the highlands of southwestern Arabia, legends, jokes, local rituals and precedent cases of customary law would have to be added to the list. Local, often orally transmitted, genres of moral examples are thus key media for passing on the standards of appropriate ethical suppositions.

Decades of secular (communist) political rule, however, entail a differing, perhaps more disenchanting impact on local moralities than has been experienced in societies where political systems and religion have been more closely entwined. Inner Asian societies have experienced the collapse of both lamaism and communism, two contrasting, formerly dominant scriptural moralities, as state doctrines. It is therefore possible that these societies presently display an even stronger emphasis on the local media of moral examples than previously. Still, these moral examples obviously have not been produced independently from literary influences but in creative interaction with them. In the Muslim context, at least, we cannot ignore the increasing, differentiated impact of 'interiorized and general moral rules' (Humphrey this volume), which appears to be absent or less present in the Inner Asian context. I have classified the historical embodiment of this general impact in local social relations and lifestyles as haramization.

POST-HARAMIZATION AND ITS LIMITS

Having identified moralities of haramization and non-haramization, I close by situating them in a broader contemporary context.

In today's Muslim world, both moralities have become exhausted, albeit at different rates of speed. As in southwestern Arabia, the codes of non-haramization have had to retreat and gradually hide or dissolve under the impact of combined expansions of haramization and the market economy, together with popularized and transformed versions of the moral norms of Islamic jurisprudence (*fiqh*). The popularized versions of *fiqh* have partly supported haramization and partly tried to overtake it and put it under pressure. Simultaneously, these versions are contradicted and undermined by some of the very groups that claim to uphold and strengthen them.

Consider the moral implications from an orthodox Muslim and *fiqh* point of view when warplanes drop bombs and poison gas on Kurdish villages to kill mainly children, young mothers and elder villagers; when the militia of one Somali warlord burns alive the unarmed families of another militia's members; when Islamist activists in North Africa attack and kill Muslim women who, by their public appearance and statements, do not conform to Islamist expectations; or when one Afghani guerrilla group rapes the sisters and daughters of members of a rival group. According to *fiqh* standards of any variant, such deeds are immoral.

Today, a growing number of systematic local atrocities, inside and outside the Muslim world, are at least partly due to putting sophisticated weapons for the first time into the hands of local groups, where they combine with transformed codes of honour. Modern war technology itself implies an anonymous enemy, and it has become virtually impossible to distinguish armed men from the rest of the population, even where such a distinction would be preferable, as the code of haramization in the Muslim world would have it. The point is that in the Muslim world such distinctions are considered less and less. In fact, women and children are often killed precisely because their deaths publicly humiliate their fathers, brothers, sons and husbands, demonstrating that their men are not men, since they are unable to protect the *haram*.

Competition for local state power and the arms market itself represent the main stimulus for the many hot, local confrontations that are taking the place of the previous single, cold and international one. Rarely are these new forms of violence carried out with the direct political support of major Euro-American or Asian political powers. Inside this general scenario, an international war technology combines with prevailing local moralities and contributes to their transformation. For the Muslim world, I argue that these local codes of honour lead to the growing destruction of the *haram*, either deliberately or unintentionally, but certainly systematically. This tendency is represented and reproduced by certain political types: transformed ex-tribal 'big men' who were analysed in their tribal form by Jamous.[6]

Jamous's tribal 'big man' attains more power than the rest of his tribe through personal achievements and skills. He gathers groups of clients who are either morally or economically indebted to him and may become his sharecroppers; he thus appropriates some of their honour for himself. His personal accumulation of power, prestige and honour has its counterpart in the dependent status of his 'little men', constituting something of a big man's enlarged *haram* sphere.

It would be below the honour of a big man to challenge someone of inferior status from his own group, but the inverse is not true. This increases internal tension for the big man: not only must he challenge other big men of equal status as a matter of his own honour, but he also has to re-channel the internal pressure of potential challenge from his own little men into loyalty against the outside world, through 'exporting violence by availing himself of mercenaries' (Jamous 1991: 175).

The emergence of this tribal type of big man may still occur infrequently, under socio-economic and political conditions allowing tribal or local rural societies to maintain an agnatic morality of male egalitarianism within the same status group. The importance of the phenomenon rises, however, in the nineteenth and twentieth centuries. Under the new post-cold-war conditions, with the international arms market invading weak or shattered states, the inherent potential of local, transformed big men to compete for state power by exporting violence against each other and committing massacres becomes a social regularity. There are peaceful forms of interplay between various moralities in the Muslim world, just as there are additional forms of violent confrontation between local moralities. Within this broader range, the transformed, post-cold-war, local big man is just one specific type. He rhetorically upholds and revitalizes haramization while undermining it in practice, through exporting violence that does not respect *haram*.

No interpretation of *jihad* justifies these deeds. From the point of view of most modern versions of *fiqh*, systematic atrocities against Muslim women, children and older people are *haram*, forbidden, and all the shame and disgrace of which scriptural Islamic morality is capable falls on those who order and commit such atrocities. However, open moral outrage remains rare within the Muslim world. What can be analysed today, and for the present context, is the contradiction between moral reinforcement of the scriptural norm to protect the *haram* and the social reality of its increasingly violent destruction. This related interplay of moral rhetoric and social practice may be classified as post-haramization. It is acted out by transformed 'big men' in the role of party leaders, warlords and generals; and it signifies a code of honour that presents the systematic destruction of the enemy's *haram* as a partial necessity – as useful and sometimes good. As the morality and lifestyle of post-haramization expand, they are reforming and subordinating haramization; re-haramizing previously modernized, de-haramized segments of society; and exhausting and destroying the remnants of non-haramization.

There are cases of explicit anti-haramization, as in some sectors of Turkish, Syrian, Egyptian, Tunisian, Moroccan, Palestinian, Eritrean or Kurdish societies. The wave of post-haramization is still rising, but its political vanguard may already have reached its zenith (Roy 1992). A number of processes have begun to challenge the self-contradictory morality of post-haramization inside the centres of its own influence. One is the growing importance of neo-haramization. Social life and moral behaviour have not come to a standstill in these centres. Women and women's groups may basically accept the imposition of (post-)haramized lifestyles, but they have also begun to launch tireless and courageous bargaining processes with the official guardians of morality. The result is their participation in a variety of activities that haramized discourses find difficult to accept, such as appearing at international sports events, publishing women's journals on the Internet, and representing themselves in political or legal procedures. Neo-haramization processes thus include a constant, small-scale questioning of dominant moralities.

In the long run, this questioning becomes a contest for redefining the limits and ranges of haramized and post-haramized routine. Although the dominant moral codes in some of these societies claim to be eternal and are defended with physical and moral force, they cannot escape the changes caused by social practice.

NOTES

1 Jahoda (1991: 120) writes of 'einer müden, resignierten Gemeinde', whereby 'Gemeinde' (literally, 'commune') is used in the Austrian administrative sense. I therefore prefer to translate it as 'community'. For further references, cf. Jahoda (1987); Jahoda, Lazarsfeld and Zeisel (1980); and Lazarsfeld (1972).

2 Acknowledgements for support for that field research are given in Gingrich (1994: 8–10). I thank Signe Howell and the participants in the 'Ethnography of moralities' panel at the third EASA Conference in Oslo (June 1994), and participants in the December 1994 Colloquium at the School of American Research, Santa Fe, especially Jill Furst (Philadelphia), for their helpful comments and suggestions. I also thank Kirsten Hastrup (Copenhagen), Jo Ann Baldinger and Joan O'Donnell (Santa Fe), Elizabeth Blowers (Madison) and Rowe Gingrich (Geneva) for their criticism and help.

3 Classifying these three exemplary versions of combination (accommodated, balanced and loose) serves the purpose of distinguishing the impact of scriptural on local moralities, legal systems and lifestyles. I do not intend to relate these three provisional versions to E. Gellner's (1990: 119–125) typology of political relations between tribes and states in the Middle East.

4 Abu-Lughod (1986: especially 78–167) does emphasize women's autonomy and the honour of the weak to such a degree that she does not mention the term *haram* itself (which might not be in use among the Awlad Ali). Women's moral inferiority, their segregation and vulnerability are nevertheless clearly specified by the author.

5 The quotations are from a passage in which Arkoun analyses a propaganda text by an Islamist ('fundamentalist') group, pointing out which elements in that text actually represent re-emphasized pieces of a dominant tradition in Islamic literature and thought. It should be added that Arkoun certainly belongs to those authors who are extremely cautious about producing stereotypes.

6 This topic was discussed with R. Jamous in the 'Anthropology of the Middle East' section, organized by Sh. Nadjmabadi, E. Orywal and myself, at the Bi-annual Meeting of German-Speaking Anthropological Societies in Leipzig (Germany), October 1993.

REFERENCES

Abu-Lughod, Leila (1986) *Veiled Sentiments: Honor and Poetry in a Bedouin Society*, Berkeley: University of California Press.

Arkoun, Mohammed (1994) *Rethinking Islam: Common Questions, Uncommon Answers* (trans. and ed. Robert D. Lee, from original 1989), Boulder: Westview Press.

Bonte, Pierre (1991) 'Egalité et Hiérarchie dans une Tribu Maure: Les Awlad Qaylan de l'Adrar Mauritanien', in Pierre Bonte, Edouard Conte, Constant Hamès, Abdel Wedoud Ould Cheikh, Al-Ansāb, *La Quête des*

Origines: Anthropologie Historique de la Société Tribale Arabe, Paris: Editions de la Maison des Sciences de l' Homme.

Bourdieu, Pierre (1972) *Esquisse d'une Théorie de la Pratique, precédé de Trois Etudes d'Ethnologie Kabyle*, Geneva: Droz S.A.

Coulson, Noel J. (1969) *Conflicts and Tensions in Islamic Jurisprudence*, Chicago and London: University of Chicago Press.

Dostal, Walter (1993) *Ethnographica Jemenica: Auszüge aus den Tagebüchern Eduard Glasers mit einem Kommentar versehen*, Vienna: Verlag der Österreichischen Akademie der Wissenschaften.

Dresch, Paul (1989) *Tribes, Government and History in Yemen*, Oxford: Clarendon Press.

Eder, Klaus (1988) *Die Vergesellschaftung der Natur: Studien zur sozialen Evolution der praktischen Vernunft*, Frankfurt a.M.: Suhrkamp.

Flick, Uwe, Kardorff, Ernst v., Keupp, Heiner, Rosenstiel, Lutz v. and Wolff, Stephan (eds) (1991) *Handbuch Qualitative Sozialforschung: Grundlagen, Konzepte, Methoden und Anwendungen*, München: Psychologie Verlags Union.

Gellner, Ernest (1990) 'Tribalism and the State in the Middle East', in Philip S. Khoury and Joseph Kostiner (eds), *Tribes and State Formation in the Middle East*, Berkeley: University of California Press.

Gingrich, Andre (1993) 'Tribes and rulers in Northern Yemen', in Andre Gingrich, Sylvia Haas, Gabriele Paleczek and Thomas Fillitz (eds)-*Studies in Oriental Culture and History: Festschrift for Walter Dostal*, Frankfurt a.M.: Peter Lang.

——(1994) *Südwestarabische Sternenkalender: Eine ethnologische Studie zu Struktur, Kontext und regionalem Vergleich des tribalen Agrarkalenders der Munebbih im Jemen*, Vienna: WUV.

——(forthcoming 1997) 'Ehre, Raum und Körper: Zur sozialen Konstruktion der Geschlechter im Nordjemen', in Hilde Diemberger, Andre Gingrich and Jürg Helbling (eds) *Die Differenz der Anderen: Beiträge zur Sozialanthropologie der Geschlechter*, Frankfurt a.M.: Suhrkamp.

Gochenour, D. T. (1984) *The Penetration of Zaydi Islam into Early Medieval Yemen*, Ph.D. dissertation, Harvard University: Ann Arbor UMI.

Godelier, Maurice (1982) *La Production des Grands Hommes*, Paris: Fayard.

Gokalp, Altan (1981) *Têtes Rouges et Bouches Noires*, Paris: Société d'Ethnographie.

Herzfeld, Michael (1980) 'Problems in the comparative analysis of moral systems', *Man* 15 (2): 339–351.

Jahoda, Marie (1991) 'Die Arbeitslosen von Marienthal', in Uwe Flick, Ernst v. Kardorff, Heiner Keupp, Lutz v. Rosenstiel and Stephan Wolff (eds) *Handbuch Qualitative Sozialforschung*, München: Psychologie Verlags Union.

——(1987) 'Unemployed men at work', in D. Fryer and P. Ullah, (eds) *Unemployed People*, Milton Keynes: Open University Press.

Jahoda, Marie, Lazarsfeld, Paul F. and Zeisel, Hans (1933) *Die Arbeitslosen von Marienthal*, Leipzig: Hirzel (reprinted Frankfurt a.M.: Suhrkamp 1980).

Jamous, Raymond (1992) 'From the death of men to the peace of God:

violence and peace-making in the Rif', in John G. Peristiany and Julian Pitt-Rivers (eds) *Honor and Grace in Anthropology*, Cambridge: Cambridge University Press.

Lazarsfeld, Paul F. (1972) *Qualitative Analysis: Historical and Critical Essays*, Boston: Allyn & Bacon.

Madelung, Wilferd (1979) 'Shi'i attitudes toward women as reflected in fiqh', in Afaf Lutfi Al-Sayyid-Marsot (ed.) *Society and the Sexes in Medieval Islam*, Malibu: Undena Publications.

Mernissy, Fatima (1975) *Beyond the Veil*, Cambridge: Schenkman.

——(1987) *Le Harem Politique: Le Prophète et les Femmes*, Paris: Albin Michel.

Müller, David H. and Rhodokanakis, Nikolaus (eds) (1903) *Eduard Glasers Reise nach Marib*, Vienna: Alfred Hölder.

Peristiany, John G. (ed.) (1965) *Honour and Shame: The Values of Mediterranean Society*, London: Weidenfeld & Nicholson.

Peristiany, John G. and Pitt-Rivers, Julian (eds) (1992) *Honor and Grace in Anthropology*, Cambridge: Cambridge University Press.

Reif, Elisabeth (1995) *Ethnopsychoanalytische Aspekte der Geschlechterbeziehungen im Islam*, unpublished Ph.D. thesis, University of Vienna.

Rosen, Lawrence (1984) *Bargaining for Reality: The Construction of Social Relations in a Muslim Community*, Chicago and London: Chicago University Press.

Roy, Olivier (1992) *L'Echec de l'Islam Politique*, Paris: Editions du Seuil.

Spellberg, D. A. (1994) *Politics, Gender, and the Islamic Past: The Legacy of 'A'isha Bint Abi Bakr*, New York: Columbia University Press.

Stewart, Charles (1994) 'Honour and Sanctity: Two Levels of Ideology in Greece', *Social Anthropology/Anthropologie Sociale* 2 (3): 205–228.

Strasser, Sabine (1995) *Die Unreinheit ist fruchtbar: Grenzüberschreitungen in einem türkischen Dorf am Schwarzen Meer*, Vienna: Wiener Frauenverlag.

Tapper, Richard and Tapper, Nancy (Lindisfarne) (1992/1993) 'Marriage, honour and responsibility: Islamic and local models in the Mediterranean and the Middle East', *Cambridge Anthropology* 16 (2): 3–21.

Taylor, Charles (1994) 'The Politics of Recognition', in Amy Gutman (ed.) *Multiculturalism: Examining the Politics of Recognition*, Princeton: Princeton University Press.

Chapter 7

The troubles of virtue
Values of violence and suffering in a Mexican context

Marit Melhuus

The Mexican film entitled *El secreto de Romelia* (Romelia's Secret) plots a story of love and revenge, of rivalry between men over specific sexual favours from women. It is a familiar tale. The story gains its particular twist by hinging the drama on the relationship between a dead man (Rafael) and his brother-in-law (Carlos) and an unusual enactment of vengeance. The deceased man's sister, the lovely Romelia, is accused of not being a virgin on the night of her wedding. What prompts this accusation forms the subtext of the film; the succession of events can only be meaningfully grasped in terms of a moral code which is based on the notions of honour and shame. The film starts with Carlos marrying Elena and her subsequent rejection of him on their wedding night. Soon thereafter Carlos receives a bundle of love letters that Elena has written to another; to the man she loves and to whom she has succumbed. Elena dies of grief. Carlos discovers that her lover was Rafael. Rafael, however, has taken his life upon learning that Elena is dead. Carlos seeks to avenge himself on Rafael by marrying his younger sister, Romelia. The day after their wedding night he sends Romelia back to her family, claiming that she was not a virgin. She was, but no one would believe her. Her sisters' bad reputations sullied hers as well. Romelia became pregnant on her wedding night. She left the village and gave birth to a daughter and did not return until the funeral of Carlos (and the settlement of the estate).[1]

What is at stake in this tale is not the virginity of the girl as such, but its symbolic value for the men who are within her immediate orbit. The story recounts an affront on a specific masculinity – a male right of precedence – which pivots on a particular perception of female virtue which is embedded in her sexuality. A virgin bride seals a bond between men, embodying both the honour of the family from which she comes and that of the family that she is about to enter. Conversely, a breach of the bond is cause for vengeance. Men will revenge themselves on other men (in this case the wife's dead brother and father) by a public act of retribution. Usually, this takes the form of direct assault but, in this instance, of returning the bride because she was not intact. Thus, a rivalry between men is provoked by the intermediary of female lack of virtue. Not only do women figure as mediators in men's relations among themselves, they also represent a threat to men in so far as their actions impinge on men's reputations, revealing the precariousness of masculinity. The dependency of masculinity on female virtue is intimately associated with notions of control, power and sexuality, often glossed as *machismo*, and underpins perceptions about gender relations. The way that these elements are interlinked is characteristic of a morality based on notions of honour and shame.

APPROACHING THE STUDY OF MORALITIES

In their pioneering book on anthropology and ethics, Edel and Edel give a very broad outline as to what the study of moralities may contribute to the field of anthropology and hence to the understanding of human societies (Edel and Edel 1959). One of their concerns is to explore 'the ways in which moral content is to be understood in the context of on-going human living' (ibid.: 18). They point to the fact that there will always be certain terms that bear the burden of moral communication (ibid.: 108) thus indicating that there may be a certain moral order that can be discerned by examining these terms. They also address the issues of consistency, compatibility and incompatibility, pointing to areas of contradiction in morality and raising the question of moral dilemmas (e.g. two goals can be desired together but cannot be achieved together).

What Edel and Edel convey throughout their book is that the content of morality (to remain within their terminology) is mediated through many different means. These are contextually determined and may be either explicit or implicit. Thus, there are many ways in which morality may be concerned with conduct. Although they insist on the importance of recognizing that moral discourses occur at different levels and are also sensitive to the kinds of generalization that are possible within the study of morality, Edel and Edel nevertheless stress the need to study whole moralities and not piecemeal separate parts. Their use of the term 'moral configuration', to convey this sense of wholeness, seems to imply a certain coherence or unity. Yet they explicitly state that a unity of pattern in any morality cannot be assumed (ibid.: 197), while pressing for an acceptance of some organizing point which 'may lie not in the obvious features of the moral content but in the role and function which morality plays in that culture' (ibid.: 198).

The recognition that the fields of morality are diverse makes it possible to approach the study of morality from various vantage points, as indeed this volume bears witness. Moreover, in contrast to Edel and Edel, I would argue that moralities can be studied piecemeal, if by that we mean limiting the focus to certain domains which are constitutive of central aspects of morality. In other words, the holistic ambition that the Edels espouse is not a prerequisite for studying moralities. On the contrary, in modern, industrialized societies, characterized by multiple life worlds, perhaps the only way to approach morality is by delineating a particular field through which moral values and their meanings can be gleaned (e.g. Archetti this volume). However, such an approach does not preclude attempts to relate various domains or fields of morality within any one society in order to explore their possible interconnectedness. Rather, such analytic attempts would permit the tracing of values and meanings, focusing on the way that they are articulated in different contexts in order to establish whether there is an underlying subtext or circuit of meaning which binds the different domains of morality together. It would also permit a recognition that several moral codes can exist in any one society at any one time.

This approximation to morality implies a perspective that shifts from a predominant concentration on moral rules constituting a mechanism for sanction, to the more complex focus on significant ideas and values as a set of cultural presuppositions which inform and create social relations, and not just sanction or maintain them. Moreover, as the meaning of moral values also hinges on imagination and emotions, morality will always be open to interpretation; it will necessarily be less than certain (e.g. Evens 1982; Wuthnow 1987; Johnson 1993). A perception of morality as multivocal does not imply that central values are not shared or recognized. It does, however, imply that their meanings may be contested. In other words, it is not necessary to agree to a set of

values or to their meanings in order to recognize their prevalence. It
follows from this that morality is not necessarily always explicit. On
the contrary, the content of morality – the moral message – is in
many instances implicit, to be gleaned from symbolic representations, metaphors and narratives. In fact, as Jacobson-Widding (this
volume) suggests, there may even be muted notions of morality
which, in contrast to more public cultural scripts, are revealed in
private contexts, in situations of confidentiality or gossip. And
Evens (this volume), in his interpretation of the feminine principle
in Genesis, introduces the concept of implicate order 'to unfold the
order enfolded in the figure of Eve'. Thus, the elements that make it
possible to trace the contours of a moral discourse may be elicited
from very different social phenomena. For present purposes, this
will be my approach. I will draw on different statements, tales and
images in order to capture what I consider to be a central field of
morality in a rural, Spanish-speaking, Catholic community in
Mexico. I will juxtapose tales of violence with comments about
suffering and motherhood and reflections on the symbolic meanings of virginity as these are articulated in the perceptions held
about the Virgin Mother. These fragments, which are extrapolated
from a wider social setting, contain the elements that I need in order
to elaborate the relation between morality and gender. More
specifically, I suggest that it is through the perceptions of sexuality,
as expressions of masculinity and female virtue, that significant
insights about the local morality can be gleaned. Moreover, the
significance of sexuality for an understanding of morality in this
community can only be meaningfully grasped within the terms set
by a moral code of honour and shame.[2]

In this local community, gender is a vehicle through which
morality speaks. Thus the representations of gendered identities
serve as an important access to the moral universe. Moreover, the
separate categories of gender are not constituted in the same way:
there is a difference in the ascription of values to men and women
respectively and hence a significant difference between the
construction of male and female identity. In other words, in the
articulation of cross-sex and same-sex relations it is possible to
discern different patterns of evaluation of men and women (cf.
Strathern this volume, for a discussion of the work of gender
differences and the implications for morality). Whereas the
masculinity of men is perceived as a continuum – you are either
more or less a man – women are perceived as dichotomous – you are

either a good woman or not (see also Carrier 1976, 1985 for a similar claim; and Melhuus and Stølen 1996). The former is relative, and can perhaps be envisioned as an evaluation of shifting power relations with respect to the relative position of men. The latter is categorical, classifying women into two kinds according to specific attributions of value.[3]In both cases, aspects of men's and women's sexuality come into play. The joint operation of these two schemata work so as to create two hierarchies or symbolic orders: one that establishes the masculine as the encompassing value and one that does exactly the opposite, namely, the feminine is seen as containing the masculine. The former is articulated through relations of dominance, between men and women and between men. The latter is articulated through the veneration of the Virgin Mother.[4] In terms of morality, it is my argument that this configuration of gender works so as to create simultaneously unambiguous and ambiguous meanings, allowing for a certain leeway in moral interpretations.

HONOUR AND SHAME

One of the few areas within anthropology that explicitly deals with morality is that of honour and shame. In the terms of the Edels, they would be concepts that carry the burden of moral communication. Nevertheless, it is worth noting that despite the central moral concerns, the ethnographies on honour and shame have not been used to probe questions pertaining to an anthropological understanding of morality in general or, perhaps even more importantly, to the implications of conflicting or coexisting moral orders. A moral code where notions of honour and shame appear to be central values is a particularistic one which implies that rules of conduct apply unequally to men and women: what is appropriate for men is not appropriate for women and vice versa. In other words, it is a code that discriminates according to gender. This is in contrast to a universal moral code which claims equality for all, irrespective of race, gender, sex and age. However, as much ethnographic material has indicated, notions of honour and shame seem to be operative in modern nation states, suggesting a historical continuity of certain values while raising questions that have to do with the distinction between different moral domains and the possibility – as well as the implications – of coexisting moralities and their mutual inclusiveness or exclusiveness. These issues demand attention in so far as anthropologists are interested in discerning the overall workings of conflicting moral orders.[5]

The concepts of honour and shame have generally been employed to characterize the value system of the circum-Mediterranean region.[6] From the evidence at hand, it can be surmised that the characteristic trait of a moral code based on notions of honour and shame is its overarching gender specificity. Moreover, much of the empirical, as well as theoretical, observations suggest that sexuality represents the nexus around which this morality pivots. It is only recently that these concepts and the underlying moral order that they seem to imply have been made relevant in a Latin American context (one notable exception is Rivière 1967; for more recent contributions see, for example, Melhuus 1990, 1992; Lancaster 1988, 1992). Yet, taking into account the impact of the Spanish and Portuguese legacy as a consequence of the conquest in combination with the profound influence of the Catholic Church, it is not surprising that these notions are echoed in certain spheres of Latin American societies. In fact, as I have argued elsewhere (Melhuus 1992), the stereotypical gender ideologies in Mexico, exacerbated *machismo* and the concomitant image of the self-denying woman (see also Stevens 1973 and Bartra 1987) can be better understood with reference to honour and shame.

Like any moral code, one based on the notions of honour and shame is founded on significant distinctions. In this local context, these distinctions are represented through gender and obtain not just between men and women (that is in cross-sex relations) but also between men and between women (that is in same-sex relations). Central to this gender differentiation is a specific division of labour, which is both spatially and occupationally reflected, and which ties notion of work to ideas of sexuality.

Briefly stated: a man is expected to work and through his work maintain his family. Concomitantly, women (and most particularly wives) are not expected to work (outside the house) but to attend to their families. In fact, a man who lives off a woman (his wife or mother) is called *un mantenido* (literally a maintained one, i.e. one who lets himself be supported) and locally this has very unmanly connotations. However, it is not work *per se* that is denied wives (they find ways of generating income from within the confines of their house) but rather employment outside the house and the ability to provide. Both these activities are associated with sexuality. The former is often explained in terms of husbands' jealousy (*los celos*), implying that paid employment potentially jeopardizes a woman's chastity. The latter is seen as a manifestation that the husband is not man enough, thereby diminishing his respect in the eyes of others. Moreover, a woman's place is in the house, but the house is not considered a respectable one if not under the protective guard of an honoured man; of course, not any man, but a man who is socially accepted as a guardian of her virtue. Women's virtue, then, is also attached to presence and, by implication, space.

In the space of a short paper it is not possible to demonstrate fully how honour and shame are lived and articulated in this local community (but see Melhuus 1992, ch. 3). Rather, in line with my initial statements about the multivocality of morality, I have chosen to provide a few fragments from my fieldwork to illustrate some situations that clearly actualize these notions and others that reveal differing aspects of the gender relation pertinent to grasping the double hierarchy indicated above. In particular, I have chosen to focus on those aspects that highlight the meanings of sexuality. I do this primarily because it seems that also in this setting it is the varying connotations attached to sexuality that underscore the moral interpretations and hence sexuality represents one organizing point for moral discourse. It may be that the excerpts that I am about to present only seem to confirm the stereotypical imagery of the Mexican macho man and the passive, subordinated woman. However, these images have been chosen precisely because they fit the stereotype while at the same time serve to subvert it, rendering a much more complex picture of the meanings and significance of gender relations for morality.

IMAGES OF VIOLENCE AND SUFFERING

In the village where I carried out my fieldwork, physical violence among men (either against other men or women) was not uncommon. In discussing violence with Don Fidel, an elderly well-educated man, he said that violence usually springs out of situations where honour has been tainted. These situations are, according to him, nearly always familial and have either to do with women or land. He used the expression *mancillar el honor* ('to taint honour' – an expression that was not common, although the meaning conveyed is) and that a man *se siente mancillado* (feels tainted, humiliated). 'In order to defend the honour of the family, they [men] seek vengeance, to rid themselves of the mark,' he said.

However, he hastened to add that this was 'before'. He said: 'Today it seems that parents are softer [*más blandos*] as if the honour of the family is losing something. No one has the right to take anyone's life.' He may be right in his observations that recourse to violence, and in particular killing, spurred by the defence of honour is no longer an accepted practice, and there are many tendencies that may indicate a change of mores. However, the example that he gave me – of a husband who throws out his wife; her brothers arriving to defend her; the husband's killing of the two brothers; his being put in jail and there receiving the threat that, once out of jail, he will be killed; his nephews, in turn, then killing his wife's nephew – was of a fairly recent date.

Other tales of violence are told. Carmen, the youngest of seven children, relates the following about the murder of her own father. The sibling immediately preceding her had died, the event caused by her mother's anger (*tenía coraje*). Her mother had been breastfeeding the baby in the evening and in the morning it 'woke up dead' (*amaneció muerto*).[7] The reason for her anger was that her husband had another woman. Carmen's mother had gone to accuse the woman (a public act of retribution among women) who had then hit her mother. Carmen's father arrived home more than indignant, scolding his wife for having gone to this woman. This is what had made Carmen's mother very angry. Right after this event, her husband was killed. The reason that her father was killed, according to Carmen, had to do with a few words exchanged between her father and one of his good friends. It seems that the friend and his wife were not able to have children. They had been married for many years. One day, Carmen's father said to his friend: 'Pass her [implying the wife] to me and she will have children.' A few days later he was struck from behind by this friend. He died from the blow. There may, of course, have been other underlying motives for this attack which were not disclosed to me. However, the point is that in explaining both tragic events (the death of her sibling and the murder of her father), Carmen chooses to do so by framing them in terms of her father's sexual prowess, thus implying that these are implicitly linked. On the one hand, Carmen starts the story by saying that they are seven children in all (thus underlining her father's virility) and also relates that her father had a mistress. It is this relationship that arouses her mother's anger, subsequently bringing on the death of her child. On the other hand, she refers to her father's challenge to his friend, which at one and the same time reduces the friend's manhood by alluding to his lack of virility, while simultaneously enhancing his own. Carmen's mother was only 34 when her husband died. She never remarried.

Ignacio, a young, dynamic man who, among other things, was in charge of a group receiving fertilizer through a local government scheme, was murdered. The motives for the murder were unclear but did not have to do with either his wife or the wife of the assailant, but appeared to be a case involving corruption. Ignacio's widow, Carlota, was left with four young children to support. She had married very young, had had no education and felt ill equipped to cope with the situation. She said she knew nothing of how he had run his affairs. He had been better off than many in the village, cultivating several hectares of land, while at the same time raising cattle and running a taxi. When I asked his brother (who was also the closest neighbour) what would become of Carlota, how she would manage, he answered: 'We will help her in what ways we can, if she behaves.' I countered: 'Behaves, in what sense?' 'That she does not remarry. She has to look after her children. If she is a good mother, we will give her a hand.' Ignacio's brother feels obliged to help his sister-in-law only in so far as she remains chaste (i.e. excluding potential partners) and thus maintaining her husband's honour. However, this is cast in terms of her being a good mother. A good mother would not remarry as it is assumed (and this I have from many people, both men and women) that a man will never care for the children of another man. Hence in remarrying, Carlota would forsake her children. She would be considered an egotist. This would not be condoned.[8]

Soon after Ignacio's murderer was apprehended and put in jail, rumours began to circulate in the village with respect to the assailant's wife, Dolores. It was said with some scorn that Dolores was claiming that she had been Ignacio's lover, implying that her intention was to change the nature of the crime (from one of corruption to one of passion). By admitting publicly that she had been the mistress of the deceased, she was obviously shaming her husband. However, she was at the same time giving her husband his legitimate grounds for having killed Ignacio: he was only defending his honour. In a sense she was offering her virtue for that of her husband (in the hope that he will be let off with a minimum charge) and thus contributing to restoring family honour. However, the rumours did not say anything about whether the husband would also feel obliged to punish Dolores, in order to restore his honour fully.

What these tales have in common, in addition to being situations of violence, are women constituted as focal objects in a struggle between men. They point to a particular construction of male virtue (which can be glossed as honour, covering local terms such as respect, being responsible) which implicates a specific construction of female virtue. Embedded in this construction is a tension, visualized through the discrete categorization of women. The virtuous woman is contrasted to the immoral woman as in the case of Carmen's mother and the mistress. The importance of chastity and loyalty to the husband (even after his death) is underscored in the case of Carlota (implying that other actions are possible, but not acceptable). Both these tales also evoke images of motherhood. However, the ambiguity of the discrete categorization of women is best illustrated in the case of Dolores, the wife of Ignacio's assailant. Her claims to lack of virtue (saying that she was the deceased's mistress) is an attempt to restore family honour, thus transforming a 'bad' act to a 'good' one. The very fact that this transformation is possible indicates that the reverse might also occur. Hence, this act highlights a potential contained in all women: an either/or becomes simultaneously a both/and. Not only do these stories reveal that some particular aspect of femininity is intrinsic to the construction of masculinity, but they also indicate that men's honour is something that has to be defended in order to be upheld. In other words, women can be seen as the keepers of men's honour, their actions impinging on men's reputations, while at the same time, men are seen as the guardians of women's virtue. Moreover, both male and female virtue are shown to hinge on different notions of sexuality – virility for men, chastity for women outside marriage.

Let me therefore present some contrasting images, in order to complicate the picture. It was Easter; the day was Good Friday. A procession was under way. The procession with its subsequent Mass are major events and the culmination of the Easter rituals commemorating the Passion of Christ. The sculptured image of Christ had been removed from the church and had spent one night (symbolizing the Last Supper) in the house of one of the villagers (who had petitioned for this honour). The image was then carried to a nearby chapel, perched on a hilltop, where it was kept until the morning of Good Friday whence the procession enacting the

stations of the cross commenced. Behind the image of Christ
followed an image of Mary, the Virgin Mother. The procession
wound down the steep and muddy path from the chapel and
proceeded up the cobbled main street towards the church on the
main plaza. At each station of the cross, the procession came to a
halt and the priest invoked a prayer. The occasion was solemn.
Tears were streaming down the cheeks of the older women who
were standing next to me as the images of Jesus and Mary passed
us. I wanted to know why they were crying. The essence of the
conversation that then ensued can briefly be recapitulated as
follows: they were crying for Mary, for the suffering that she
experienced at witnessing the death of her own son. Their tears
were not for Jesus who suffered on the cross and died for our sins.
In their understanding of this central religious ritual, it is the
suffering that the son bestows on his mother that is focused upon.
His suffering becomes her suffering. *She suffers for him* and not
vice versa.

This brief encounter contributed to throwing light on something
that had, until then, puzzled me. I had continually been confronted
with statements (by women) that in some form or other expressed
suffering. Suffering was explicitly stated and referred to in everyday
speech, and commentaries on life situations (one's own or others')
nearly always included comments on the degree of suffering
involved. A typical statement would be: 'Como sufrí, como sufrí
por mis hijos' ('how I have suffered, how I have suffered for my
children') or 'ella ha sufrido mucho' ('she has suffered a lot'). It was
difficult to ascertain the significance of these remarks as the
statements did not necessarily refer to concrete events or processes
of suffering (although that was also the case; maltreatment of
women, for example, is common). The context for the statements
and the way that they were phrased pointed both to a certain
conventionality (a manner of speaking, and hence not meant to be
taken seriously) and to a certain obviousness. To tease out the
meaning of suffering appeared, on the one hand, unnecessary (being
just casual remarks), while on the other hand of utmost importance,
as the self-evident often constitutes the very 'kitchen of meaning' (to
borrow a term from Roland Barthes).

The events of the Easter procession, however, locked into other
local representations of feminine identity and served to recontex-
tualize the reiterations about suffering. They appeared as a
culturally significant indication of local notions of women's self-

esteem. They also shed another light on the meanings attached to sexuality, to which I will return below. It became evident that not only is the notion of suffering understood as explicitly tied to motherhood, but also that suffering represents a particular moral quality regarded as good or meritorious. Seen in this light, it was possible to reassess the women's discourses on suffering as both a way of reflecting a life experience, and as reflecting aspects of a local morality. These aspects are best captured in the notion of the suffering mother,[9] and can only be grasped by considering the symbolic meanings of the Virgin of Guadalupe.

In the course of my fieldwork it was inevitable that the conversation broached the subject of the Virgin of Guadalupe.[10] The following are a few representative excerpts drawn from various dialogues in different situations which somehow touch on the Virgin of Guadalupe. In a conversation that I had with Don Felipe about the situation in the world, he comments: 'If she [the Virgin] had not intervened, we human beings would have been punished by God in unimaginable ways.' In my talks with Doña Luisa, it emerged that her son was serving time in jail. In order to earn some money to cover some of his expenses, the son had dedicated himself to making images of the Virgin of Guadalupe, which his mother sells. Commenting on the Virgin, Doña Luisa says: 'We all come from her. She is the mother of God. She is our mother. She gave us life.' Doña Teresa echoes these sentiments: 'She intervenes on our behalf. That the father almighty may not punish us. Like a mother who on behalf of her children asks that the father does not punish them .... We are all sinners. It is our sins she wished to eliminate. She is the mother. We all have a mother and God does too.'

Leaving aside what these statements imply with respect to a view of humans as children and sinners, and the father as inherently the one who metes out punishment, what can be elicited is an image of the mother as powerful, as the one who in fact is saving us from our (just?) punishment, as a life-giver and as representing an intermediate – or perhaps a separate (and uncontested) – space. She is perceived as a (our?) saviour, in that she has the means to influence God. She is also held to be the mother of God. In these representations it seems that both men and women concur. The imagery revealed with respect to the symbolic representations of the Virgin is telling in more ways than one. It not only points to the significance of the mother, and by implication the value of motherhood (see also Martin 1991), but also to the powers with which the mother is endowed (cf. also Evens this volume on the power of reproduction as creative and procreative).

That the Virgin is a motivated symbol for women will not be further argued.[11] (She is so also for men, but obviously in a different way.) Rather, I wish to draw attention to the ambiguities inherent in this symbol of femininity and their implications for the understanding of female virtue, as this is conveyed through the imagery of the Virgin Mother. I opened this chapter by evoking an image of virginity in the bonding of relationships between men. However, virginity also has a symbolic meaning for women, which is contingent upon but also different from that which is actualized in male-to-male relations. Virginity is an expression of female sexuality and fertility, as well as chastity, and represents the potential transformation from 'virgin' to mother, implied by the act of penetration. It is the meanings embedded in this transformation that are significant for an understanding of female virtue and which the Virgin helps to elucidate.[12]

Motherhood is socially institutionalized through marriage (which in the local context includes consensual unions). It is marriage that serves to legitimize sex for women, and hence also her offspring. Children born out of wedlock are not considered legitimate, unless the father is willing to recognize them and give them his name. Sexual intercourse for women before marriage is strictly sanctioned and parents are mindful of their daughters' reputations. The term used locally to denote a woman who has fallen from grace is *fracasada* which, literally translated, means 'failed' and implies having sex before marriage. Yet, and this is the crucial point, despite the negative connotations associated with pre-marital or extra-marital sex and illegitimate children (for women; the converse is the case for men), it appears that motherhood *per se* is the ultimate confirmation of womanhood, no matter what the circumstances.

To be a mother and to be a virgin are mutually exclusive states. Hence, the Virgin, through her transcendence of sexuality, being a virgin mother, makes visible the carnal state of women, and the ambivalence embedded in women as sexual beings, as women can only become mothers by losing their virginity. In order that motherhood *as such* can become a virtue, this ambivalence must be overcome. The point in this connection is not that marriage serves to legitimize sex (for women) and render redundant any consideration of the tension between these two states. The point is, rather, to grasp in what ways the symbol of the Virgin Mother appeals to women; how the meanings of this symbol are linked to virtue and can be understood in terms of the overarching significance of motherhood *per se*.

The link that works to bridge the ambivalence of asexual and sexual and also represents the shared experience between women and the Virgin is suffering – or more precisely, the suffering inherent in motherhood (both in becoming a mother and being a mother). In a metaphorical transformation, 'virginity' comes to be 'like the Virgin' by virtue of the suffering that they have in common. The notion of suffering, then, operates on different levels. At one level, and more implicitly, suffering serves to cancel out sexuality; yet at another more explicit level, sexual activity appears to be equated with suffering. Of all the women to whom I addressed the topic of their sexuality, only one talked about sex as pleasurable, and phrased it in terms of her husband understanding her. Most other women would either not want to talk explicitly about sex, or phrased it in terms of 'his will'.

FEMALE SEXUALITY: AN AMBIVALENT SOURCE OF VIRTUE

The importance of these images for envisioning a domain of morality is that the elements of maternity and suffering conjoin in a single concept, that of the suffering mother, *la madre sufrida*. It is not possible to understand this composite notion without looking again to the symbolic meaning of the Virgin, as virgin and mother. As mentioned, virginity has a symbolic meaning which carries particular significance in the relationships between men. It is also that aspect of female virtue that serves to summarize the categorization of women into two kinds: the moral and the immoral woman. This aspect is brought forth in the tales of violence. However, it is important to point out that in this local context it is not so much virginity *per se* that is stressed, as that of being a respected, decent woman (with all that this entails locally).[13] Nevertheless, girls are not only brought up to be mothers; they are in a sense also brought up to be virgins (see also Le Vine *et al.* 1986 and Le Vine 1993). In all important ceremonies where girls are involved allusions to virginity, or chastity, are overtly demonstrated.

It is through the particular suffering evoked by the Virgin that the basis for women's chastity is generated.[14] It is suffering, explicitly expressed in a form of self-sacrifice, that serves to transcend sexuality and becomes the mark of motherhood. In this transformation, the children are crucial as they create the mother, as it were, in bestowing upon her motherhood and hence her legitimate grounds for suffering. She will suffer for them, as through her suffering she can enhance her virtue and make it visible – to herself and to others. Women share this ideal of martyrdom and recognize it when they see it. They are the ones who, first and foremost, evaluate and condone the degree and kind of suffering to be acknowledged. Men are excluded from this moral community of suffering and self-sacrifice but are necessary and conducive to its maintenance.

Because suffering is perceived as a female virtue, it is *ipso facto* a moral issue. It forms part of a moral discourse which is exclusive to women and serves to enhance their self-esteem. The gist of the logic is that the more you suffer, the better you are, albeit within the limits as to what is perceived as the morally right source of suffering. Not all suffering qualifies as virtuous. The suffering involved in being abandoned by your children does not enhance a woman's public esteem. Nor does rape. Whereas the former is interpreted as a sign of having been a poor mother, rape is framed in terms of being a loose woman, i.e. being where you are not supposed to be or doing what you are not supposed to be doing. Overall perhaps, the point is not necessarily to suffer, but to be able to frame your life experiences in terms of suffering, in what you have forfeited for the sake of others (in contrast to what you could have done for yourself, and thus be labelled an egotist, something that is not condoned; see, for example, Melhuus 1993). There are life experiences that clearly represent sources of suffering and feed into explicit discourses on suffering: maltreatment, being abandoned by your husband, having to fend for your children on your own, having to accept your husband's infidelity, not receiving enough money for the upkeep of the children, not being allowed to work, toleration of jealous husbands, even problems with your in-laws.

A wife will rarely leave her husband despite continued maltreatment, because of the children. She knows that she will receive no support for them. In fact, a mother will not, under most circumstances, act in any way that can be interpreted as being a poor mother (e.g. remarrying if widowed), usually understood as putting yourself before your children. For a woman her children are her being and she is, in the broadest sense of the word, responsible for them. Not only does motherhood seem to be coterminous with womanhood, but to be a poor mother is to be a poor woman.

It seems that, at one level, a prerequisite for determining virtue in terms of suffering is that you are a mother. Not only is a good mother by definition a suffering one, but more importantly, mothers suffer by definition. That being the case, to be a mother is good enough. Implied in this statement lies the recognition that for women to have children – irrespective of whether they are legitimate or not – overrides the categorical division of woman into two kinds – the moral and the immoral woman. If this is correct, and my empirical evidence would substantiate this, it has implications not only for the meaning of children but also for the meaning of sexuality for both men and women.

CONTINUOUS MEN AND DICHOTOMOUS WOMEN

Within the terms set by the indigenous moral constructions, women are categorized into two kinds: 'the decent woman' (*la mujer decente*), 'the one that does not lack respect' (*que no le falta el respeto*), 'the one that has shame' (*que tiene vergüenza*); and the women lacking these qualities. Varying terms are used to denote the latter kind. The most common are: that she has no shame; that she is open; that she does not maintain her distance. All these expressions have sexual connotations, alluding to the availability or accessibility of the woman. They are all definitely negative and imply some degree of voluntariness; that such indecent women are exposing their sexuality and 'asking for it' (as we would say). That women are thus dichotomized is intrinsic to this morality and springs directly out of the emphasis placed on female sexuality as a locus for her virtue. Nevertheless, which women fall into which category is contextually determined and not given a priori.

In contrast to the discrete categorization of women, men are perceived as more or less 'men', implying that there are degrees of masculinity. Hence, masculinity can be continually contested.[15] Moreover, what robs a man of his masculinity more than anything else is an ascribed femininity.[16] The defining link that orders the relationship *between men*, then, rests on a particular perception of the feminine. In other words, embedded in the construction of same-sex relations (between men) lies a negative inscription of femininity (which is conducive to demasculizing men, and hence, within the terms of the discourse, not considered flattering!).[17] At one level, then, it may appear that the feminine as such has negative connotations, and this in turn may help to explain the positive valuations of masculinity and the notions of male dominance so prevalent throughout Mexico. However, the contingencies between attributes of maleness and femaleness, as pertaining to either sex is much more complex. In the mutual constitution of same-sex and cross-sex relations, same-sex relations appear as both contingent upon and independent of cross-sex relations in their making. There is a double edge to this.

As the tales of violence have revealed, female virtue is valued precisely because it enhances a man. Thus in the articulation of cross-sex relations, the virtue of a woman figures as a positive attribute of a man. Inscribed in this view is the very categorizing of women in two kinds: the decent or good woman and the immoral or bad woman. This categorization of women is shared by both men and women, although the meaning attached to it is different for the two sexes. For men, the discrete categorization of women is inscribed in the continual estimations of masculinity, underscoring the precariousness of being a man; for women this categorization serves as a continual reminder of the fragility of their virtue. To oversimplify: whereas a man needs the bad woman to remain a man, a woman needs the bad woman to remain good. Moreover, there is no analogous category of men that plays the same role with respect to both women and men. In other words, there is no categorization of good and bad men linked to sexuality.[18]

This dual categorization of women – and its differing implications for the two sexes – represents an important access to grasp the link between gender and morality. In fact, in moral terms we could say that the particular dichotomous definition of women is necessary in that it creates morality out of sexuality, for both men and women. For men their sexuality is tied to virility, to penetration, which in turn symbolizes their ability to be in command. For women, their sexuality is tied to motherhood and to chastity. However, as has been indicated, the very positing of women as an either/or implies the possibility of slipping from one category to another, with seemingly clear-cut moral implications. In other words, the discrete categorization of actual women points to the potential transformation of all women, and thus an either/or is in a sense elevated to a both/and. Women have to live with this dilemma: that they are to be, or perceived to be, at one and the same time asexual and sexual, virgins and mothers. Their femininity is defined through these opposite poles, which are incompatible, though reconciled in the same person. Men also have to live with the dilemma of women's ambiguous nature and the fact that women's sexual behaviour may encroach on their own reputations as men. The fate of the lovely Romelia is a case in point. However, they are at least able to sort it out with regard to different women. Or to put it another way, the dilemma is articulated in different relationships: son–mother; husband–wife; lover–mistress. As the father's sexual purity is not an issue, the fact of being a father, a husband and a lover at the same time does not represent any categorical confusion. On the contrary, it only serves to increase his manhood. Hence, it is the mother who comes to represent the focal point around which these varying notions gravitate.[19]

THE WORK OF VIRTUE AND THE MAKING OF THE DOUBLE HIERARCHY

There is a local male discourse that is associated with violence and a particular form of self-assertion which, more than anything, implies being in control, being in command, having authority not only, or primarily, over women, but over other men. This discourse is tied to local notions of power, which is assumed to be a male prerogative and which glosses all those attributes denoted as masculine. It is associated with notions of sexuality and represents a space for contesting masculine identity. In addition, values such as generosity, honesty and independence all constitute part of the masculine make-up and will influence a man's reputation, as will his political connections, the number of god-children he has and his general character. Together these aspects connote what it means locally to be a *macho* – a true man.

Parallel to a male discourse of dominance and power, there is a female discourse on suffering and motherhood. Both discourses pivot around notions of sexuality; in both discourses women's virtue is at stake, but with differing implications. Whereas in the former, the virtue – or lack of virtue – of women is used as a schema for evaluating both men and women, it nevertheless serves primarily to uphold men's honour. Women are thus inscribed in a discourse of male dominance and are perceived as central to it – so much so that they can in fact, by their own actions, impinge on the reputations of men. In the latter discourse, the distinction between the moral and immoral woman is reduced to the very ambiguity that women contain. By making a virtue of suffering and motherhood its ultimate expression, women's sexuality is transformed and comes to represent an empowerment. Thus it seems that the very notion of female virtue works so as to encompass different meanings of women's sexuality – so much so that women seem to accept the loss of 'virtue' (in the first sense), which is so precious to men, only to recuperate it in another sense: by becoming mothers. In other words, the evaluation of women according to degrees of suffering is not necessarily coterminous with the distinction of women into moral and immoral. Returning to Romelia and her secret: this is perhaps what she 'knows'. Although publicly shamed by being exposed as a *fracasada*, she nevertheless is a mother. Hence, her secret is not what people assume it to be, and which is reflected in the doubt cast about her virginity and who the father of her child really is (a fact that only she would know). Her secret is the knowledge that ultimately *that* secret does not make a difference.

Before closing this section on women's virtue it should be added that suffering is not the only way to articulate chastity. Different aspects of chastity are signalled in various ways. They are expressed through a woman's daily conduct, in particular what she refrains from doing – paid work, casual visiting, loitering or even gossiping (*andar de metiche*) – and through what she is expected to do, preparing meals, doing housework and taking care of children. Ideas of virtue are expressed through notions of not being an egotist, which in local terms would imply putting herself before her children (re the issue of Carlota's remarrying). Moreover, women are extremely mindful of their reputations, especially in situations where there are no men to defend their virtue. Gossip is an effective sanction as women are sensitive to what people might say (*el que dirán*). Most importantly, a woman is judged on whether she knows how to treat people (*saber tratar a la gente*). This would apply especially to women who have somehow fallen from grace, who can, to some extent, compensate by showing the proper decorum, showing deference and not being presumptuous.

One way of grasping the workings of this configuration of gender is to picture it as two hierarchies or symbolic orders: one that establishes the masculine as encompassing and subordinating the feminine; and one that does exactly the opposite: the feminine is seen to contain the masculine. These two hierarchies coexist and are at work at the same time. Dominance is expressed through the local discourse on *machismo*, through men's overt control over women and contested control over other men. It is also expressed through the idea that women are the keepers of men's honour, while men are the guardians of women's virtue. Although reflecting a mutual interdependence of the sexes, it is nevertheless framed in a male idiom. The complementarity between male and female is illustrated by the contradiction between dominance (male) and value (female), i.e. between powerful men versus sacred women. This latter could be envisioned as the Virgin, mother of God, eclipsing the image of God the almighty father, where the female, as complete, singular and separate, is the encompassing value. The non-sexual woman represented as mother is an all-embracing value, which is expressed through men's honour – and hence their vulnerability – being contingent upon female sexuality. Thus femininity is placed simultaneously both within and without the confines of the male.

I stated initially that I would approach morality by focusing on significant ideas and values as a set of cultural presuppositions that inform and create social relations. Moreover, I suggested that it is possible to elicit the content of morality by tracing the contours of a moral discourse as this is articulated in disparate social phenomena. The purpose of this endeavour would be to establish whether there is an underlying circuit of meaning, an organizing point or certain terms that carry the burden of moral communication. Focusing on sexuality and notions of honour and shame, the thrust of my argument has been directed not only at establishing the significance of gender for this local morality, but more importantly at illustrating how the ambiguities inherent in the gender configuration implies a multivocality in the moral interpretations, rendering a moral configuration which is at one and the same time both unequivocal and equivocal.

The configuration of gender in this local community is embedded in a moral code which permits a double structuring for both dominance and complementarity, for both male and female at the same time. This morality contains the elements that inform the structuring principles of the gender relation and by implication its meaning as a significant bearer of cultural values. It also contains the elements that make both male and female equivocal categories, in that both masculinity and femininity are open to continuous interpretation, albeit within certain parameters. Not only are men and women constituted differently, but their significance for each other and for themselves is different. This becomes all the more evident when the constitution of same sex-relations and cross-sex relations are examined and juxtaposed, revealing the varying implications of sexuality for the evaluation of men and women. The local morality based on notions of honour and shame not only buttresses these different evaluations of gendered identities, but also accommodates these differences and hence the ambiguities to which they give rise. Or to twist this once more: the representations of gender spring out of a gender configuration which in itself is ambiguous and can thus only be grasped within the terms set by that very ambiguity. These terms, in turn, are intrinsically moral and can only be understood with reference to a moral discourse. Moreover, it is the workings of this gender configuration that represent the subtext or the very glue that keeps the moral imagination going.

ACKNOWLEDGEMENTS

I wish to thank Signe Howell and Tordis Borchgrevink for very insightful comments on earlier drafts of this article.

NOTES

1 I saw this film at a Mexican film festival in Oslo in 1990. Needless to say, the significance of its plot was hard to grasp for a Norwegian public, as it would perhaps be for anyone not familiar with the strict codes of honour and shame. I was reminded of this film through Annick Prieur's book on homosexuality in Mexico (Prieur 1994) where she uses its theme to introduce the notions of honour and shame in Mexico.

2 Fieldwork which was funded by the NFR (Norwegian Science Council) and the Department and Museum of Anthropology, University of Oslo, was carried out over a period of a year in 1983–1984 and a shorter follow-up visit in 1989. It must be remembered that Mexico is a multi-ethnic, markedly stratified society, encompassing vast differences in socio-cultural and economic conditions. Mexico is a modern, industrializing nation, a secular state, and the majority of the population is Catholic. There are competing political discourses as there are competing moral discourses, grounded in different world-views. These differences will necessarily influence the construction of gender relations in one way or another and thereby also the representations of gender and their wider significance. For other gender configurations, see for example Le Vine (1993) and Behar (1993).

3   These are the overriding classifications. They do not entail that there are no 'bad' men or that there are no continuous evaluations of degrees of femininity. The point is that as classifications of men and women they are different, both with respect to the aspect or quality that is being evaluated (the implications of being less a man are not the same as being defined as an indecent woman) and with respect to the qualities used to evaluate women and men.

4   My discussion does not take into consideration the relevance of the doctrines of Catholicism for the local gender imagery. However, Evens' (this volume) interpretation of the Fall in Genesis, arguing for the primacy of the feminine principle, represents very interesting parallels to mine and the two papers can fruitfully be read in tandem.

5   I have treated this issue at some length elsewhere (Melhuus 1990, 1992). However, for a more in-depth discussion see Borchgrevink (1990) and also Berger (1974: 85 ff.) for a discussion of the contrasting notions of honour/chastity and dignity.

6   Not only have the relevance of these concepts as possible universals for the region been contested, but several authors also stress both the androcentric and ethnocentric bias that has permeated the use of these terms. See, for example, Peristiany (1974), Schneider (1971), Herzfeld (1980), Wikan (1984), Lever (1986) and Gilmore (1987).

7   It is a common assumption that a mother's anger when breastfeeding will cause the baby harm.

8   The condition that she is not to remarry can also be interpreted as an expression of the brother's wish to have control over Ignacio's land, as a new husband would automatically assume this right. Hence there appears to be an interesting link between access to land and access to women.

9   Cf. Evens (this volume) on the explicit storyline of Genesis where 'Eve is made to suffer much in childbirth'.

10   The Virgin of Guadalupe is the most important religious symbol in Mexico. She is also a national symbol. She is omnipresent: stickers of her image can be found in cars, buses, taxis; poster images on walls; statuettes in homes; her image is on banners held high in her honour and on medallions worn close to the body. She moves people in very visible ways. For a further substantiation of her importance see, for example, Paz (1977), Campbell (1982), de la Maza (1981), Wolf (1979) and Lafaye (1977).

11   I use the term 'motivated symbol' in order to convey the double movement in the ascription of meaning to symbols: both the impelling power of the symbol (which appears to reside in the symbol itself) and the impetus that women themselves represent in investing the symbol with particular meanings. These processes work together so as to induce certain overarching perceptions of the Virgin.

12   These meanings cannot fully be understood without also taking into account the symbolic meanings of penetration. There are many indicators that penetration – or the ability to penetrate – is one of the central metaphors of *machismo*. Conversely, to be penetrated is associated with the feminine. With reference to homosexual relations,

for example, the homosexual is defined as the one who is penetrated. The man penetrating is still a man – a *macho* (Prieur 1994, Prieur forthcoming; also Paz 1988). Archetti (1992) makes a similar argument with reference to Argentina and football.

13   In fact, it is common that a young couple will elope, rather than go through the formal procedures of engagement and marriage. In local terms they refer to this arrangement as 'she was robbed', *fue robada*. Consensual union is a very common form of marriage.

14   For a much more detailed argument see Melhuus (1992: 150 ff).

15   The exception being perhaps the man who is defined and defines himself as being homosexual.

16   There are many examples that confirm this statement both in my own ethnography and in that of others, e.g. Prieur 1994 (on notions of homosexuality in Mexico), Lewis 1966, Lancaster 1992 (on Nicaragua), Archetti 1992 (on Argentina) and Limón 1989 (Chicanos in Texas).

17   The fact that feminine attributes are considered derogatory is, of course, an empirical finding and not a universal. It is not at all necessary or obvious that *not* to be man (as a man should) implies being feminine. However, the implications of this type of structuring and the use of gendered attributes as constitutive of the construction of same-sex relations has some important ramifications which I have not yet been able to pursue in full.

18   Some might argue that the homosexual man could play this role. But the category 'homosexual', which in the Mexican context is defined as the man who lets himself be penetrated by another man, although necessary to define the true man, does not seem to have any implications for the definition of the good woman. See Prieur (1994) and also Bartra (1987).

19   I have argued elsewhere that, with respect to gender relations, it is the mother–son relation that takes on commanding significance. This contention is supported by other research from Mexico. See, for example, Arizpe (1989).

REFERENCES

Archetti, E. (1992) 'Argentinian Football: A Ritual Violence?', *The International Journal of the History of Sport* 9 (2): 209–235.

Arizpe, L. (1989) *Cultura y Desarollo: Una etnografía de las creencias de una comunidad mexicana*, Mexico: UNAM/El Colegio de Mexico/Grupo Editorial Miguel Angel Porrua.

Bartra, R. (1987) *La juala de la melancolía: Identidad y metamorfosis del mexicano*, Mexico: Editorial Grijalbo.

Behar, R. (1993) *Translated Woman: Crossing the Border with Esperanza's Story*, Boston: Beacon Press.

Berger, P. (1974) *The Homeless Mind*, New York: Vintage Books.

Borchgrevink, T. (1990) *Kjærlighetens Diktatur: Kjønn, arbeidsdeling og modernitet*, Oslo: Oslo Occasional Papers in Social Anthropology, 21, University of Oslo.

Campbell, E. (1982) 'The Virgin of Guadalupe and the female self-image: a Mexican case history', in J. Preston (ed.) *Mother Worship: Theme and Variations*, Chapel Hill: University of North Carolina Press.

Carrier, J.M. (1976) 'Cultural factors affecting urban male homosexual behaviour', *Archives of Sexual Behavior* 5 (2): 103–124.

——(1985) 'Mexican male bisexuality', in F. Klein and T. Wolf (eds) *Bisexualities: Theory and Research*, New York: Haworth Press.

de la Maza, F. (1981 [1953]) *El guadalupanismo mexicano*, Mexico: Fondo de Cultura Economica.

Edel, M. and Edel, A. (1959) *Anthropology and Ethics*, Illinois: Charles C. Thomas.

Evens, T.M.S. (1982) 'Two concepts of "society as a moral system": Evans-Pritchard heterodoxy', *Man* 17: 205–218.

Gilmore, D. (ed.) (1987) *Honor and Shame and the Unity of the Mediterranean*, *American Anthropologist* 22, special publication.

Herzfeld, M. (1980) 'Honour and shame: problems in the comparative analysis of moral systems', *Man* 15: 339–351.

Johnson, M. (1993) *Moral Imagination: Implications of Cognitive Science for Ethics*, Chicago: University of Chicago Press.

Lafaye, J. (1977) *Quetzalcóatl y Guadalupe: La formación de la consciencia nacional en Mexico*, Mexico: Fondo de Cultura Economica.

Lancaster, R.N. (1988) 'Subject honor and object shame: the construction of male homosexuality and stigma in Nicaragua', *Ethnology* 28 (2): 111–126.

——(1992) *Life is Hard: Machismo, Danger, and the Intimacy of Power in Nicaragua*, Berkeley: University of California Press.

Le Vine, S. (1993) *Dolor y Alegría: Women and Social Change in Urban Mexico*, Madison: University of Wisconsin Press.

Le Vine, S.E., Correa, C. and Uribe, F.M. (1986) 'The marital morality of Mexican women: an urban study', *Journal of Anthropological Research* 42 (2): 183–202.

Lever, A. (1986) 'Honour as a red herring', *Critique of Anthropology* 6 (3): 86–106.

Lewis, O. (1966 [1961]) *The Children of Sánchez*, Harmondsworth: Penguin.

Limón, J. (1989) '*Carne, carnales*, and the carnivalesque: Bakhtinian *batos*, disorder, and narrative discourses', *American Ethnologist* 16: 471–486.

Martin, J.A. (1991) 'Motherhood and power: the production of a women's culture of politics in a Mexican community', *American Anthropologist* 17 (3): 470–490.

Melhuus, M. (1990) 'A shame to honour – a shame to suffer', *Ethnos* 1–2: 5–25.

——(1992) '*Todos tenemos madre. Dios también.* Morality, Meaning and Change in a Mexican Context', unpublished Ph.D. thesis, University of Oslo.

——(1993) ' "I want to buy me a baby!" Some reflections on gender and change in modern society', in V. Broch-Due, I. Rudie and T. Bleie (eds)

Carved Flesh, Cast Selves: Gendered Symbols and Social Practices, Oxford: Berg.

Melhuus, M. and Stølen, K.A. (1996) 'Introduction', in M. Melhuus and K.A. Stølen (eds) *Machos, Mistresses, Madonnas. Contesting the Power of Latin American Gender Imagery,* London: Verso.

Paz, O. (1977) 'Preface', in J. Lafaye, *Quetzalcóatl y Guadalupe: La formación de la consciencia nacional en Mexico,* Mexico: Fondo de Cultura Económica.

——(1988 [1955]) *El laberinto de la soledad,* Mexico: Fondo de Cultura Economica.

Peristiany, J.G. (ed.) (1974 [1966]) *Honour and Shame: The Values of the Mediterranean,* Chicago: University of Chicago Press.

Prieur, A. (1994) *Iscenesettelser av kjønn,* Oslo: Pax Forlag.

——(1996) 'Domination and desire: male homosexuality and the construction of masculinity in Mexico', in M. Melhuus and K. A. Stølen (eds) *Machos, Mistresses, Madonnas. Contesting the Power of Latin American Gender Imagery,* London: Verso.

Rivière, P. (1967) 'The honour of Sánchez', *Man* 2 (4): 569–583.

Schneider, J. (1971) 'Of vigilance and virgins: honour, shame and access to resources in Mediterranean societies', *Ethnology* 10: 1–24.

Stevens, E. (1973) 'Marianismo: the other face of machismo in Latin America', in A. Pescatello (ed.) *Female and Male in Latin America,* Pittsburgh: University of Pittsburgh Press.

Wikan, U. (1984) 'Shame and honour: a contestable pair', *Man* 19: 635–652.

Wolf, E. (1979) 'The Virgin of Guadalupe: a Mexican national symbol', in W.A. Lessa and E.Z. Vogt (eds) *Reader in Comparative Religion: An Anthropological Approach,* New York: Harper & Row.

Wuthnow, R. (1987) *Meaning and Moral Order: Explorations in Cultural Analysis,* Berkeley: University of California Press.

Chapter 8

Eve
Ethics and the feminine principle in the second and third chapters of Genesis

T.M.S. Evens

To banish his loneliness, Lilith was first given to Adam as wife. Like him she had been created out of the dust of the ground. But she remained with him only a short time, because she insisted upon enjoying full equality with her husband. She derived her rights from their identical origin. With the help of the Ineffable Name, which she pronounced, Lilith flew away from Adam, and vanished in the air.

(Ginzberg 1909)

The serpent pushed Eve against the tree, and said:
  Thou seest that touching the tree has not caused thy death. As little will it hurt thee to eat the fruit of the tree. Naught but malevolence has prompted the prohibition, for as soon as ye eat thereof, ye shall be as God. As He creates and destroys worlds, so will ye have the power to create and destroy. As He doth slay and revive, so will ye have the power to slay and revive.

(Ginzberg 1909)

METHOD

There are at least two sides to every story. I wish to examine the role of Eve in the Book of Genesis in light of this old saying. One can detect in the second and third chapters of Genesis a latent or implicit as well as an explicit storyline. The explicit is, I propose, by and large the one that the Yahwist redactors intended and which has preoccupied much of standard exegesis. It concerns the creation of man, the act of disobedience and man's expulsion from paradise, the so-called Fall ('so-called' because the story itself makes no direct mention of a fall). The implicit storyline is, as its name suggests, largely submerged or even repressed, although some commentators, preeminently the gnostics and Milton, either elaborated or intimated versions of it. Playing on the text's many ambiguities, this storyline pictures the Fall as fortunate, indeed, an elevating movement.[1] In making this distinction and recounting the two storylines sequentially, I do not mean to imply that they are perfectly separate and distinct. Rather, they are interpenetrating, a point to which I will return in conclusion. They are related as if each were the mirror image of the other, such that they form chiasmic contraries and present themselves simultaneously. And, like all such contraries, the boundary between them, and between the implicit and the explicit, is no less relative and fluid than it is plain.

Before recounting the storylines themselves, it is well to comment on my 'method' of interpretation and the nature of my argument. Biblical criticism is a notoriously rich scholarly tradition, and I do not claim to be an expert in it. Rather, I have been trained in the discipline of social anthropology. Accordingly, I approach Genesis as a myth projecting a 'logic' of a particular socio-cultural tradition. In recent decades the most distinguished anthropological approach to myth has been forged, of course, by Claude Lévi-Strauss, and was applied to Genesis, with characteristic aplomb, on the English side of the Channel, by the late Sir Edmund Leach (e.g. 1969).

Regarding the structuralism of their approach as edifying but too formal to do justice to the existential aspect of myth, I have sought here to ground structure in existence. I take Genesis not primarily as an intellectual exercise but as an endeavour of self-construction. By that I mean that the intellectual questions to which the story might be thought to answer – questions concerning the nature of religious, political, economic, domestic and biological relations – all stand finally in the service of a quintessentially practical question: where do I stand in the world, or who am I? What makes this question practical is that in forging a response, whether or not one enlightens oneself about oneself, one virtually constructs the self that one is.

The logic that I seek to determine, then, is an instrument of, not thought as such, but human existence; it is an elevated but intensely practical expression of how it feels to be a self-conscious being, a being that is in exceptional measure its own construct. For purposes of getting at this sort of logic, since it is definitively culturally particular, the history and origin of the story, the ethnic tradition(s) in which the story originated, the functions of the story within that tradition and technical mastery of the story's native language(s) are all critical contextual aids. But they remain distinctly secondary to the context provided by the powerful impression made by the story in its own meaningful roundness, considered concretely, in the telling.

The impression that the story tends to give is, surely, for one thing, that there is something very deep about its picture of humanity and the world. I try here to project that something, for more detached viewing. I do so by interpretively referring the meaningful contents of the story to the profoundly existential question of self-identity, and by focusing my 'translation' on, rather than the cognitive stuff of the story's answer, the lived, 'bodily' experiences registered therein. Given the eccentric focus of my translation, the picture I see is something that the story acquires from the impression that the story makes on me and others, examined in relation to not only whatever technical knowledge and skills I possess, but also and especially, inspired here by Wittgenstein's interpretive genius, 'the thought of man and his past, from the strangeness of what I see in myself and in others, what I have seen and have heard'.[2] As regards the question of self-identity, the response of Genesis is, despite the text's scriptural foundationalism, startlingly postmodern: humans have the identity of non-identity, or, put less tendentiously, they are those creatures who are specially given to giving themselves their own identity. It so happens, then, that the logic projected by Genesis is peculiarly the very one on which I have pinned my interpretive enterprise, namely: self-construction. Given the universalizing thrust of Genesis, this working correspondence, between my approach as an anthropological reader and the text's practical point, is not altogether surprising. What is more surprising is that the correspondence suggestively defines the text as (for all and whatever its objectionable contents) a source of anthropological instruction as well as an object of investigation, and, correlatively, my project as an exercise in self-construction as well as in interpretation.

In relation to method, it is also important to mark that my approach supposes as a matter of course that the story of Genesis is bound to deceive or contradict itself. The reason for this easy supposition has to do with the consideration that the endeavour of self-construction makes up, as the story itself propounds, a fundamental paradox: the self as innately other (non-identical) to itself. Accordingly, in as much as it itself amounts to the practice of this paradoxical endeavour, the endeavour of self-constructing, the story of Genesis may be expected to betray themes that run contrary (other) to those that it proclaims. In short, as I began, it may be expected to yield a story with at least two sides.

With this expectation, my reading takes a turn toward deconstructionism. Consistent with this school of criticism, by fastening onto the story's self-deceptions, I aim to unmask the story's received claims. But as against deconstructionism (or at least some practitioners of it), and all the more so for ineradicable difference, my approach supposes that there is something to be said for foundations.

My reason for thinking so is that, while the logic of self-construction is indeed paradoxical, it is also intrinsically hierarchical. This truth strikes me as self-evident. For as the component sides of the paradox are always encompassed by the practice of the paradox, in so far as one of the sides is somehow privileged in relation to the practice, it too must enjoy the primacy of encompassment. So long as they are considered solely from the standpoint of their opposition to one another, the sides of a story remain axiological equals, locked in rhetorical combat by power. But once the perspective of the encompassing dynamic is assumed, in any particular context there is bound to obtain between the sides an asymmetrical relationship of value.[3]

In the present case, to preview my thesis and argument, taking a fortuitous feminist turn, my interpretation of Genesis accords to the existential principle that Eve enfigures, as a general rule, the axiological primacy at point.[4] Cued by Merleau-Ponty's philosophy of ambiguity, I conjecture that we are predisposed to grant this primacy to the feminine principle. The conceptual axis of this French thinker's eccentric phenomenology is the paralogical idea of bodily perception. I propose that as a matter of perception of this kind, the feminine principle best brings to mind precisely that which cannot be phenomenologically reduced. And what cannot be thus fixed and made to appear, what must remain basically ambiguous, is the practice of self-construction itself – in a word, genesis.

As might be expected from the special association of the feminine with ambiguity that is irremissible, what is also remarkable about the predisposition to privilege this principle is that, while it gives direction, it does not secure compliance. For, by definition, basic ambiguity conditions essential difference rather than utter identity, including the difference or relative openness that we call moral choice and exhibit as the conduct of self-construction in the face of the other. In effect, although the predisposition is well and truly given, it has the selective force of – contrary to the biblical story's most conspicuous and influential picture of woman – not nature as such, but ethics; which is why the predisposition can be consequentially thwarted, and we can be ill disposed to what it predisposes.

INTERPRETATION

To begin, then, with the explicit storyline, Eve is pictured especially in her association with the serpent and as a temptress. As will be recalled, God makes an authoritative pact with Adam. He commands him that of the trees of the garden he planted for him, Adam may eat of every one but 'the tree of the knowledge of good and evil'. This tree he forbids to man on pain of death: 'in the day that you eat of it you shall die'. Owing, however, to the serpent's guile (the serpent being 'more subtle than any other wild creature'), and then to Eve's essential concupiscence (being inclined to give way to her appetites, 'the woman saw that the tree was good for food, and that it was a delight to the eyes, and that the tree was to be desired'), Adam proved unequal, or, as we shall see, in view of the implicit storyline, more than equal, to temptation.

Eve, thus, is a crucial instrument of the Fall. In this connection it is important to realize that the woman is literally part of the man: 'the rib which the Lord God had taken from the man He made into a woman'. 'This at last is bone of my bones and flesh of my flesh,' declares Adam. Remarkably, therefore, Eve's temptation of Adam must amount to Adam's temptation of himself.

There is more to this point. Recall that Adam has a two-sided constitution. God forms him of 'dust from the ground' and gives life to him by means of divine inspiration: He 'breathed into his nostrils the breath of life; and man became a living being'. It would appear that right from the start man has a dual nature – he exists tensionally, as between a more material and a more vital or spiritual side.

Now, as 'bone of his bones and flesh of his flesh', the woman must represent one side of Adam's dual nature in particular – the more bodily side. A psychoanalytical interpretation of Adam's 'rib' as a euphemism for his penis is inviting here (Rubenstein 1971: 52). But even if one does not wish to entertain this sort of conjecture, the one-sided identification of Eve with Adam remains textually compelling. Judging from the standard biblical Hebrew and English lexicon (Brown, Driver and Briggs 1975) and from Rashi's famous commentary (1949), the most authoritative gloss for *tsela*, the Hebrew for 'rib', is 'side'. It would appear, therefore, that Adam's temptation of himself by way of Eve amounts to the seduction of his more spiritual by his more carnal nature.

Thus Eve represents a divisive process whereby a side of Adam is alienated from him, establishing a condition of temptation. Given Adam's disunited state, Eve constitutes the attraction of completion, a deeply gravitative attraction; through her, Adam is capacitated to fulfil himself, to make himself whole again. The idea of fit in God's declaration 'I will make a helper fit for him', finds its most graphic meaning here. The Hebrew at point, *ezer k'negdo*, literally 'helper as against him', plainly has the sense of 'complement', and makes the woman out as serving, dialectically, to complete the man. This impelling, bodily sense of 'fit' is given linguistically in Adam's proclamation 'she shall be called Woman, because she was taken out of man', the word 'woman' (Hebrew *ishah*) being, in the text, the feminization of the word 'man' (Hebrew *ish*) (Levinas 1969a: 34). And it is given more directly in the story's comment that when a man 'cleaves to his wife, ... they shall become one flesh'. Rashi, whom Jews tend to regard as the commentator *par excellence* on the Hebrew Bible, took this to mean that they become one flesh in the child of their union, an interpretation that finds remarkable support in certain present-day ethnographic literature.[5] Eve's role as temptress may also be read from the remark that, owing to the creation of woman, 'a man leaves his father and his mother and cleaves to his wife'. From the perspective of modern anthropology, the passage may be seen to suggest that the principle of marriage is at odds with the principle of descent. The reason for this incompatibility is that Eve's capacity for reproduction gives to Adam a certain independence from his creator, his father. Whereas Adam is absolutely dependent on God for his creation in the first place, because of Eve he is enabled to recreate himself independently. This autonomy marks a certain separation from his father. In this way the passage pictures woman as a representative means by which flesh cannot help but draw away from spirit.

Here, however, a distinct ambiguity comes to light. For the passage is not normally read in this way. Instead it is typically interpreted to the contrary, as emphasizing the sanctity of marriage and of the incest prohibition. It is argued that 'a man leaves his father and his mother and cleaves to his wife' because the incest prohibiton so demands (see Rashi 1949, also Kasher 1953: 117–118).

Ambiguity is even plainer when it comes to interpreting the symbolism of the serpent. The serpent seems to represent both the forces of darkness and chaos and at the same time the capacity of creation. It seems only fitting that this distinctly phallic figure, whose earthly character could scarcely be more complete (it is fated to crawl on its belly and eat dust), should tempt the woman. In a crudely formal sense, it is the serpent to whom the woman is fit. This sense was not lost on Rashi, who held that the serpent actually desired Eve (see also Rubenstein 1971: 54). Although the text uses the Hebrew (*nachash*), the Aramaic for 'snake' is *chivia*, and it is worth noting that the rabbis play on the linguistic relation of this word to the Hebrew *chava* 'Eve'.[6] Yet, as a phallic figure, the serpent also shares in the identity of Adam.[7] And since it partakes of the identity of both the man and the woman, it naturally obtains between them. It is thus a mediatory figure *par excellence*. Furthermore, since the serpent is identifiable with Adam, as in the case of Eve's temptation of Adam, so in the case of the serpent's cunning deed, it is Adam in his dual construction inciting himself. Hence, as the serpent obtains representatively between the man and the woman, so it obtains between the two sides of Adam's nature, the spiritual and the material. It should follow that the kind of mediation at stake here is self-mediation, an involutionary, and therefore profoundly creative, movement.

The serpent's capacity for mediation of this kind is perhaps nowhere better told than in the fact that it has no need to eat of the fruit of the forbidden tree – it already possesses the knowledge in question. Indeed, it might appear that the serpent has partaken even of the tree of life, as symbolized by this creature's habit of renewing itself each year by shedding its skin. It has been established that ancient Near Eastern peoples commonly associated the figure of the serpent with recurrent youthfulness, thus taking it as a picture of self-mediation (Joines 1974: 17–21).

At any rate, it is plain that the story endows the serpent with an esoteric and mediatory knowledge of life ('But the serpent said to the woman, "You will not die. For God knows that when you eat of [the tree of knowledge] your eyes will be opened"'). Given an association of deep-sightedness with the serpent, the very locomotion of this creature smacks of subtlety and indirection, and its coiled repose presents an image of the tensile force of intuition and imagination. The serpent implants in Eve's mind an image of self-enlightenment ('You will be like God'), interposing between her and the Edenic reality the possibility of her very own self, a self-mediating being that develops for the sake of itself.

In the figure of the serpent, then, we see the imagination pressing back against the pressure of reality, against the *status quo*. However much the serpent stands for an evil inclination and chaotic force (as has been the preeminent theme of traditional exegesis), it is also acutely representative of a certain kind of knowledge, knowledge born of fancy and implicit in action. No less concrete than ethereal, such knowledge is fundamentally mediatory, unfolding creatively, as if by magic, from the material action in which it is somehow contained.[8]

Whatever the ambiguities, the explicit storyline receives its logical consummation in the punitive measures that God levels at each of the culprits. The serpent is made to go on its belly all the days of its life and to enter into a relationship of enmity with man ('he shall bruise your head, and you shall bruise his heel'); Adam is made to toil for a living and is condemned to mortality ('you are dust and to dust you shall return'). And for her part in the deviant act, Eve is made to suffer much in childbirth but also to want the precondition of her pain, namely, her mate ('in pain you shall bring forth children yet your desire shall be for your husband'). In addition, she is subordinated to her husband's will ('he shall rule over you'). In effect, the limitations of all three as contingent, creaturely beings are given added emphasis. For their failure to observe the limits God had set for them originally, the man, the woman and the serpent are all brought down to earth, so to speak. They are made to take a fall. Man's spiritual nature, or, what amounts to the same thing, his capacity of self-determination, is fixed absolutely according to the limits of his material nature, ironically the very nature that prompted him to exceed his God-given limits in the first place. Measure for measure, the punishments fit the crime.

To turn now directly to the implicit storyline, the text leaves no doubt that the ejection and fall from the garden describe also an inward and upward movement. 'Behold,' says God, 'the man has become like one of us', and, so that he does not 'put forth his hand and take also of the tree of life, and eat, and live forever', God expels him from the garden. Evidently, as the serpent divined, for reasons of his act of disobedience man becomes god-like, and he does so to such an extent that he poses a substantial threat to God's dominion, moving God to drive him from the garden. If man becomes god-like and the figure of God epitomizes what is inclusive and on high, then in taking an outward-bound fall, man must have taken an inward and upward turn.

To elucidate this paradox it is necessary to disclose the sense in which man becomes like God. The diacritical difference between man and God in Genesis may be understood in terms of the capacity to create: whereas God creates absolutely, man does so only relatively, on behalf of Creation. This difference is given ineradicably in the fact that man could not have created himself in the first place. Therefore, an increase in man's likeness to God must indicate an increase in man's capacity to create on his own behalf, that is, in his autonomy relative to his maker.

Now, the effective power to create on one's own behalf, to choose for the sake of oneself, implies that one is present to oneself – witting choices entail self-consciousness. In other words, the enrichment of Adam and Eve's creative capacity amounts to a rise, or even leap, in consciousness. That this is so is evidenced in the story perhaps nowhere more plainly than in the treatment of the first couple's nakedness. Before having eaten of the forbidden fruit, 'the man and his wife were both naked, and were not ashamed'; but afterwards, 'The eyes of both were opened, and they knew that they were naked.' Obviously, it is not the nakedness as such that is significant, but the awareness of it: 'Who told you that you were naked?' God asks. God wants to know how Adam and Eve became self-conscious.

Self-consciousness may be understood, however, in terms of self-creation or 'reproduction'. To be conscious of oneself is to have at least two selves, one to think with and one to think about. 'To wonder', with the poet (Emily Dickinson), 'what myself will say' is to indulge this split between the self-as-subject and the self-as-object. To be conscious of oneself is to duplicate or reproduce oneself.

This is a difficult and involved matter. But that what is at stake in Adam's and Eve's amplified resemblance to God is the capacity to recreate or reproduce themselves is given in the story in a number of ways. Let me mention two. First, why does God expel them from the Garden? ' " [L]est [Adam] put forth his hand and take also of the tree of life, and eat, and live for ever" – therefore the Lord God sent him forth from the garden'. That is to say, Adam's advance toward immortality had to be checked. And second, just before expelling them, God 'made for the man and his wife garments of skins, and clothed them'. Following Sir James Frazer (1984), we may interpret this award to augur their rebirth, a new or second life on which Adam and Eve were about to embark: they assume the serpent's power to renew itself by slipping into a new skin.

Where, then, does Eve fit into this picture of the ascent of man, of the raising of his consciousness? Although she clearly represents Adam's concupiscent aspect, it should not be forgotten that she is also identified as the 'mother of all living'. Indeed, her very name is 'life' – in Hebrew 'Eve' is *chava*, from the root *chay*, for 'life.' She is named, then, after her power of reproduction. But on the latent storyline, this power appears to be creative as well as procreative, to be god-like. Her vital power reproduces in worldly fashion God's power of creation. Therefore, she affords Adam the resources necessary to compete with God. We can now see why the passage 'a man leaves his father and his mother and cleaves to his wife' is subject to apparently contradictory interpretations: at the same time as the conjugal relationship opposes Adam to his maker, its fundamental association with creativity makes it next to godliness.

But I wish to claim more than simply that Eve may be construed in a positive light. I wish also to claim that she, or the feminine principle for which she stands, enjoys a certain primacy in Genesis.

Recall here that the serpent is acutely ambiguous: on the one hand, it represents chaos and darkness, on the other, a vital, esoteric knowledge, a godly gnosis. If one were to ask how it is that the serpent already possessed the knowledge of good and evil and had no need to eat of the forbidden tree, the answer would have to be, perhaps inescapably, that the serpent is peculiarly identifiable with the absolute, with God. Allow me to quote from the great biblically inspired novel *Moby Dick*, in which Melville gives that answer and makes that identification:

> But in the great Sperm Whale, this high and mighty god-like dignity inherent in the brow is so immensely amplified that gazing on it, in that full front view, you feel the Deity and the dread powers more forcibly than in beholding any other object in living nature.

Biblically, the leviathan (the word is a direct transliteration of the Hebrew) is a sea-serpent, a serpent of the deep; and, like its

Edenic namesake, it represents the powers of chaos and disorder (Joines 1974).

Eve and the serpent, however, present a dynamic duo. Together they constitute the story's fundamental and integral structure of attraction and desire – the bodily but creative force of gravity that sets humankind in worldly motion, towards moral order. If, then, the serpent is peculiarly identifiable with the First Principle, Eve must be similarly privileged. Doubtless, the name of 'Eve', 'the mother of all living', bespeaks both the generative power and the continuing encompassment characterizing a first principle. But there is an even more directly compelling indication of Eve's primacy. It is singularly telling that *adamah*, the Hebrew for 'earth' or 'ground' and from which the name of 'Adam' is derived, is feminine in gender. Evidently, the conspicuous derivation of woman from man in the story is an inversion of a prior and more fundamental birthing whereby man is derived from woman.

One must take care in determining what to make of this sort of etymological connection. But the warrant here for taking it as evidence for the primacy of the female principle is multiple.[9] For one thing, when Eve is baptized 'Woman [*ishah*], because she was taken out of Man [*ish*]', the text itself establishes the relevant linguistic rule of determination. For another, at the beginning of Chapter 2, we are told that immediately after God made the earth and the heavens, 'there was no man [*adam*] to till the earth [*adamah*]'. This passage, using an erotically charged language of agrarian production, metaphorically establishes the relevance of gender to the distinction between *adam* and *adamah*, as well as the belatedness of the male principle. And finally, most telling, like the relation between figure and ground in Gestalt psychology, the nominal emergence of *adam* from *adamah* is not discursive (as in 'she shall be called Woman, because she was taken out of Man') but is simply taken for granted, ingenuously exhibiting – in relation to the generative primacy of the female principle – the essentialist nature with which the story is wont to credit names. In short, the identity 'man' in the story is implicitly and categorically grounded in the feminine.

ARGUMENT

I have distinguished two storylines in relation to Eve's image in Genesis 2–3. If this interpretation of ambiguity is compelling, then, given the foundationalist designs of the biblical text, the question might be put as to which of the two storylines truly deserves the greater respect. Providing that one still thinks that the idea of foundations cannot be absolutely unfounded,[10] this question merits attention. No one will doubt that the unhappy image of Eve as the instrument of Adam's downfall has been the prevailing image in Western thought. Indeed, that image has largely been received as the only story that Genesis has to tell in connection with Eve. If the redactors of Genesis are themselves regarded as readers of a kind, then, plainly, they interpreted their tradition primarily in terms of a negatively valorized Eve. That is why that image of Eve constitutes the explicit storyline.

But the implicit storyline recommends itself in very powerful ways. Indeed, the received interpretation presupposes the one that it conceals. The questions left dangling by the straightforward account of Eve as Adam's weak side – questions such as how can Eve, who is born of Adam, be the mother of all that lives?, or how can the serpent, the most creaturely creature in all of creation, be omniscient? – point unavoidably to the dependence of the explicit on the implicit storyline. The explicit storyline is erected on certain presuppositions – the likes of an all-knowing serpent and a primordial mother – which, for the sake of the explicit storyline's consistent intelligibility, must remain in shadow.

The two storylines are, then, interpenetrating. It is evident that they stand to each other as positive and negative. But the systematic ambiguity that they present comes to more than an easy play of chiasmic reversals. The hermeneutic decision of the redactors notwithstanding, the ambiguity intrinsically affords a certain privilege to the positive projection of Eve. As the implicit account, the positive projection is encompassing and in this special sense hierarchically superior. Put another way, the explicit storyline is nothing but one explication or unfolding of the order enfolded in the figure of Eve, an 'implicate order'. The concept of implicate order is due to the physicist David Bohm who, in his own iconoclastic cosmological account of genesis, uses it to grasp the 'unbroken wholeness of the totality of existence as an undivided flowing movement without borders', a wholeness that permeates everything, 'from the very outset'.[11] Eve's name as encompassment – 'the mother of all living' – associates her directly with an order of this kind; it serves to identify her with the centreless centre of everything, that perfectly unique and inexhaustible dynamic which, precisely because it always stands outside itself, because it always comes to more than it is, cannot really be specified. Such is a name of genesis or the whole, or of God or the creator. Exactly why the feminine principle is thus privileged is a gem-hard question. The text, as I have argued, largely runs the association of Eve with the implicate order implicitly, as a structural feature. In addition, the overt description of Eve as the fitting, natural environment for the serpent's ruptive seed treats her rhetorically as interior possibility, which is to say, again, an implicate order.

This biblical sense of the female principle can be suggestively drawn in terms of Merleau-Ponty's oxymoronic notion of bodily perception (Merleau-Ponty 1962). Obviously, a perceiving body implicates a phenomenal world in which consciousness is not radically differentiated from matter. In such a relatively undifferentiated world, the female anatomy can only be considered with a view to its existential involvement with the world. And when it is, that anatomy exhibits a prepossessing susceptibility to 'know' itself and be 'known' as representatively embodying the paradoxical meaning of an unstructured structure or gravid negativity.[12] The literature of psychoanalysis lends strong support to this phenomenological construction.[13] But much of this literature invokes naturalism, and I am anxious to avoid any suggestion that my thesis of privilege denies the essential historicity of the story. Indeed, my interpretation of the story as a question of creative but less than conscious choice – what I call moral selection – as between a text and a subtext leaves no doubt as to the story's fundamentally historical or constructed nature. I am committed to the idea that structure and history ground each other (that neither obtains outside the originary intertwining of both), such that the moral selection of which I speak must prevail somehow between natural selection and choice in the strict sense, the sense keyed to entirely conscious agency. Natural selection may be thought of as a mechanical process that produces an agentless unfolding, an evolution, whereas choice in the strict sense bespeaks selection so utterly unconstrained that it projects the idea of movement that is wholly directed, sheer history.

There is no room here to develop these hard ideas.[14] I can say, however, that what I intend by the understanding of a fundamental association of the figure of Eve with the implicate order is in the way of a bodily prepossession and precondition, neither a nomological determinant nor a pure choice. Consistent with my appeal to Merleau-Ponty's non-dualist sense of 'bodily', the claim is not that our body imposes on us definite instincts but that it gives general form and continuity of disposition to our existence.

To propose that the feminine principle is phenomenologically privileged, then, does not preclude the possibility of an association of that principle with an explicit storyline. Rather, such privilege suggests that whatever its contents, the overt axiological configuration will presuppose an even deeper, encompassing association between femininity and the implicate order.[15] This expectation is no more implausible than, say, the consideration that an association of evil with the direction upwards presupposes an association between upwards and the good. The association between upwards and evil is given transparently in the biblical identification of a sinful Adam with God ('Behold,' says God, 'the man has become like one of us'). But that of upwards and the good is the more elementary association, by virtue of, to follow Erwin Straus's ingenious phenomenological argument, the veritable embodiment of the possibility of moral choice in upright posture (Straus 1966: ch. 7).

The axiological configuration of femininity and interiority, however, presents an even more remarkable and ontologically exciting association. For this association is embodied – perversely, according to our received metaphysics of flesh and blood – not in the individual as such, but in the transcendent form of female–male. Whereas, on the face of it, if the body is regarded indexically, as an axis of direction, upwards demands for its experiential realization only a single body, femininity as a cardinal bearing is phenomenologically rooted in a bodily structure that defies final reduction to sheer material unicity.

If the finding that Eve is really a privileged figure in Genesis redeems the feminine principle from the overriding opprobrium of the explicit storyline, it also provides small comfort to a reversed gender dualism. For in this projection of Eve, her identity naturally exceeds the feminine *qua* feminine. As a privileged cipher of the implicate order, she is identified with both sides of the story, the divisiveness signified by the opposing projections of man and God as well as the intertwining or chiasm of these projections. Now taking the perspective of the implicit storyline (the more intuitive perspective), if we apprehend opposition in Genesis primarily in terms of the male principle, then Eve paradoxically embodies that principle also.[16] But, to come now to the main point about foundations, if Eve is the embodiment of both opposition and continuity, then she must configure, rather than any fixed principle, a basically ambiguous one – which is to say, a foundation that is not a foundation. What makes such logically and ontologically strange fruit in the story is the possibility of choice. Through her image and actions the story manages to engender an ethical, in addition to a paradisical, order, an order based on expressly self-responsible, rather than simply providential, choice. For, as the territorial chiasm where opposition and continuity cross, she marks, in the highly encompassing terms of gender, all the oppositionality in the story. That oppositionality is given its most compact and potent iconic representation in the tree of knowledge. Obviously, as the essence of difference, the radical and representatively moral difference between the values of good and evil, the fruit of this tree comes to the very stuff of choice.

But Eve does more than merely subsume within her image all difference and therewith the possibility of choice. She not only represents choice but also presents it; she constitutes the difference that makes a difference; she is creation at its most creative, a bodily void of consciousness in which self-conscious existence, that is, the life of moral consciousness, can take root. In her capacity as the mother of all living, she is indistinguishable from the enclosed garden: an ultimately self-fecundating interiority not only in which the tree of knowledge grows, but also, I venture, in view of the equivalence between such enchanted interiority and the First Principle, from which the tree issues. Indeed, at this point we can see that, given her dynamic character as an implicate order, an open or involving whole, Eve is even more closely identifiable with the other prominent tree in the garden – the tree of life. By contrast to the tree of knowledge, which enjoys an exterior presence in the story, this tree is twice mentioned (at the beginning as prohibited and at the end as guarded) but never made to appear for any practical or creaturely purpose. That is because, as the tree in the midst of the garden, it points to a centreless centre, a pregnant void, filled with concealed imaginings. As such, in spite of its nominal representation as a tree, an exteriority that is phenomenally unmistakable and of towering force, it cannot but remain phenomenologically unavailable.

The disclosure of Eve's privileged position suggests that in forging the explicit storyline the biblical redactors were less than frank with themselves. One suspects that they were suffering from a terrible anxiety, a dread of incorporation, brought on by the implicit apprehension that, since they could not have created themselves in the first place, their power of self-fashioning was constitutionally and finally limited.[17] By holding Eve peculiarly accountable for humankind's failed integrity, they managed to secure, consequentially, her subjugation to her husband's authority.[18] In the event, in view of their implicit dependence on woman, a positively vital dependence that serves to identify the female principle with God, they managed to turn the tables, symbolically but also consequentially, on their most embracing and significant other. As a result, as contrary as it may seem to say so in relation to such ungodly god-like action, they introduced the power of patriarchy into an inherently anarchical and ethical order. If the name of Eve traces peculiarly, among other things, no-thing, then, ethically speaking, it precludes the priority of identity and exteriority or full presence on which patriarchy thrives (see below, note 4).

All this strongly suggests that the explicit storyline's negative valorization of Eve is linked to a terrific conceit, ironically the central conceit, as the redactors well knew, against which the story tells. In his trenchant essay about the poet Paul Celan, 'Shibboleth', Jacques Derrida makes midrashic play with the arbitrary mark of the Jew (Derrida 1986). To take a hint from him, if there is an altogether round caution in Genesis 2–3, surely it is that the will to uncircumscribed/-cized power founds a worldly exercise in self-deception.

ACKNOWLEDGEMENTS

This essay is based on a wider study of Genesis 2–3, in which I concentrate more generally on the ambiguity of the Fall as a rise, and on the manner in which the tale constitutes an account of man's development as a moral being. I have benefited here substantially from the insights of David Halperin, Ruel Tyson, Peter Kaufman and Sima Godfrey, the first three of the Department of Religious Studies at the University of North Carolina at Chapel Hill, and the last, formerly of the Department of Romance Languages at that same institution. Versions of this paper were presented at meetings of the American Ethnological Society, the International Oral History Conference, the International Society of Phenomenology and Literature, the European Association of Social Anthropologists, to the Social Science Faculty at Jawaharlal Nehru University in New Delhi and to the Department of Social Anthropology at the London School of Economics. Comments that I received on these occasions have moved me to clarify my argument at several points, and I remain grateful for the provocation. Finally, I owe Signe Howell for helpful suggestions on this the published version.

NOTES

1   In his classic study, *The Gnostic Religion*, Hans Jonas tells us that Genesis 'exerted a strong attraction upon the Gnostics', whose conception of the story amounts to a 'comprehensive revision' (Jonas 1963: 92, 93). 'Gnostic allegory', he writes [ibid.: 91–92], 'is in its most telling instances of a very different nature [from orthodox allegory]. Instead of taking over the value-system of the traditional myth, it proves the deeper "knowledge" by reversing the roles of good and evil, sublime and base, blest and accursed, found in the original. It tries, not to demonstrate agreement, but to shock by blatantly subverting the meaning of the most firmly established, and preferably also the most revered, elements of tradition. The rebellious tone of this type of allegory cannot be missed .... Of the three examples we shall discuss, two concern subjects from the Old Testament, which supplied the favorite material for gnostic perversions of meaning.'

Regarding Milton, it was, according to Paul Cantor (1984: 2–3), 'the paradox of the fortunate fall' that made Milton's task so difficult in *Paradise Lost*. Milton, he argues, 'could not admit to any defects in the original paradise, for that would be to impugn divine providence .... Nevertheless, like Eve, we may feel dissatisfied with Eden, and Milton himself seems uncomfortable with the idea that man was to live in such a dependent condition forever. Hence, although Milton cannot openly approve of the disobedience which led to the fall, he does view the event as part of a larger providential scheme for the development of the human spirit.'

2   The quotation is from Wittgenstein's scathing critique of Sir James Frazer and profound examination of the anthropological problem of how we understand stories of the Beltane fire festival, in which the theme of human sacrifice makes itself felt (Wittgenstein 1991: 18e). Wittgenstein's argument seems to have radical implications for the problem of translation. But whatever these implications, he expressly points to an existential context of significance that makes possible but, ironically, is fundamentally inconceivable to theoretical and explanatory description and analysis (cf. Zengotita 1989). In addition to Wittgenstein, I might cite also the authority of Walter Benjamin's discussion (1968), in which he talks about translation that aims at imparting, not the sense of the original, as if what is at stake were basically information, but rather what remains when the information is stripped away – an ultimately untranslatable significance or 'pure language'.

3 The anthropological notion of hierarchy as encompassment is, of course, due to Louis Dumont, whose penetrating clarifications of power and value as social phenomena, and of what it means to take the perspective of the whole rather than the part, have profoundly influenced my thinking here (e.g. Dumont 1980, 1986). However, my picture of the whole as a matter of practice, a fundamentally open and uncertain dynamic, derives from existential phenomenology. This sort of (definitively ambiguous) holism, though still beholden to Dumont's ideas about the logic of hierarchy, moves in a direction different from his. Dumont has himself employed the biblical opposition of Adam and Eve to illustrate hierarchy, picturing Adam in terms of the superior or encompassing pole of the holistic structure (Dumont 1980: 239–241). However, once the whole is regarded as dynamic, not simply in that it allows for reversals at subordinate levels of the hierarchy but, more disconcerting still, in that it remains ever ambiguous, always escaping final circumscription, Eve rather than Adam becomes pre-eminently identifiable with the finally encompassing pole of the hierarchy. For, to anticipate my textual argument, as the mother of all living, she presents a principle of creation or generation rather than structure, of uncertain practice rather than ideological logic, even if such logic is (as Dumont says) so self-inconsistent as to be scandalous. It seems to me that this reconception of the idea of the whole addresses some of the important problems raised by Melhuus, in her probing interrogation of Dumont's approach to gender in relation to the problem of hierarchy (Melhuus 1990).

4 Even so, my reading of Genesis 2–3 does not accord well with some of the feminist biblical interpretation I have seen. In view of the direct relevance of this literature to my enterprise, it seems important to set out here, as a substantial note, significant differences. Both Trible's *God and the Rhetoric of Sexuality* (1978) and Meyers' *Discovering Eve* (1988) set out to 'depatriarchalize' Genesis, thus giving readings that would have to cast serious doubt on my own. However, although their studies are expert in the field, highly provocative, and at points furnish interpretations compatible with my own, I do not find their key arguments concerning Genesis and patriarchy compelling. Take, for example, Trible's claim that the initial absence of a sexual counterpart for 'him' implies that the prelapsarian Adam was sexually undifferentiated (Trible 1978: 80–81 and 141, n. 17). It seems clear that before the arrival of Eve on the scene, Adam was indeed androgynous. Androgyny, though, is not synonymous with absence of sexual differentiation. The story plainly places emphasis on the relatively undifferentiated nature of things during the prelapsarian phase. But, if only in view of Adam's decidedly ambiguous constitution (he is formed of the earth's dust and vitalized by God's breath) and the river that 'flowed out of Eden to water the garden' there to divide into four rivers, differentiation, including sexual differentiation, is hardly missing prior to Eve's emergence. Like the mist which came before it, the river is designedly fecundating (Kaplan 1982). Prior to Eve's arrival on the scene, Adam's sexual differentiation may be contained,

but it is nevertheless in place. In view of such pendent differentiation, as well as the consideration that the human figure next to appear is female, although from one perspective the *ha-adam* of the first episode may have an androgynous reference, from another its reference is indubitably male. Both perspectives are included in the text, that from a perfect garden in which there is no well-developed divide, and that from a creaturely world in which effective division is the rule and perfect gardens the imaginary. As long as the story is deemed to be 'authored' by human beings, how could the imaginary garden fail to reflect the imperfect nature of its maker?

Again, for example, take Meyers' claim that, since the word 'fall' does not appear in the text, 'the Fall' is a mistaken idea ascribed to the story by post-biblical exegetes (Meyers 1988: 77). There can be no doubt that the story explicitly features an (expulsive) movement from inside to outside rather than from above to below, and the formal concept of the Fall is a spin put on the story by post-biblical Christian commentators. Nevertheless, the experience of falling is recorded in the story in a number of ways, for instance, most conspicuously, in the savage punishment of the serpent, who is brought so low that it is made to crawl on its belly and eat dirt.

Finally, take the question of gender equality. Both Trible and Meyers are keen to show that Eve is not pictured as basically subordinate to Adam. In relation to this aim, as I see it, Trible seems not to explain but to explain away the hierarchical and derivative nature of Eve's birth, while Meyers' functionalist interpretation (in terms of a subordination that is exclusively a question of fertility, wisely mandating an increased procreative role for the woman and intensifying her contribution in the labour-intensive agrarian setting of early Israelite society) seems sorely strained (Meyers 1988: 105). But even if I am wrong in these critical judgements, it is plain that both scholars omit to consider another, more genial, interpretive possibility. That the story describes between Adam and Eve a fundamental mutuality and equality is plain (Trible 1978: 101). But, although it is logically insensitive, in fact in practice there is nothing anomalous about the hierarchical organization of equals, so long as hierarchy is conceived of – as it is in Genesis – in terms of encompassment. Dumont has given a reading of Adam and Eve along these lines (Dumont 1980: 239–241; cf. also Melhuus 1990). And, if I read Emmanuel Levinas's phenomenological and talmudical scholarship correctly (Levinas 1969a), he finds that Eve is depicted, on one plane, as essentially equal to Adam (Eve was greeted by Adam 'precisely as an equal being'), and on another, as fundamentally secondary to him (the masculine enjoys 'a certain priority' and 'remains the prototype of the human').

Trible's and Meyers' claims about Adam's androgyny, the Fall and Eve's gender equality are made in defence of the thesis that the story does not promote patriarchal hierarchy. They make a multiplicity of such supporting claims, many of which seem no less narrowly conceived than the three that I have just cited. The trouble is that the particular way these two scholars grind the (many-sided) axe of feminism, the meaning that they extract from the story, though usefully redirective, is unhappily impoverished. By rendering the story's meaning as unambiguous, they make it impossible to understand the extraordinary force of the story for the moral practice of self-construction. In interpreting Eve as a strong character, Trible and Meyers are monitoring a vital, if also narratively hard to tap, pulse of the story. But the presence of this pulse does not so much imply the destruction as the deconstruction (the exposing of the limits) of the venerable and received interpretation of Eve as Adam's 'rib' and subordinate. Perhaps Aschkenasy, whose brief interpretation of the figure of Eve in Genesis seems to owe much to Trible, is making a similar point when she argues that 'the rabbinic exegetes and storytellers picked up some of the strains of the biblical story, while at the same time they tried to suppress other elements of the ancient story that did not conform to their patriarchal norms' (Aschkenasy 1986: 40–43). Certainly, Exum, in her strong, feminist study of women in the bible, rejects directly Trible's and Meyers' thesis that the biblical story of Genesis does not constitute a piece of patriarchal literature (Exum 1993: 9).

One can learn much from Trible's and Meyers' close and skilful readings. But, although Trible may save the biblical figure of God from being held accountable for misogynism, and Meyers' may do the same for Judaism, in so doing, I suggest, both scholars serve to perpetuate at its deepest level the very patriarchal order that they want to abolish. For, as Kristeva has argued (Kristeva 1986: ch. 6), the principle of patriarchy virtually thrives on the priority of identity and full presence inscribed in that high and mighty figure of ancient Judaism. In short, neither Trible's nor Meyers' reading is radical enough.

5 I have in mind the Nuer of East Africa, among whom (as among so many 'primitive' peoples) a marital union is not regarded as consummated until a child is born of it, and, even more to the point, the existence of that child creates, retroactively, blood kinship (i.e. 'one flesh') between the father's kin and the mother's kin; in our terms, between in-laws. Hence, by virtue of the child, sexual relations between the father and the wife's sister are regarded as incestuous (Evans-Pritchard 1951; see also Evens 1989).

6 Professor David Halperin, personal communication; see also Joines (1974: 18).

7 It is not surprising, then, that the serpent has been identified as both male and female. According to Rubenstein (1971: 54), the rabbinic traditions take the male identity of the serpent for granted. 'The most interesting tradition is an old Palestinian legend that the serpent originally possessed the upright posture of a man. He was destined to rule over all the other animals save man. In consequence of his sin God cut off his arms and legs.' The Freudian significance of the punitive modification of the serpent's posture, from erect to prostrate, is unmistakable. As Rubenstein says (1971: 56), 'There is no explicit reference to castration. Nevertheless, the mutilation of all of the

serpent's appendages can hardly be interpreted in any other light.' Yet, as Elaine Pagels reports, in the gnostic text called *Reality of the Rulers*, Eve rather than Adam is represented as the 'higher principle', and this principle reappears 'in the form of the serpent' (Pagels 1988: 66f., see also 68ff.).

8 Compare the gnostic view of the serpent and its role in inducing Eve to eat of the forbidden fruit (Jonas 1963: 93): the serpent 'came in a whole group of [gnostic] systems to represent the "pneumatic" principle from beyond counteracting the designs of the Demiurge [the leader of the powers of darkness and the world, i.e. the biblical God], and thus could become as much a symbol of the powers of redemption as the biblical God had been degraded to a symbol of cosmic oppression'; the serpent's seduction of Eve 'is the first success of the transcendent principle against the principle of the world, which is vitally interested in preventing knowledge in man as the inner-worldly hostage of Light: the serpent's action marks the beginning of all gnosis on earth which thus by its very origin is stamped as opposed to the world and its God, and indeed as a form of rebellion'; finally, 'The Peratae [a gnostic cult] ...did not even shrink from regarding the historical Jesus as a particular incarnation of the "general serpent", i.e., the serpent from Paradise'.

9 Cf. Trible (1978: 80), who simply proclaims, 'Grammatical gender ['*adam* as a masculine word] is not sexual identification.' Later (ibid.: 98), however, she draws a structural parallel between the way that the story employs the units *ish* (man)/*ishah* (woman) and *adamah*/*adam*, but restricts the correspondence to the idea of playful 'origination' (of sexuality and humanity respectively), although the chiasm of grammatical gender the units constitute is hardly less conspicuous a structural and linguistic feature than that of punning. Levinas, too, cites the 'Sages' as seizing on the etymological account of *ish* and *ishah* to affirm the association of (the Hebrew) language with creativity ('the mystery of creation'). But he also argues that what is being talked about is the 'quasi-grammatical derivation' of 'woman' from 'man' (1969a: 34). In view of Barr's authoritative study (1961), I should make clear, though, that I am not arguing that grammatical gender in biblical Hebrew may be taken to reflect Hebrew thought in general. My point is that in the case at hand the weight of the textual evidence is such as to suggest strongly that the linguistic difference of gender between *adam* and *adamah* is not at all logically haphazard in relation to the story's axiological representations of femininity.

10 As deconstructionists must mean but cannot say (since they cannot coherently embrace any foundation, including that of anti-foundationalism (Caputo 1987).

11 To cite more fully (Bohm 1980: 172): 'Throughout this book, the central underlying theme has been the unbroken wholeness of the totality of existence as an undivided flowing movement without borders .... It seems clear from the discussion ... that the implicate order is particularly suitable for the understanding of such unbroken wholeness in flowing movement, for in the implicate order the totality

of existence is enfolded within each region of space (and time). So, whatever part, element, or aspect we may abstract in thought, this still enfolds the whole and is therefore intrinsically related to the totality from which it has been abstracted. Thus, wholeness permeates all that is being discussed, from the very outset.'

12 See here Iris Marion Young's critically thoughtful and revealing phenomenological account of women's experience of pregnancy, in which she observes about herself (Young 1990: 163): 'Pregnancy challenges the integration of my body experience by rendering fluid the boundary between what is within, myself, and what is outside, separate. I experience my insides as the space of another, yet my own body.' 'The pregnant subject', she suggests (ibid.: 160), 'is decentered, split, or doubled ....' In other words, she describes the experience of pregnancy in the paradoxical terms of fluid boundaries, crossings that creatively smear, without obliterating, the difference between inside and outside, self and other, body and thought, giving the pregnant subject a 'privileged relation to this other life' (ibid.: 163). In connection with the picture of Eve as implicitly creative and Milton's revision of the meaning of the biblical creation and fall, consult Patricia Parker's rich phenomenological reading of Eve in *Paradise Lost* as the figure for 'pendency' and 'a twilight space of "creation" in and for itself' (Parker 1987). Finally, see Emmanuel Levinas's phenomenological reflections on the feminine element in Jewish thought, in which he associates woman with the 'interiority of "the house"', with 'habitation itself' (Levinas 1969a: 33; see also 1969b: 154–158). Arguing on the basis of the classical Jewish sources, he finds that, without woman, the world would be merely an 'outdoors', a space without place, characterized only by the alienation resulting from the 'masculinity of the universal and conquering logos'.

13 For a Freudian picture, see Erikson's famous study (1965: 97–98) in which he finds that 'If "high" and "low" are masculine variables, "open" and "closed" are feminine modalities', as well as Bardwick's more recent study (1971: 15; cf. also Jessica Benjamin 1988: 129–131) in which, emphasizing the positive character of inner space, she claims that 'it is not the absence of the penis but the presence of creative inner space that is important for girls'. For a Jungian perspective see Neumann's analysis of the feminine principle (Neumann 1963: chs 3 and 4), in which he finds a special symbolic association of the Feminine with the 'uroboros' (the circular snake eating its own tail); with the inside or 'vessel par excellence' ('Woman as body-vessel is the natural expression of the human experience of woman bearing the child "within" her and of man entering "into" her in the sexual act'); with containment as both destructive or limiting and transforming or generative; and with the 'unconscious' or 'original situation of the psyche'.

14 I have begun to do so systematically in Evens 1995.

15 Nor does this privilege preclude the possibility of cultural settings that present themselves with little or even no thematic regard for femininity (a possibility brought to my attention by Alfred Gell, whose

ethnographic researches in Papua New Guinea made him mindful of it). Following my argument, it would indeed be hard not to suspect such settings of 'self-deception'. But the argument leaves the question of the authenticity of such a setting to empirical determination, and does not rule the question out of court.

16 Levinas appears to imply something of the sort when he links femininity integrally to 'the miracle of social relations', and argues that such relationships are superordinate to merely sexual or biological ones (Levinas 1969a: 35). In effect, as he interprets the feminine principle, it seems to go beyond being, to incorporate, for ethical purposes, the creaturely difference between male and female. But his formula may well belittle sexual difference, which is not what I intend. Moreover, in sharp contrast to my reading of the principle enfigured by Eve, Levinas makes it very clear that, although the masculine world depends on maternity for conversion to goodness, ethics as such remains the preserve of masculinity. 'The dimension of intimacy is opened by woman', he writes (ibid.: 37), 'not the dimension of loftiness.' Evidently buying into the patriarchal bias of the Hebrew scriptures, Levinas ties the divinity of the Other, the transcendence of being, to the father–son relationship: 'The I breaks free from itself in paternity without thereby ceasing to be an I, for the I is its son' (ibid.: 278, see also 274–277). In his powerful appreciative commentaries on Levinas, Derrida has ingeniously critiqued this profound thinker's apparent patriarchalism (Derrida 1978, 1991; see also Critchley 1991, Chalier 1991, Irigaray 1991; cf., however, Cohen 1994: ch. 9). I hasten to add here that, in reading Levinas, I have found very helpful my own son's exegesis of Levinas's *Totality and Infinity* (A. Evens 1991).

17 The voice of Harold Bloom echoes here, despite his speculation that J ('the Yahwist'), the putative author of Genesis 2–3, was a woman (Bloom 1990; see also Bloom 1973).

18 This conclusion is complicated by Rubenstein's work on the meaning of anxiety in Rabbinic Judaism. In his fascinating essay (Rubenstein 1971: ch. 5), he isolates and identifies in Judaism an unmeasured terror of the 'pre-Oedipal mother', whose power of incorporation represents cannibalism and annihilation. Where he expressly takes up the question of the 'strong masculine bias' in the Bible and Rabbinic Judaism, however, he offers a more sociological account (ibid. ch. 3): 'No explanation which fails to include the stresses of defeat, conquest, and minority status upon male Jews will have any degree of adequacy. Jewish masculinity was decisively challenged by the defeat of Roman times and perhaps earlier. After defeat by the Romans and the alienation of the Jewish community from its ancestral territory, Jewish men lacked the capacity to defend or assure possession of their own women .... The Jew reacted to the external threat to his masculinity by asserting it with extra insistence within his own community.'

REFERENCES

Aschkenasy, Nehama (1986) *Eve's Journey*, Philadelphia: University of Pennsylvania Press.

Bardwick, Judith M. (1971) *Psychology of Women*, New York: Harper & Row.

Barr, James (1961) *The Semantics of Biblical Language*, Oxford: Oxford University Press.

Benjamin, Jessica (1988) *The Bonds of Love*, New York: Pantheon Books.

Benjamin, Walter (1968) *Book Illuminations*, New York: Schocken.

Bloom, Harold (1973) *The Anxiety of Influence*, Oxford: Oxford University Press.

——(1990) 'The author J.', in *The Book of J.*, trans. David Rosenberg and interpret. Harold Bloom, New York: Grove Weidenfeld.

Bohm, David (1980) *Wholeness and the Implicate Order*, London: Routledge & Kegan Paul.

Brown, F., Driver, S.R. and Briggs, C.A. (eds) (1975) *A Hebrew and English Lexicon of the Old Testament*, Oxford: Clarendon Press.

Cantor, Paul A. (1984) *Creature and Creator: Myth-making and English Romanticism*, Cambridge: Cambridge University Press.

Caputo, John D. (1987) 'The economy of signs in Husserl and Derrida', in John Sallis (ed.) *Deconstruction and Philosophy*, Chicago: University of Chicago Press.

Chalier, Catherine (1991) 'Ethics and the feminine', in Robert Bernasconi and Simon Critchley (eds) *Re-Reading Levinas*, Bloomington: Indiana University Press.

Cohen, Richard A. (1994) *Elevations*, Chicago: Chicago University Press.

Critchley, Simon (1991) ' "Bois": Derrida's final word on Levinas', in Robert Bernasconi and Simon Critchley (eds) *Re-Reading Levinas*, Bloomington: Indiana University Press.

Derrida, Jacques (1978) 'Violence and metaphysics: an essay on the thought of Emmanuel Levinas', in Jacques Derrida, *Writing and Difference*, Chicago: University of Chicago Press.

——(1986) 'Shibboleth', in Geoffrey H. Hartman and Sanford Budick (eds) *Midrash and Literature*, New Haven: Yale University Press.

——(1991) 'At this very moment in this work here I am', in Robert Bernasconi and Simon Critchley (eds) *Re-Reading Levinas*, Bloomington: Indiana University Press.

Dumont, Louis (1980) *Homo Hierarchicus* (revised English edn), Chicago: University of Chicago Press.

——(1986) 'On value', in *Essays on Individualism: Modern Ideology in Anthropological Perspective*, Chicago: University of Chicago Press.

Erikson, Erik H. (1965) *Childhood and Society*, Harmondsworth: Penguin.

Evans-Pritchard, E.E. (1951) *Kinship and Marriage among the Nuer*, Oxford: Oxford University Press.

Evens, Aden L. (1991) 'Writing ethics', unpublished manuscript.

Evens, T. M. S. (1989) 'The Nuer incest prohibition and the nature of kinship: alterlogical reckoning', *Cultural Anthropology* 4 (4): 323–346.

——(1995) *Two kinds of rationality*, Minneapolis: University of Minnesota Press.

Exum, J. Cheryl (1993) *Fragmented Women: Feminist (Sub)versions of Biblical Narratives*, Sheffield: JSOT Press.

Frazer, James G. (1984 [1923]) 'The fall of man', in Alan Dundes (ed.) *Sacred Narrative: Readings in the Theory of Myth*, Berkeley: University of California Press.

Ginzberg, Louis (ed.) (1909) *The Legends of the Jews* Vol. 1, trans. Henrietta Szold, Philadelphia: Jewish Publication Society of America.

Irigaray, Luce (1991) 'Questions to Emmanuel Levinas: on the divinity of love', in Robert Bernasconi and Simon Critchley (eds) *Re-Reading Levinas*, Bloomington: Indiana University Press.

Joines, Karen R. (1974) *Serpent Symbolism in the Old Testament*, New Jersey: Haddonfield House.

Jonas, Hans (1963) *The Gnostic Religion* (2nd edn, rev.), Boston: Beacon Press.

Kaplan, Aryeh (1982) *Waters of Eden* (2nd edn), New York: National Conference of Synagogue Youth/Union of Orthodox Jewish Congregations of America.

Kasher, Menahem M. (1953) *Encyclopedia of Biblical Interpretation, Vol. 1: Genesis*, trans. and ed. Harry Freedman, New York: American Biblical Encyclopedia Society, .

Kristeva, Julia (1986) *The Kristeva Reader*, Toril Moi (ed.), New York: Columbia University Press.

Leach, Edmund (1969) 'Genesis as myth', in *Genesis as Myth and Other Essays*, London: Jonathan Cape.

Levinas, Emmanuel (1969a) 'Judaism and the feminine element', *Judaism* 18 (1): 30–38.

——(1969b) *Totality and Infinity* trans. Alphonso Lingis, Pittsburgh: Duquesne University Press.

Melhuus, Marit (1990) 'Gender – and the problem of hierarchy', *Ethnos* 55 (3–4): 151–168.

Merleau-Ponty, M. (1962) *Phenomenology of Perception*, trans. Colin Smith, London: Routledge & Kegan Paul.

Meyers, Carol (1988) *Discovering Eve: Ancient Israelite Women in Context*, New York: Oxford University Press.

Neumann, Erich (1963) *The Great Mother* (2nd edn), trans. Ralph Manheim, New York: Bollingen Foundation Inc.

Pagels, Elaine (1988) *Adam, Eve, and the Serpent*, New York: Random House.

Parker, Patricia (1987) 'Eve, evening, and the labor of reading in *Paradise Lost*', in Harold Bloom (ed.) *John Milton's Paradise Lost*, New York: Chelsea House Publishers.

Rashi (1949) *The Pentateuch and Commentary: Genesis*, trans. Abraham Ben Isaiah and Benjamin Sharfman, Brooklyn, N.Y.: S.S. & R. Publishing.

Rubenstein, Richard L. (1971) *The Religious Imagination*, Boston: Beacon Press.

Straus, Erwin W. (1966) *Phenomenological Psychology*, New York: Basic Books.

Trible, Phyllis (1978) *God and the Rhetoric of Sexuality*, Philadelphia: Fortress Press.

Wittgenstein, Ludwig (1991) *Remarks on Frazer's Golden Bough*, (ed.) Rush Rhees and trans. A.C. Miles, Yorkshire: Brynmill Press.

Young, Iris M. (1990) *Throwing Like A Girl and Other Essays in Feminist Philosophy and Social Theory*, Bloomington: Indiana University Press.

Zengotita, Thomas de (1989) 'On Wittgenstein's remarks on Frazer's golden bough', *Cultural Anthropology* 4 (4): 390–398.

Index

Abu-Lughod, L. 156, 175 n.4
Adam and Eve 19, 207–18
Alexander, F. 49
altruism 17, 33, 42
American Anthropological
    Association 10
Archetti, E.: (1992) 200 n.12; (1995)
    114; (this volume) 4, 8, 12, 15–16,
    34, 74, 94 n.4, 95 n.12, 180
Ardener, E. 56
Argentina 12, 15–16, 98–120
Aristotle 38–9
Arizpe, L. 200 n.19
Arkoun, M. 158
Aschkenasy, N. 221 n.4
Avatip, New Guinea 137, 141–2

Bardwick, J.M. 224 n.13
Barr, J. 223 n.9
Barthes, R. 188
Bartra, R. 183, 200 n.18
Bateson, G. 95 n.11
Battaglia, D. 146
Bayer, O. 108–9, 113, 114, 116
Behar, R. 199 n.2
Benjamin, J. 224 n.13
Benjamin, W. 219
Berger, P. 199 n.5
Bible 13, *see also* Genesis
Bloom, H. 225 n.17
body posture 58–9
Bohm, D. 214, 223 n.11
Bonte, P. 156
Boon, J. 17, 75, 89–91

Borchgrevink, T. 199 n.5
Borofsky, R. 3
Bourdieu, P. 27–8, 155, 156
Bourne, E. 50
Brady, I. 95 n.10
Briggs, C.A. 208
Brown, F. 208
Brown, P. 146 n.1
Buddhism 30, 33, 35

Campbell, E. 199 n.10
Cantor, P.A. 219
Caputo, J.D. 223 n.10
caring, ethic of 135
Carrier, J.M. 182
Carrithers, M. 16, 33–4, 45 n.5
caste system 5
Catholicism 13, 18–19, 34
causality 16
Celan, P. 218
Chalier, C. 225 n.16
Chinese 26, 40–1
Chingghis Khaan, Emperor 26, 29,
    35, 38, 42
choice 16
clans, Hagen 131–2, 137–8, 141
Clarin Deportivo, El 121 n.6
Cohen, A. 96 n.16
Cohen, R.A. 225 n.16
Communist Party 33, 40
Condorcet, Marquis de 38
Confucianism 226
conscience 16, 50
control 50–1

Cornwall, A. 121 n.3
Coulson, N.J. 157
Critchley, S. 225 n.16
Cultural Revolution 41
customs 25, 28

Damon, F. 130
D'Andrade, R. 44 n.3
de la Maza, F. 199 n.10
Declaration of Human Rights 10, 69
Derrida, J. 218, 225 n.16
desire 101
Devereux, G. 96 n.18
Dickinson, E. 211
Dieterlin, G. 6
dignity 13, 50, 67–8
Dinka people 6
Dogon people 6
dominant models 52–7
Dorjlham, T. 39
Dostal, W. 163
Dresch, P. 157, 162
Driver, S.R. 208
Dumont, L. 8, 50, 220 n.3, 221 n.4
Durkheim, E. 7–8, 93, 100–1, 112

Edel, M. and A. 2–3, 8, 100, 101,
    179–80
Eder, K. 154
edicts 28
Elvin, M. 36
England 12, 17–18, 74–94
Erdene-Ochir, G. 37
Erikson, E.H. 49, 224 n.13
ethics: applied 8, 10; communist 33;
    comparative 7; meta- 8; personal
    25; sociology of 7
Evans-Pritchard, E.E. 6, 222 n.5
Eve 19, 181, 207–18
Evens, A.L. 225 n.16
Evens, T.M.S.: (1982) 180; (1989)
    101–2, 222 n.5; (1993) 113; (1995)
    224 n.14; (this volume) 13, 16, 19,
    128, 180, 181, 190
exemplars 4, 12, 34–8; Maoist 40–5;
    negative 39–40
Exum, J.C. 222 n.4

farming 76–9

farting 50
Flick, U. 167
Fontanarrosa 111
football 12, 15–16, 98–120
forgiveness 16
Forssen, A. 50
Fortes, M. 51
Foucault, M. 18, 26–7, 44 n.1
Frazer, J.G. 212, 219 n.2
Fulani people 50–2, 70

Gaadamba, M. 29, 30
Gahuku-Gama people 7
Geertz, C. 50, 69, 94 n.3, 155
Gell, A. 224 n.15
Gellner, E. 155, 157, 175 n.3
gender: female poisoning cases
    129–30; Hagen men and women
    131–2; law and morality 127–8;
    Manyika men and women 59;
    Mexican morality 13, 181–98; sex
    and morality 18–20
generosity 195
Genesis, Book of 13, 16, 19, 181,
    203–18
George, Mr 60–8
gifts 64–9
Gilligan, C. 135–6, 148 nn.11, 12
Gillison, G. 143
Gilmore, D. 199 n.6
Gingrich, A. 6, 14, 20, 157, 162, 175
    n.2
Ginzberg, L. 203
Giordano, H. 122 n.9
Glaser, E. 163–4
Gluckman, M. 6
Gochenour, D.T. 159
Godelier, M. 153
Godfrey, S. 218
Gokalp, A. 160
Goldman, L. 142, 147 n.8
good and evil 16
gossip 4, 12, 57, 196
grace 155, 156, 167
Gráfico, El 106, 107, 121 nn. 2, 4, 7
Greeks, Homeric 14
Griaule, M. 6
grievance, petitions of 31
Guadelupe, Virgin of 19, 189–91

guilt 4, 13, 49–50, 70

Habermas, J. 28, 154
Hagen people 13, 14, 15, 19, 129–46
Halperin, D. 218, 222 n.6
Hampshire, S. 39
happiness 12, 15, 102–3, 118
haram 4, 14, 20, 155–8;
    haramization 159–62; non-
    haramization 163–6; post-
    haramization 171–4
Harman, G. 8, 10
Harrison, S. 137, 141–2, 148 n.16
Heelas, P. 16
Hem, H.S. 121 n.1
Herzfeld, M. 155, 199 n.6
hierarchical systems 52–7
Hill, J. 48
Hinduism 5
honesty 195
honour 4, 6, 13, 16, 18, 19; men's 18,
    195; Mexican code 13, 18–19,
    181–4; Muslim concepts 155–6,
    160; shame and 182–4; women's
    166–9
Howell, S.: (1992) 96 n.17; (1994)
    11; (1995) 9–10; (this volume)
    128, 145, 154
Humphrey, C. 12, 17, 33, 105, 145,
    171
Hyer, P. 45 n.7

immoral acts, responsibility for 15
independence 195
indigenous moralities 6–9
individualism 16–17
individuality 36
insiders 17
intentionality 16
Irigaray, L. 225 n.16
Islam 14, 18, 20, 154–74
Isono, F. 45 n.8

Jacobson-Widding, A.: (1990) 56;
    (1991) 56; (this volume) 6, 11,
    12–13, 16–17, 34, 158, 181
Jagchid, S. 28, 42, 45 n.7
Jahoda, M. 152, 175 n.1
Jamous, R. 155–6, 173, 175 n.6

Johnson, M. 9, 119, 180
Joines, K.R. 209, 213, 222 n.6
Jonas, H. 219 n.1
Josephides, L. 128, 149 n.20
justice: ethic of 135; Mongol idea 31

Kanaq people 6
Kaplan, A. 220 n.4
Kasher, M.M. 209
Kaufman, P. 218
kinship 32, 67, 70–1, 137–8, 160
Kirkpatrick, J. 50
Kondo, D. 48
Kripke, S.A. 27
Kristeva, J. 222

La Fontaine, J. 52
Lafaye, J. 199 n.10
Lancaster, R.N. 183, 200 n.16
landownership 74–94
Langness, L.L. 141
Lattimore, O. 45 n.8
law 6, 13; customary 170; gender
    issues 13, 127; Islamic 157, 160,
    172; legal systems 170
Lázaro 114
Lazarsfeld, P.F. 175 n.1
Le Vine, S. 191, 199 n.2
Leach, E. 204
Leenhardt, M. 6
Lei Feng 40–1
Lessing, D. 9
Lever, A. 199 n.6
Lévi-Strauss, C. 55, 204
Levinas, E. 208, 221 n.4, 223 n.9,
    224 n.12, 225 n.16
Lewis, O. 200 n.16
Libonatti, J. 116
Lienhardt, R.G. 6
Limón, J. 200 n.16
Lindisfarne, N. 121 n.3
Lock, A. 16
Lorenzo, R. 105
Lukes, S. 7–8, 100
Lutz, C. 48
lying 50

machismo 18, 179, 197
Madelung, W. 160

madness 15
male: identity 18, 195; virtues 12,
   99, 102, 118–20, 193–4
Malinowski, B. 6
Manchester School 6
Mannheim, B. 48
Manyika people 48, 53–71
Mao Zedong 40–1
Maradona, D. 116, 121 n.6
Marsella, A. 50
Martin, J.A. 190
Marzolini, S. 113
Maswera, J. 60–3, 64
Mauritania 156
Mauss, M. 36, 51, 55
mediation 137–8
Melanesia 130
Melhuus, M.: (1990) 183, 199 n.5,
   220 n.3; (1992) 183, 184, 199 n.5,
   200 n.14; (1993) 192; (this
   volume) 6, 13, 18–19, 20, 100, 155
Melpa language 129
Melville, H. 212
Menotti, C.L. 115–16, 117–18, 122
   n.8
Merlan, F. 132, 147 nn.4, 5, 149
   n.20
Merleau-Ponty, M. 206, 215–16
Mernissy, F. 155, 156
Methodist church 58, 64
Mexico 13, 18–19, 20, 178–98
Meyers, C. 220–2 n.4
Midgley, M. 14
Milton, J. 203, 219 n.1, 224 n.12
modernity 58
modesty 156
Mongolian people 17, 25–44;
   language 12, 25
Monti, L. 108
moral: choices 101–2; codes 6–7, 11,
   34, 100; person 16–18; reasoning
   14–16; relativism 10
morality, moralities: defining and
   locating 12–14; definitions 2–6,
   49; exemplary 34; of football
   103–18; indigenous 6–9; in
   Muslim societies 154–6; sex and
   18–20
Morgenthaler, F. 50

Morocco 155–7, 162
motherhood 190, 192–3, 195–6
Müller, D.H. 163
Mutasa myth 54–5, 65

nature 28–9
Needham, R. 5, 44
Neumann, E. 224 n.13
New Guinea 13, 15, 19, 129–46
Nilsson, P. 119
Nuer people 6, 14, 222 n.5

Obelkevich, J. 44
O'Hanlon, M. 143, 148 n.10, 149
   nn.17, 20
Okada, H. 29
Olympic Games 99, 108
Ortner, S. 43
outsiders 17, 74–5, 89–93
Overing, J. 148 n.13

Pagels, E. 223 n.7
Panzeri, D. 121 n.7
Parin, P. 50
Parin-Matthey, G. 50
Parker, P. 224 n.12
Parkin, D. 3, 5, 7, 145
Paternoster, F. 122 n.9
Paz, O. 199 n.10, 200 n.12
Pedernera, A. 122 n.9
Peristiany, J.G. 6, 155, 199 n.6
personhood: collective/individual,
   17, 52; different cultural
   traditions 17; indigenous notions
   7; Kanaq 6; Muslim doctrine
   158; social 13, 17, 51–3, 59, 67
Piers, G. 49, 70
Pitt-Rivers, J. 155
Pocock, D.F. 8, 14
politics 9
Prieur, A. 198 n.1, 200 nn.12, 16, 18
punishment: crime and 16; fear of 6;
   Mongol view 32

Quinn, N. 43

rape 192
Rapport, N.: (1987) 94 n.5, 95 n.9;
   (1993) 94 nn.1, 6, 96 n.15;

(1994a) 94 n.1; (1994b) 95 n.9;
(1994c) 96 n.18; (this volume) 12,
17, 100, 119
Rashi 208–9
Rashidondog, S. 31
Read, K.E. 7, 148 n.13
reasonableness 30–1
Reif, E. 159
relations, mediated/unmediated
137–41
respect 4, 48, 58
responsibility 15, 16, 17
Rhodokanakis, N. 163
Ricoeur, P. 55–7
Riesman, P. 50–1
rights 5, 16
Rivière, P. 183
Rosen, L. 154
Rothschild, E. 39
Roy, O. 174
Rubenstein, R.L. 207, 209, 222 n.6,
225 n.18
rulers 28, 30–1
rules 16, 25, 27–30, 34
Rumsey, A. 132, 147 nn.4, 5, 149
n.20
Russell, J. 48

Sábato, E. 105, 106
sanctions 16
Sanz 111
Sapir, E. 94
Schneider, J. 199 n.6
Secret History of the Mongols, The
42
self 36, 49
self-mastery 51
sexuality 4; cross-sex and same-sex
relations 4, 132–5, 181, 193–4;
Mexican division of labour
183–4; Mexican female 191–3;
sex and morality 18–20; sex and
politics 9
shamanism 28
shame 4, 6, 13, 16, 17, 19;
Argentinian football 16; guilt and
49–51, 70; honour and 160,
182–4; Mexican code 19, 181–4;

Muslim concepts 160; Shona
society 13, 17
Shirendev, B. 33
Shona-speaking people 12–13, 17,
48
Shweder, R.A. 50
sin 16
Singer, M. 49, 70
Smart, C. 13, 127, 131, 135, 146 n.2
Smith, N. 43, 45 n.9
Spellberg, D.A. 159
Spiro, M. 48
Stalin, J. 40
Stevens, E. 183
Stewart, C. 155
Strasser, S. 160
Strathern, A. 134, 143, 147 n.8, 149
n.17
Strathern, M.: (1981) 96 n.16, 147
n.9; (1982) 96 n.16; (1988) 138,
143, 147 n.4, 148 n.13; (1994)
129–30, 138, 147 n.5, 148 n.15;
(1995) 136; (this volume) 13, 15,
19, 94 n.2, 102, 170, 181
Straus, E.W. 216
surtakhuun 12, 25
Sweden 69, 114–15
sympathy 17, 33, 137
Szwed, J. 94 n.4

Tapper, R. and N. 160
Taylor, C. 10, 27–9, 45 n.9, 152
teachers 35–8
theft 50–1
Thompson, J.J. 8, 10
tradition 102
tribes, Yemeni 162
Trible, P. 220–2 n.4, 223 n.9
Tserensodnom, D. 29, 30
tsika 12, 48, 53–4, 58, 62–3, 65–8
Turner, B.S. 7
Tuzin, D.F. 148 n.16
Tyson, R. 218

Valdano, J. 106
Van Baal, J. 140
Veit, V. 31
violence and suffering 184–91,
195–6

virginity 178–9, 190–1
virtue: female 193–5; male 12, 102, 118–20, 193–4

Wagner, R. 130
Walzer, M. 96 n.16
Weber, M. 154
Western philosophical tradition 8, 10
White, M. 50
Wierzbicka, A. 48
Wikan, U. 199 n.6
Williams, B. 33, 49
Wittgenstein, L. 27, 44 n.2, 205, 219 n.2
Wolf, E. 199 n.10

women: female poisoning cases 128–30; female virtue 193–5; good/bad 18–19; motherhood 190, 192–3, 195–6; in Muslim societies 156, 157, 162; virginity 178–9, 190–1
World Cup 16, 99, 106, 108–11, 115
wulya 15, 134, 142–5
Wuthnow, R. 180

Yemen 14, 20, 161–9
yos 12, 25, 28, 30, 39
Young, I.M. 224 n.12

Zeisel, H. 175 n.1
Zengotita, T. de 219 n.2
Zimbabwe 12, 48–71, 53